PITTSBURGH SERIES IN
COMPOSITION, LITERACY,
AND CULTURE

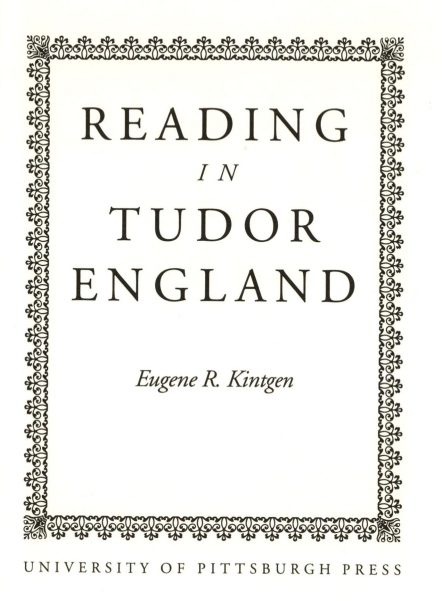

READING
IN
TUDOR
ENGLAND

Eugene R. Kintgen

UNIVERSITY OF PITTSBURGH PRESS

Published by the University of Pittsburgh Press, Pittsburgh, Pa. 15260
Copyright © 1996, University of Pittsburgh Press
Manufactured in the United States of America
Printed on acid-free paper

Kintgen, Eugene R.
    Reading in Tudor England / Eugene R. Kintgen.
        p.   cm. — (Pittsburgh series in composition, literacy, and
culture)
    Includes bibliographical references (p.   ) and index.
    ISBN 0-8229-3939-8 (cl. : alk. paper)
    1. Reading—England—History—16th century.   2. Cognitive
learning—England—History—16th century.   I. Title.   II. Series.
LA631.4.K56   1996
428.4'071'04209031—dc20   95-53193

Portions of chapters 1 and 2 and the appendix previously appeared in *Studies in English
Literature 1500–1900* 30, 1 (Winter 1990) and are reprinted here with permission.

A CIP catalogue record for this book is available from the British Library.
Eurospan, London

For Elaina, Gene, and David

CONTENTS

PREFACE

A word about the organization of this book: to introduce readers more immediately to the main topic—the reading strategies of Tudor readers—I have relegated my discussion of the theoretical underpinnings and affiliations of my method to an appendix; those who are curious will find there a fuller discussion of my assumptions and evidence that similar conceptions were current in Tudor England. For those more interested in Tudor reading, in the first chapter, the introduction, I survey the education provided in grammar schools organized according to Erasmian principles to determine how schoolboys thus educated would have learned to interpret a text. Facility in Latin was a primary goal of these schools, and I make the operational assumption that readers who could read Latin texts would have internalized this method of reading (including those who had been tutored, since the tutors would have attended a university where these principles were assumed). An important corollary is that for evidence about other methods of reading we will have to examine texts in the vernacular. The second chapter explores three examples of these educated readers: Gabriel Harvey, the E. K., whoever he was, who provided the editorial apparatus for Spenser's *Shepheardes Calendar,* and Sir John Harington, who presented his translation of Ariosto's *Orlando Furioso* in an opulent scholarly edition. The third chapter considers those who learned to read without having attended grammar school (and thus did not learn Latin): I argue that the church services they were mandated by statute to attend (and various religious guidebooks) would have provided, in addition to the obvious religious instruction, a model of reading for them to use. In the fourth chapter I discuss a number of books of self-help (in English) to see what sort of advice they offered about reading. A brief conclusion relates the various methods of reading, and the appendix provides the theoretical bases of the historical study of reading.

I want to thank those who read this manuscript in various stages—Pat Brantlinger, Kathryn Flannery, Don Gray, and anonymous reviewers for the University of Pittsburgh Press. Until I wrestled with their comments I thought that the typical authorial thanks and exculpation of readers from blame for the remaining mistakes was a literary trope, a little like my friend from Louisiana who confessed that until he moved to Wisconsin he thought all those poems welcoming spring had purely literary sources. But confronting their comments and objections has made me formulate more explicitly (and, I hope, more clearly) what I believe, even when it is not what they believe. To return to the trope, they will have no trouble discerning their influence even when they think I would have been wiser to have accepted more of it.

I would also like to thank the participants of the seminars with whom I explored many of these ideas for the first time, and the members of the Indiana University Literacy Forum for their stimulating discussions. The Office of Research of Indiana University granted me a summer faculty fellowship to pursue research related to this book, and the Office of Academic Affairs, a sabbatical.

The part my family—Elaina, Gene, and David—has played in this project exceeds the possibilities of verbal acknowledgement. They provided the continuo for these variations, and watching the boys resist constructions of reality recommended by others (including parents and teachers as well as friends) has constantly reminded me how much what we read and write in books needs to be checked against (what I perhaps naively continue to believe in as) outside reality.

READING IN TUDOR ENGLAND

CHAPTER 1

INTRODUCTION

Before I went into Germany, I came to Broadgate in Leicestershire to take my leave of that noble Lady Jane Grey, to whom I was exceeding much beholding. Her parents, the duke and the duchess, with all the household, gentlemen and gentlewomen, were hunting in the park. I found her in her chamber reading *Phaedon Platonis* in Greek, and that with as much delight as some gentleman would read a merry tale in Boccaccio. After salutation and duty done, with some other talk, I asked her why she would lose such pastime in the park. Smiling she answered me, "Iwis [Truly], all their sport in the park is but a shadow to that pleasure that I find in Plato. Alas, good folk, they never felt what true pleasure meant." "And how came you, madame," quoth I, "to this deep knowledge of pleasure, and what did chiefly allure you unto it, seeing not many women, but very few men, have attained thereunto?" "I will tell you," quoth she, "and tell you a truth which perchance ye will marvel at. One of the greatest benefits that ever God gave me is that he sent me so sharp and severe parents and so gentle a schoolmaster. For when I am in presence either of father or mother, whether I speak, keep silence, sit, stand, or go, eat, drink, be merry or sad, be sewing, playing, dancing, or doing anything else, I must do it, as it were, in such weight, measure, and number, even so perfectly as God made the world, or else I am so sharply taunted, so cruelly threatened, yea, presently sometimes, with pinches, nips, and bobs, and other ways which I will not name for the honor I bear them, so without measure misordered, that I think myself in hell till time come that I must go to Master Aylmer, who teacheth me so

3

gently, so pleasantly, with such fair allurements to learning, that I
think all the time nothing whilst I am with him. And when I am
called from him, I fall on weeping because whatsoever I do else
but learning is full of grief, trouble, fear, and whole misliking
unto me. And thus my book hath been so much my pleasure,
and bringeth daily to me more pleasure and more, that in respect
of it all other pleasures in very deed be but trifles and troubles
unto me.[1]

Roger Ascham's moving anecdote about Lady Jane Grey presents,
it seems to me, a fitting emblem for this study. The juxtaposition
between the solitary lady in her chamber, deriving pleasure from
her private reading, and the rest of the household collectively
pursuing courtly pleasures (and other game) suggests two realms,
interpenetrating to be sure, but distinct enough at times to allow
separate discussion. Her tale of physical encouragements to proper
courtly behavior provides an objective correlative for the psychological pressure many courtiers must have felt about elegant and
graceful courtliness, and her retreat into the pleasures of solitary
reading (itself something of an anomaly at a time when reading
was a more social activity than it is today) suggests that it might be
useful and illuminating to complement the extraordinary efflores-
cence of studies of what Erving Goffman some time ago referred
to as the presentation of self in everyday life, and Stephen Greenblatt has more recently popularized in a slightly revised version
as Renaissance self-fashioning,[2] with some consideration of how
these people conducted themselves in the more private sphere of
literacy. Lady Jane's tragic later history—through no desire or fault
of her own queen of England for nine days, and then subsequently
beheaded for treason—reminds us how easily the balance of power
shifts from the private to the public realm, at least for the socially
prominent, and thus perhaps explains at least partially our own
fascination with the construction of social identities, often en-
gagingly vivacious and flamboyant, and absorbed in public affairs,
and our consequent neglect of the lesser ostentations of relatively
private activities like reading.

4

As one (synecdochic) example of this fascination we might consider the case of George Puttenham, whose *Arte of English Poesie* I scrutinize below for the light it sheds on reading practices. Until recently, Puttenham's treatise had often been considered, in Derek Attridge's words, "as a charming but unsophisticated and inconsistent potpourri of Renaissance commonplaces" (18); he is mentioned only in passing in Margaret W. Ferguson's *Trials of Desire: Renaissance Defenses of Poetry,*[3] and at that only three times, twice in reference to a single quote about allegory. In 1976, Daniel Javitch devoted a chapter of *Poetry and Courtliness in Renaissance England* to demonstrating that "to be a good poet entails being a proper courtier":[4]

> Puttenham encouraged indirection and ambiguity in language because he realized that the pleasures derived from poetry are related to the way it obscures and retards the disclosure of its meaning.
> . . . He knew that the courtier delighted and appeared to best advantage by disguising himself in a manner that disclosed less than what was really there, more than was apparent. It was an extension of this knowledge that made him assert that the poet's chief skill was to delight with metaphor, leaving his audience to discover the larger meaning of his suggestions. (66)

The emphasis on metaphor and the disclosure of meaning sounds promising for somebody interested in the process of reading, and I use Javitch in my discussion of Puttenham, but his treatment concentrates on the parallels between "the poet's small devices and the courtier's deceptive ploys" (76) as social strategies to be employed, and so provides little information about how either metaphor or meaning is to be understood. This general approach is expanded to consider the use of art as both simulation and dissimulation by Frank Whigham, Heinrich Plett, and Louis Montrose.[5]

Derek Attridge's Derridean reading of Puttenham concentrates on the relation between nature and art, more specifically, on the instability of their relation: art is a supplement to nature, curing ills and adding to what is already complete, but the best art is in itself a kind of nature.[6] Jonathan Crewe focusses on Puttenham's history of dramatic forms to argue that it "implies a view of theater as a major hegemonic institution of the state. . . . public drama—and hence public theater—alone possesses the ability to institute hegemonic control in a situation otherwise insusceptible to 'enlightened' or 'lawful' rule."[7] For Rosemary Kegl, Puttenham's "riddling disclosure is a form of politic courtliness which reproduces courtly relations and, in the process, offers the court's internal struggles as a model for larger struggles over gender and class."[8]

For all of these recent studies, Puttenham's treatise functions socially; as Louis Montrose says, "by representing the world in discourse, texts are engaged in constructing the world and in accommodating writers, performers, readers, and audiences to positions within it."[9] I think it would be more accurate to say that we (the people who write and read books like this one or articles like Montrose's) are so implicated in a textual world, especially in dealing with events that occurred centuries ago, that texts (and how we manipulate them) do in fact constitute the historical world for us. Whether this was true for the people who lived out their lives in that world—whether even Lady Jane Grey, who was more interested in private reading than most of her contemporaries, would see her life as constructed by texts—is an altogether different question, and one I will not venture into here. Suffice it to say that in our textual reconstruction of past ages it is possible to distinguish (or perhaps construct) two complementary realms or domains of experience, one corresponding roughly to the social, the other, to the private, and that to understand the past it is necessary to attempt to understand both.

There are, naturally, limitations to any such project:

> Any attempt to examine the ways in which the question of literary language was conceived of and discussed in a period as historically and culturally distant from our own as the English Renaissance involves difficulties that cannot finally be overcome. We cannot step outside the structures of thought and habits of mind with which we perceive the past, nor can we make ourselves fully

conscious of the motivations and assumptions that propel our investigation and determine what we see and what we give weight to. However, as long as we recognize that our findings can never be verified, and that many "historical" readings have come to look, with the further passage of history, like little more than the enlisting of past texts in current theoretical and ideological battles, we ought to be able to muster sufficient skepticism and scrupulousness to perform a useful task of recovery and revaluation.[10]

Though my topic is reading rather than literary language, Derek Attridge has so gracefully anticipated what I would have said about the limitations of such a study that I cannot forbear using his words. I am especially conscious that the structures of thought and habits of mind with which I perceive the past are different from— and, I hope, interestingly complementary to—those of many engaged in Renaissance (or early modern) studies; the cognitive approach I take is explained in the appendix (as is Reddy's toolmakers paradigm, of which Attridge's comments are an example). My conception of the relation between the individual and the group is informed (and perhaps even formed) by general approaches in the field of cognitive science, the intersection of linguistics, psychology, computer science (particularly artificial intelligence), and philosophy. Although there are (as might be expected) a number of different schools constituting this enterprise, we might characterize them as generally subscribing to the view called by George Lakoff and his associates "experiential realism" or "experientialism":

The experientialist approach is very different: to attempt to characterize meaning in terms of *the nature and experience of the organisms doing the thinking.* Not just the nature and experience of individuals, but the thinking and experience of the species and communities. "Experience" is thus not taken in the narrow sense of the things that have "happened to happen" to a single individual. Experience is instead construed in the broad sense: the totality of human experience and everything that plays a role in it— the nature of our bodies, our genetically inherited capacities, the

modes of our physical functioning in the world, our social organization, etc.[11]

Lakoff's attempt to relate meaning to those who experience (or
better: construct) it includes attention to social organization, yet I
think one should be wary of abstracting too quickly from the
experience of individuals to that of "species and communities." I
would argue that whatever social groupings one belongs to, their
influence on behavior must be mediated through individual psychological mechanisms.[12] Thus although one might derive individual interpretive strategies from the practice of the interpretive
community to which one either belongs or aspires to belong, it is
the individual interpretive strategies, internalized and represented
in perhaps idiosyncratic ways, that are the source of behavior. The
relation between individual and social roots of behavior has become a site of contention, and it would be wise to explain my own
approach as clearly as possible. It stems from relatively straightforward observations: for instance, I stop my car at a red traffic light.
This is clearly socially or culturally situated behavior—traffic lights
don't exist naturally, and their significance derives from the social
semiotic in which they are embedded—and yet at the time of
stopping, my car often contains only me. There is nobody physically present to remind me of the social expectations or my obli-
gations in the situation; instead I abide by them because of some
internal representation I have previously constructed.

My conception of the relation between the individual and the
group is thus similar to Bourdieu's habitus ("the durably installed
generative principle of regulated improvisations"):[13]

the habitus could be considered as a subjective but not individual
system of internalized structures, schemes of perception, conception, and action common to all members of the same group or
class and constituting the precondition for all objectification and
apperception. . . . Since the history of the individual is never anything other than a certain specification of the collective history of
his group or class, *each individual system of dispositions* may be

8

seen as a *structural variant* of all the other group or class habitus. "Personal" style, the particular stamp marking all the products of the same habitus, whether practices or works, is never more than a *deviation* in relation to the *style* of the period or class so that it relates back to the common style not only by its conformity . . . but also by the difference which makes the whole "manner." (86)

These individual structural variants, or personal styles, are the result of idiosyncratic experience of the possibilities available to the class or group:

> The principle of these individual differences lies in the fact that, being the product of a chronologically ordered series of structuring determinations, the habitus, which at every moment structures in terms of the structuring experiences which produced it the structuring experiences which affect its structure, brings about a unique integration, dominated by the earliest experiences, of the experiences statistically common to the members of the same class. Thus, for example, the habitus acquired in the family underlies the structuring of school experiences (in particular the reception and assimilation of the specifically pedagogic message), and the habitus transformed by schooling, itself diversified, in turn underlies the structuring of all subsequent experiences (e.g. the reception and assimilation of the messages of the culture industry or work experiences) and so on, from restructuring to restructuring. (86–87)

Bourdieu nicely captures the complex interaction between the internalized and that which has not yet been internalized: the external is never confronted directly, but only through the mediation of the *habitus,* which is itself the result of previous negotiations between the internal and the external. Interpretive strategies are constructed, at least in part, from already existing strategies. Of critical importance for this study is the insistence that schooling, or rather the habitus as transformed by schooling, forms the basis for the structuring of all subsequent experience.

9

Attractive as I find Bourdieu's view, my own differs from it in an extremely important way. Bourdieu valorizes the social over the individual—the history of the individual is a specification of the history of the group, which is primary, and individual style is thus (only, secondarily) a deviation from the style of the group. The view I advocate is visible in passing in the second quotation, where Bourdieu allows that the habitus integrates "the experiences statistically common to the members of the same class," and perhaps more fleetingly in the first in the reference to the "collective history of his group." The key words here are "collective" and "statistically": each member of the class or group either has an experience or doesn't have it, and either does or doesn't have it frequently enough for it to be internalized. For each member of a class, the individual experiences are primary, and there is nothing statistical or collective about them. "Statistically common," like "collective," is a concept available only from the deferred perspective of the outside observer; it is part of the apparatus for constructing groups out of individuals, for abstracting away from individuals and their individual experiences. It allows us to account for similarities in individual behavior, but it should not be allowed to obscure the fundamental point that people actually have experiences, while groups are only post hoc constructions. In discussing the method of reading that grammar school students learned I do in fact argue that all students internalized the same method because each had the same relevant educational experiences, but I understand that to be my conflation of a large number of individual internal representations based on a large number of individual experiences.

Clifford Geertz makes a more sophisticated attempt to subsume the individual in the group in distinguishing his own semiotic view of culture from that of the cognitive anthropologists.[14] Using a Beethoven quartet as an "admittedly rather special but, for these purposes, nicely illustrative, sample of culture" (11), he argues that

> no one, would, I think, identify it with its score, with the skills and knowledge needed to play it, with the understanding of it possessed by its performers or auditors, nor, to take care, *en pas-*

10

sant, of the reductionists and reifiers, with a particular performance of it or with some mysterious entity transcending material existence. The "no one" is perhaps too strong here, for there are always incorrigibles. But that a Beethoven quartet is a temporally developed tonal structure, a coherent sequence of modeled sound—in a word, music—and not anybody's knowledge of or belief about anything, including how to play it, is a proposition to which most people are, upon reflection, likely to assent. (11–12)

One can agree with his initial exclusions while still noticing how dependent is his final definition—whether we assent to it or not—on individual human perceptions. Without individual perceivers, there is no tone, no structure, no sound, and certainly no coherent structure or music; there are only sound waves, though without human agency it is difficult to see how even the waves that could potentially be perceived by a human as an excerpt from a Beethoven quartet could exist. It is experientialist rather than unnecessarily reductionist to observe that even the notion of "sound waves" presupposes a particular kind of observer, without whom all that would exist would be energy perturbations. One might notice the parallels with the TV and radio waves available in the atmosphere that only become TV or radio signals, and finally TV or radio, in the presence of the proper kind of receiver, and with the energy bursts, undetectable by humans, that dogs and other animals can perceive as signals. Geertz's example, despite his disingenuous presentation of it, is hardly innocent, since the ontological status of aesthetic objects has been debated for centuries, but if it indicates that some cultural manifestations cannot be identified entirely with knowledge of them, it also suggests how dependent they are on some kind of individual knowledge—the Beethoven quartet would not exist if *nobody* knew anything about it.

Whatever one's views about manifestations of culture in general, reading—the mental construction of meaning based on external written cues—constitutes a rather special case. Unlike a cock fight or matrimonial strategies (to cite two of the examples Geertz and Bourdieu discuss) reading is radically individual: while one

11

must participate with others in the cock fight or the matrimonial negotiations, reading must be done alone. If I read aloud to another person, only one of us is reading; if my wife wants to read something interesting to me, I have to stop my own reading to listen to her. As Walter J. Ong has observed, an audience loses its identity as a group when the lecturer asks it to read a handout and becomes instead a collection of individuals each pursuing an individual activity.[15] I should note in passing, without pursuing (as unnecessary for the present point), that the experientialist mentioned above would surely observe that the notion of an audience is itself only an illusion, the result of the same kind of belated aggregation Bourdieu and Geertz practice, since strictly speaking each audience member registers physically distinct stimuli even during the lecture—the sound waves that enter my ears are unavailable for yours.

Of all cultural practices, reading is generally seen as most similar to knowledge of a language, and for good reason. Both are socially situated but individually instantiated, and reading is quite clearly parasitic on the perception of language. But in an important respect they are utterly different: Noam Chomsky has repeatedly argued that the speed with which all normal children learn a language based on exposure to different (and possibly degenerate) samples of it suggests a large innate component, which might be conceived as a biological capacity for language which (like other biological organs) is triggered and shaped by the proper environment without being caused by it.[16] Reading is quite different: it does not develop naturally and universally, and there is no particular reason to think that it is part of a biological endowment. It is learned behavior, and thus culturally or socially inculcated in a way language is not. At the same time, it is radically individualistic, since—with the minor exception of beginning readers pronouncing aloud in unison—it can be pursued only by ignoring any others who happen to be around.

The similarity between language and reading suggests my approach to reading (or, more properly, interpretation, since I do not deal with decoding). Developing the Saussurian distinction between *langue* and *parole,* Chomsky has argued that linguistic competence—the internalized knowledge of language—must be distinguished from linguistic performance—the external manifestations of that internalized knowledge.[17] Competence may be represented as a series of rules, the specific details of which depend upon the particular brand of transformational theory one subscribes to, while performance is the result of applying these rules. Performance thus assumes a distinctly secondary role, important only insofar as it illuminates competence. My conception of reading, explained in greater detail in the appendix, is very similar: I conceive of reading as the application of a series of cognitive rules; the result of this activity is a "reading" or "interpretation" of a text or passage. These rules are what Jonathan Culler and Stanley Fish (and others discussed in the appendix) call "interpretive strategies," and they are derived from external models of reading provided both overtly (as in schools) and covertly (as in sermons). The goal of a historical study of reading, I would argue, should be the reconstruction of these interpretive rules which enable the performance of any particular reading.

In emphasizing the cognitive representation of a learned behavior, I have tried to present a relatively unified picture of reading processes. Sites of contestation are ubiquitous nowadays, and it would be surprising if reading were the only exception, but I have preferred to emphasize what my various sources share rather than where they differ, for two reasons. First, there is quite general agreement on the advice they give about reading. Whether this is due to actual agreement or to a limited vocabulary with which to discuss the topic is a nice distinction which I cannot resolve; in any case it should be clear from the outset that I am necessarily dealing with discourses about reading and not with what readers actually did. I think there is a close connection between the two—as I explain in the appendix, I believe that models are required for any behavior, and in Tudor England I simply have not discovered many competing models for reading—but it is naive to expect absolute identity.

Second, I have found Frank Whigham's notion of apparent

conflicts or even contradictions being homogenized in actual practice very appealing:

> I propose to homogenize the conceptual materials of courteous practice one step further, by arguing that most of the major texts were *formally* pliant to incremental use in social debate and self-presentation. . . . the arguments made in these texts were actively (not contemplatively) read, repeated, and enacted in a thoroughly discontinuous way that makes contradictions within or between individual texts insignificant, if not irrelevant. (27)

Whigham's topic is guidebooks to courtly behavior, such as Castiglione's *The Book of the Courtier,* but even making allowance for the differences between reading and the presentation of self in everyday life, it is clear that they are similar in their orientation toward praxis: manuals about both reading and behavior provide models for future action, and what appear from a modern perspective to be contradictory instructions may simply have been accepted at the time as complementary precepts applicable on different occasions (27).

In any case, as far as I can tell, I am embarking on relatively uncharted territory in this study, and it makes sense to me to try to provide a general map (see the appendix for a discussion of Bourdieu on maps and paths) before exploring hidden byways. In the introduction to *Renaissance Self-Fashioning,* Stephen Greenblatt remarks that "there is no such thing as a single 'history of the self' in the sixteenth century, except as the product of our need to reduce the intricacies of complex and creative beings to safe and controllable order" (8), but much as I sympathize with the democratic impulse behind this approach, I am not at all convinced that it is applicable to an instrumental practice (like reading) codified by a number of contemporary theorists. Instead of a need to impose controllable order I prefer to think of the kind of harmonization of sources I have engaged in as providing support for the strongest form of a hypothesis so that it is most vulnerable to empirical refutation and thus most stimulating to further research.

As a further stimulus, I quote liberally from these sources so readers can decide for themselves where my simplifications and selections have become vicious.

Simplification and selection are especially necessary in any study of literacy, since it is a topic which impinges on all areas of life; those who study it know how difficult it is to limit the focus of inquiry in any natural or even satisfying way. In particular, it may seem counterintuitive not to consider in some detail the content of what was read, especially in an age when reading so easily became a subversive activity and there was widespread religious and political censorship. My argument throughout this book, however, is that while there may have been many kinds of texts to be read, there were not many models of reading available for the Tudors; books or tracts were perceived as dangerous (which particular ones depending on one's situation) precisely because they were expected to be read in the serious and relatively utilitarian way I describe. Reading (of all kinds) was expected to have practical repercussions; reading the wrong sorts of texts could lead to the wrong sorts of actions. Roger Ascham's famous attack on romances and Italianate literature underscores this point:

> In our forefathers tyme, whan Papistrie, as a standing poole, covered and overflowed all England, fewe bookes were read in our tong, savyng certaine bookes of Chevalrie, as they sayd, for pastime and pleasure, which, as some say, were made in Monastaries, by idle Monkes, or wanton Chanons: as one for example, *Morte Arthure:* the whole pleasure of which books standeth in two speciall poyntes, in open man's slaughter, and bold bawdrye. . . . What toyes, the dayly readyng of such a booke, may worke in the will of a yong gentleman, or a yong mayde, that liveth welthelie and idlelie, wise men can judge, and honest men do pitie. (230–31)

Italian books are even more dangerous because they are more subtle: "they open, not fond and common wayes to vice, but such subtle, cunnynge, new, and diverse shiftes, to cary yong willes to vanitie, and yong wittes to mischief, to teach old bawdes new schole poyntes, as the simple head of an English man is not hable to invent, nor never was hard of in England before" (231).

Behind Ascham's denunciation is a set of assumptions about the efficacy of reading that are explored in this study, in particular the assumption that the effects of reading on the will and wit are all but unavoidable, propelling the reader irresistibly into practical application. Today "pastime" and "pleasure" have an innocently detached air about them, separate from the serious and important responsibilities of life, but—remembering Lady Jane Grey's distinction between the shadow pleasures of the court and the real pleasures of reading—it is not at all clear that this was true for the Tudors; indeed, I will argue that it was not.[18] And this renders questions of content less relevant: it was dangerous, politically and religiously, to read suppressed texts precisely because they would be read the same way authorized texts were, and would have analogous (but politically or religiously deleterious) effects.

Finally, I have taken seriously Robert Darnton's observation that reading practices exhibit a wide range of variation both temporally and geographically,[19] and have assumed that reading in Tudor England would be quite different from what it is today. This assumption may in fact be wrong, but I think it unlikely that one will be sufficiently vigilant to recognize differences without making it. To help others adopt this perspective I discuss numeracy in the appendix and return to it throughout the text as a kind of touchstone example of a skill mastered by all my readers, but one whose theoretical underpinnings remain more or less opaque to most of them. Perhaps even those with some interest in the theoretical foundations of mathematics may be able to use this comparison to catch themselves when they are about to object that the Tudors must surely have done (or thought) something or other by asking themselves whether they do (or think) something similar when a mathematical problem is involved (e.g., the apparently commonsensical assumption that readers have different strategies for reading religious and secular texts begins to seem somewhat less commonsensical when we ask ourselves whether the methods of addition and subtraction we use to balance our checkbooks differ from those we use to figure our deductions at tax time or to compute the grades for a course). This comparison also reminds us what it is like to have only one model for a skill: those who have not learned to add or subtract have not learned another method; they have simply not learned addition or subtraction. Students today arrive in secondary school and college with many models for making sense of texts, so it is an easy (and apparently natural) assumption that failure to master any particular method simply requires falling back on a different one. Mathematics reminds us what happens when there is no different one.

CHAPTER 2

EDUCATION AND READING IN TUDOR ENGLAND

In trying to reconstruct the reading practices of a previous era, the obvious place to start is the educational system of the time. In Tudor England, this was a various enterprise, with basic reading—decoding—in the vernacular taught in petty schools, dame schools, and by tutors, priests, parents, and friends (Edmund Coote provides some perspective when in the preface to *The English Schoole-Maister* [1596] he addresses "such men and women of trades [as Taylors, Weavers, Shop-keepers, Seamsters, and such other] as have undertaken the charge of teaching others"[1]). The kinds of interpretive skills engendered in the segment of the population that learned reading only at this level is a question considered in the chapters below treating religious instruction and the various books for self-improvement. In this chapter, we consider the kind of interpretive skills taught in the grammar schools, keeping in mind the fact that very few Tudor children actually had this experience. But the benefit of this defect (from the point of view of providing information about interpretive practices) is that the education provided for this minority was conducted with an intensity and thoroughness unparalleled today, and so—we may assume—its effects were more permanent.

T. W. Baldwin, who has provided a magisterial description of this system in *William Shakespere's Small Latin and Lesse Greeke*, characterized it as "simple but inhumanly thorough—at least on

18

paper. No wonder the masters had to flog the boys through it. One wonders how a human being, either teacher or boy, endured it. Not even Sunday was ordinarily free."[2] Students in grammar school were occupied from 6 in the morning until 7 or 8 at night with their schoolwork, with short breaks for meals and "beverage" (353–58). Memorization was emphasized, and rote learning was justified as appropriate for the age of the students. As Richard Mulcaster explained in *Positions* (1581), "*Reason* directs years, and *rote* rules in youth, *reason* calls in sense and feeling of pain, *rote* runs on apace and mindeth nothing else but either play in the end or a little praise for a great deal of pains."[3] Though there was variety in content, as different forms (or grade levels) used different texts, there was less variety in approach: everything was read and digested in more or less the same way. It is reasonable to think, it seems to me, that students who had been systematically drilled in a single kind of reading for several years would retain that kind of reading in their lives after school, just as with numeracy today.

In this chapter we first survey the field of educational theory, relying primarily on Erasmus and Vives, with occasional expansions from Eliot, Ascham, Mulcaster, and others, to determine what can be deduced about the teaching of interpretation from the best contemporary theory. We then consider various criticisms of contemporary teaching for the modifications they suggest in this picture. Finally, in this and the next chapter, we look at a number of practical examples of reading—Palsgrave's schoolroom translation of *Acolastus,* E. K.'s notes on *The Shepheardes Calendar,* Harvey's marginal notations and *Ciceronianus,* and finally, Harington's translation and notes to *Orlando Furioso*—to see how the characteristics of reading as inculcated in the grammar school appear in productions by adults for adult audiences.

Four aspects of this survey need special emphasis. First, though I will refer to "grammar school education," it cannot be assumed that every grammar school in England followed the same curriculum or inculcated precisely the same interpretive skills. Indeed, Baldwin's careful treatment of the differences in curricula indicates that the schools did not teach precisely the same texts, though

19

there is still reason to believe that they approached whatever texts they taught the same way. But even this assumption must be qualified, since Jo Ann Hoeppner Moran has recently argued (in *The Growth of English Schooling 1340–1548*) that before about the midpoint of the century—and in particular, the foundation deeds for York, Malton, and Hemsworth in 1547 and for East Retford in 1551—there is generally "no hint of any humanist influence" or curriculum in earlier foundations recorded in wills in the York diocese.[4] The spread throughout England of the educational practices I discuss thus cannot simply be assumed, and the reading practices I derive from a grammar-school education must be understood to be the practices of students who attended grammar schools organized along the lines of the Erasmian principles I discuss. Later in the chapter I consider the likely effects on students of teachers who employed other methods. Second, these educational theorists do not treat interpretation directly; for them it was simply a means to the end of writing and speaking elegant and persuasive Latin. The interesting educational consequences of this presupposition rather than teaching of interpretation will be treated below. Third, I do not intend to provide an outline of humanist education, which has already been done;[5] I only wish to highlight those elements of it that concern the method of reading. Finally, I do not think the students exposed to this kind of Erasmian education formed a "textual community" in Brian Street's sense of a "microsociet[y] organized around the common understanding of a script,"[6] any more than numerates today form special subsocieties: they had internalized highly similar procedures for understanding written texts, but unless they were in close contact after school, this ability alone would not have united "individuals who previously had little else in common . . . around common goals" (37).

"In the treatise *De Ratione Studii* by Erasmus is the fundamental philosophy of the grammar school in England. On these general principles it was organized and by these methods it was taught." So claims T. W. Baldwin (94), probably the greatest authority on Elizabethan secondary education, and so it is fitting to turn to Erasmus, and in particular to *De Ratione Studii* and *De Copia*[7] (actually, *De duplici copia verborum ac rerum commentarii duo*), the textbook on abundance of style dedicated to John Colet and the schoolboys at St. Paul's School, for an explanation of the aims, benefits, and methods of reading. *De Ratione* was originally written as a guide for Thomas Grey, one of Erasmus's students (665, fn 1). In it Erasmus intended to outline "an ordered course of study so that, following it like Theseus' thread, you may be able to find your way in the labyrinths of letters" (665); the treatise is thus an explanation of what a tutor should know about the method of teaching letters (it should come as no surprise that Erasmus's methods have a long history: see Grafton and Jardine, 1–28 and 210–20, for Renaissance and classical antecedents; and Baldwin for the English influence of Erasmus). For boys, Erasmus argues, "the true ability to speak correctly is best fostered both by conversing and consorting with those who speak correctly and by the habitual reading of the best stylists" (669). After listing the authors he considers the best for this, he concludes by recommending that the teacher become completely familiar with "Lorenzo Valla, the extremely elegant arbiter of elegant Latin" so that he will be able to recognize and pass on to his students (for both speaking and writing) the ingredients of correct Latin and Greek:

> Aided by his precepts you will notice much for yourself; for I would not like you to follow Valla's precepts slavishly in everything. It will be an additional aid if you learn off the grammatical figures set out by Donatus and Diomedes; memorize the rules of poetry and all its patterns; have at your fingertips the chief points of rhetoric, namely propositions, the grounds of proof, figures of speech, amplifications, and the rules governing transitions. For these are conducive not only to criticism but also to imitation. (670)

Here we find the typical Erasmian combination of memorization and independence: the teacher (who is himself first a student) begins by memorizing the various aspects of rhetoric (just as modern students memorize the addition tables), and this internalized knowledge allows him to "notice much" for himself. Erasmus's advice on this introductory rote learning of the necessary tools anticipates Mulcaster's and suggests how such memorization can be made almost subliminal:

> It will be of considerable help if you take things which it is neces-
> sary but rather difficult to remember—place names in geography,
> for instance, metrical feet, grammatical figures, genealogies, and
> so forth—and have them written as briefly and attractively as pos-
> sible on charts and hung up on the walls of a room where they are
> generally conspicuous even to those engaged in something else. In
> the same way, you will write some brief but pithy sayings such as
> aphorisms, proverbs, and maxims at the beginning and at the end
> of your books; others you will inscribe on rings or drinking cups;
> others you paint on doors and walls or even in the glass of a win-
> dow so that what may aid learning is constantly before the eye.
> (671)

Surrounded as they are by reminders of the earnestness of education, students are in the pedagogical equivalent of the Forest of
Arden, with its tongues in trees, books in running brooks, and
sermons in stones; whether they responded as enthusiastically as
the duke is another question. And while it strikes us as unlikely
that many classrooms were decorated in this Erasmian style, we
must remember that students were often taught their letters by
being presented with cookies in alphabetic form which they could
eat when they had exhausted their pedagogical value,[8] and that
cups and walls were often painted with moral lessons, as they are
in Erasmus's colloquy entitled *Convivium Religiosum*.[9] In any case,
the very suggestion testifies to the seriousness with which memorization of the basic elements of education was approached. Knowledge of metrical feet and figures of grammar, as well as of genealo-
gies, maxims, and so forth, was a prerequisite for reading, just as
today knowledge of the addition tables is required for the activities
of adding and subtracting. And since what has been memorized is

what becomes noticeable in the future, we should expect Tudor readers to "see" metrical feet, figures of grammar, maxims, and so on when they read, even though our different training has rendered other aspects of the text more salient for us.

However, there is a limit to the utility of memorization. Rote may rule in youth, but for more mature students, the emphasis is on understanding, something made clear in one of the sample letters in *De Conscribendi Epistolis*.[10] Although originally an independent letter, in the treatise on letter writing it immediately follows a letter originally written to a former student, Christian Northoff (see Fantazzi's note on the letter, vol. 26, pp. 543–44) and so appears to contain advice applicable to more mature students, such as Northoff or Grey. It also contains Erasmus's most concise explanation of the method of reading he recommends for older students, perhaps those (such as Northoff or Grey) who are preparing themselves to tutor others:

> Some people's primary and almost sole anxiety is to learn things by heart, word for word. I do not approve of this as it involves much work and is practically useless. For what is the point of repeating parrot-fashion words that are not understood? There is a more suitable method. Review immediately a reading you have heard in such a way that you fix the general meaning a little more deeply in your mind. Then, go back over it, starting at the end and working back to the beginning, examining individual words and observing only points of grammar in the process: take note of any word that is obscure or of doubtful derivation, or belongs to a mixed conjugation, trace the formation of its supine and its past tense, its roots and derivatives, construction, meaning, and matters of this sort. After doing this, run through the passage completely again with particular attention to points of rhetorical technique. If any phrasing seems to have special charm, elegance, or neatness, mark it with a sign or an asterisk. Examine the arrangement of words, and the fine turns of expression. Analyze the author's purpose, why he phrased things in a certain way. When you find something particularly pleasing . . . ask yourself the rea-

23

son for being so taken by that expression and why you did not derive equal pleasure from the rest as well. You will find that you
have been impressed by the incisiveness of the language, or some
rhetorical embellishment, or harmonious arrangement or, not to
rehearse them all, for some similar reason.

But if there is some saying, maxim, old proverb, anecdote,
story, apt comparison, or anything that strikes you as being
phrased with brevity, point, or in some other clever way, consider
it a treasure to be stored carefully in the mind for use and imitation. When you have attended to those things carefully, do not be
reluctant to go over the passage a fourth time. . . . seeking out
what seems to relate to philosophy, especially ethics, to discover
any example that may be applicable to morals. . . .

If you do all this, you will end up learning the reading by heart
even though that was not your original purpose. Then if you like
you may turn to the task of learning by heart, which by that time
will either be non-existent or surely minimal. (194–95)

In his four readings (or hearings, if the master read the text aloud
to the class) of the text, the student first considers grammatical
questions, then rhetorical ones. The third reading is devoted to
finding matter worth saving, while the fourth provides the moral.
By the end of the fourth reading, the student will have extracted
whatever is useful from the passage, and further memorization is
nugatory. However, if the student insists on it, the understanding
gained from the successive readings will render it almost painless,
much as the lessons on drinking cups and walls were absorbed as
a normal part of everyday existence. But we should notice that
learning at this stage can no longer be considered rote, since understanding is a necessary condition.

The aspiring teacher, who has memorized the necessary preparatory material and read a text in the prescribed Erasmian fourfold
way, is predisposed to notice certain aspects of whatever he reads:

Informed by all this you will carefully observe when reading
writers whether any striking word occurs, if diction is archaic or

novel, if some argument shows a brilliant invention or has been skillfully adapted from elsewhere, if there is any brilliance in the style, if there is any adage, historical parallel, or maxim worth committing to memory. (*De Ratione*, 670)

Although Erasmus is here prescribing a reading method for the teacher rather than for the students, what the teacher notices is what he will be prepared to pass on to his students. From the point of view of reading practices, the most important aspect of this method is the habit of treating texts as collections of individual and potentially noteworthy segments. Words, arguments, adages, historical parallels, and maxims are what attract the reader's attention, not the overall structure of a text, its cohesive features, its macrostructure. Naturally, in presenting a text for discussion a teacher must segment it into manageable sections, but humanist education consistently emphasized the habit of seeing texts as collections of segments, particularly stories or examples. Commenting on Guarino's treatment of Cicero, Grafton and Jardine observe:

> It is as if the teacher had on his desk a beautiful completed jigsaw puzzle—the text. Instead of calling up his students to look at the puzzle, he takes it apart, piece by piece. He holds each piece up, and explains its significance carefully and at length. The students for their part busy themselves writing down each explanation before the piece in question vanishes into the box. And the vital question we have to ask ourselves is whether the accumulation of fragments which the student made his own could ever take the shape of the whole from which they originated. (20)

One might ask the same question about the students educated in England in an Erasmian system.

The second noteworthy aspect of Erasmus's method is that reading is an active engagement with the text; the reader does not simply absorb what is there, he questions both it and his own responses, even at the simplest levels of grammar and rhetoric.

25

Doubtful or difficult words are removed from the text so that their grammatical features can be considered. Arresting phrases are similarly treated, as the reader actively compares them with less successful expressions in the hopes of uncovering the author's purpose. Arguments are compared with their antecedents to see how they have been adapted. Finally, the reader must somehow personalize the text by marginal notations to reflect his involvement with it. In the letter this takes the form of asterisks, but in *De Ratione* Erasmus suggests a larger variety of signs: "Such a passage [i.e., containing a striking word, etc.] should be indicated by some appropriate mark. For not only must a variety of marks be employed but appropriate ones at that, so they will immediately indicate their purpose" (670). This advice, expanded in the compilation of commonplace books (the effects of which will be discussed below), suggests at least the beginnings of the kind of transactive approach to reading discussed in the appendix. The reader is not conceived as a passive recipient of a meaning already contained in the text, but as an active interrogator of every aspect of the text.

This interrogation leads naturally to the third important aspect: the fact that reading is always necessarily intertextual. Words, phrases, maxims, arguments, whatever the reader finds in the text, are related to their uses elsewhere. Even individual words are not seen simply as parts of a text, but rather as independent entities with grammatical characteristics the reader takes care to review. Any given text is thus radically intertextual, and reading becomes inherently comparative.

The aspiring teacher must apply this method of reading to a wide variety of texts: "even someone who is preparing to teach a very little is very widely read. He must, therefore, range through the entire spectrum of writers so that he reads, in particular, all the best, but does not fail to sample any author, no matter how pedestrian" (672), and Erasmus is happy to provide a list of the most necessary authors. The knowledge gained through this reading is preserved in a commonplace book: "And in order to enhance the value of that enterprise, he should have at the ready some commonplace book of systems and topics, so that whenever something noteworthy occurs he may write it down in the appropriate column" (672–73). We shall discuss the significance of these books below.

Thus prepared by at least four readings, not only of the text under consideration, but of all the necessary background texts as well, the teacher actually presents the text to his students. Erasmus is again worth quoting in full here, since it is this method that students would be exposed to incessantly during their years at grammar school.

> In the first place, the teacher should give a brief appreciation of the writer on whom he proposes to lecture, in order to win over his audience. Next, if (as is frequently the case) the tenor of the argument should offer a variety of applications, he should explain these and distinguish between them. For example, take a comedy of Terence. Before translating this he should first of all discuss briefly the author's circumstances, his talent, the elegance of his language. Then he should mention how much enjoyment and instruction may be had from reading comedy; next the significance of that form of literature, its origins, the number of types of comedy and its laws. Next he should explain as clearly and concisely as possible the gist of the plot. He should be careful to point out the type of meter. Then he should make a simple arrangement of these points and explain each one in greater detail. In this respect he should draw their attention to any purple passage, archaism, neologism, Graecism, any obscure or verbose expression, any abrupt or confused order, any etymology, derivation, or composition worth knowing, any point of orthography, figure of speech, or rhetorical passages, or embellishment or corruption. Next he should compare parallel passages in authors, bringing out differences and similarities—what has been imitated, what merely echoed, where the source is different, where common, inasmuch as the majority of Latin works have their origin in Greek. Finally he should turn to philosophy and skillfully bring out the moral implications of the poets' stories, or employ them as patterns, for

example, the story of Pylades and Orestes to show the excellence
of friendship; that of Tantalus the curse of avarice. (682–83)

How widely these instructions were followed is a question I address later; for now, let us consider Erasmus's method to see how a
child exposed to the kind of interpretation he suggests would
conceive of reading a text.

Erasmus distinguishes between the teacher's introduction to the
text and his interpretation of it. The initial suggestions are designed to make the students more receptive to what they read:
in good Horatian fashion, the pleasure of the argument is first
stressed, and then its utility. After a brief introduction to the
author, the pleasure and benefit of the form are explained; later in
his treatise, Erasmus returns to "the nature of the argument in the
particular genre, and what should be most closely observed in it"
(687). Epigrams should be studied for their "pointed brevity,"
tragedies for "the emotions aroused, and especially, indeed, . . . the
more profound," comedies because they show "decorum . . . and
the portrayal of our common life . . . the emotions are more
subdued: that is, engaging rather than passionate" (687). Other
forms are noted—"epic poetry, history, the dialogue, the fable,
satire, the ode, and other literary genres"—but Erasmus leaves it
up to the teacher to remind pupils of their "essential nature" (689).

Only after this introduction does the teacher turn to the text at
hand, providing first "the gist of the plot," which may be more a
statement of the argument than an actual plot summary, as the
example of Palsgrave's *Acolastus*, discussed later, indicates. The
meter, the various types of which the schoolboys had memorized
(perhaps from their drinking cups) is given a prominent place.
How seriously meter was taken can be judged by Ascham's anecdotes about it:

One man in Cambridge, well liked of many, but best liked of
himself, was many times bold and busy to bring matters upon
stage which he called tragedies. In one, whereby he looked to win
his spurs, and whereat many ignorant fellows fast clapped their

28

hands, he began the *protasis* with *trochaiis octonariis,* which kind of verse, as it is but seldom and rare in tragedies, so is it never used save only in *epitasi* when the tragedy is highest and hottest and full of greatest troubles. . . . Master Watson had another manner care of perfection, with a fear and reverence of the judgment of the best learned; who to this day would never suffer yet his *Absalom* to go abroad, and that only because *in locus paribus anapestus* is twice or thrice used instead of *iambus.*[11]

When the teacher finally reaches the text itself and begins to provide an interpretation, the basic division is between expression and content. First the selection is scrutinized for purple passages, archaisms, derivations, etymologies, and so forth, features of the text deriving from the first and second readings which might be useful for the schoolboys either to employ or to avoid in their own compositions. Students who used the first book of *De Copia,* which deals with abundance of expression, would be especially aware of the possible alternatives to the expressions chosen by the author.

Although Erasmus does not mention it here (perhaps because he feared its abuse; see below), at this stage also presumably comes the learned commentary on the personages and places of the passage. Vives is quite clear about this aspect of the presentation:

It is a mistake to suppose that a subject has been taught sufficiently, when the teacher follows the Stoic manner, by indicating a few points. If the name of a man be stated, and he is renowned for warlike deeds, or for wisdom and is distinguished for his knowledge of things, or even if the man named was notorious by his hateful deeds, let it be shown where he was born, who were his parents, and the principle matters which have connection with his reputation, at any rate those things which chiefly are necessary for the understanding of the passage. Let the teacher deal thus both with what is praiseworthy and what is blameworthy. Let the teacher state the most important chronological dates. . . . Then he will point out, so as to make all things easy, those things which have connexion with the subject-matter about which he is speak-

29

ing: the city, mountain, river, fountain; where is the site, how far
it is distant from some well known place, e.g. from the Alps,
Pyrenees, from the city of Rome . . . ; what noble men the place
has produced, what special products are to be found there, then if
anything remarkable has happened in that place. An animal, or
plant, or stone should be briefly described, and anything concerning its nature and qualities should—as far as possible and in the
most attractive way—be noted and described.[12]

Though Vives continues, this passage sufficiently indicates that
the medieval tendency toward encyclopedic commentary is not
entirely dead in humanist education.

What we might be tempted to call intertextuality is the second
concern, as the teacher turns to identifying parallel passages and
discussing their significance (this is the result of the third reading, which identified interesting maxims, anecdotes, etc.). Ascham
provides more detail about how this comparison is to be accomplished. The method, which he derives from Cheke and Sturm, is
simple:

But if a man would take this pain also, when he hath laid two
places of Homer and Virgil or of Demosthenes and Tully together, to teach plainly withal after this sort:
　1. Tully retaineth thus much of the matter, these sentences,
these words.
　2. This and that he leaveth out, which he doth wittily to this
end and purpose.
　3. This he addeth here.
　4. This he diminisheth here.
　5. This he ordereth thus, with placing that here, not there.
　6. This he altereth and changeth either in property of words, in
form of sentence, in substance of the matter, or in one or other
convenient circumstance of the author's present purpose. In these
few rude English words are wrapped up all the necessary tools and
instruments wherewith true imitation is rightly wrought withal in
any tongue. (118)

Although the procedure is simple, its pedagogical effects are not insignificant. First we might note again the dissociation of the passage from its location in the text under consideration: what is important is not the function of the passage, but its literary affiliations. More important, however, is the habit thus inculcated of seeing each passage—for Erasmus (though not necessarily Ascham) implies that each passage will be treated this way—as a representation of material already extant. *Nihil sub sole novum*—and the student is led to think of reproduction rather than production; everything (or almost everything) read is expected to be *imitatio,* as Ascham explains it, either *dissimilis materei similis tractatio* or *similis materei dissimilis tractatio* (117). Again, this is a characteristic of humanist education that can be traced to Guarino:

> Classical Latin vocabulary, like that of any sophisticated literary language, is highly complex. Any word has a broad range of more or less unexpected connotations; for, once a major author has used it in a particularly attractive extended sense, or made it part of an elegant metaphor, others will make a point of imitating him. The great Roman writers—the authors who formed the backbone of the curriculum—pitched their work at a small and highly literate audience, trained to detect and enjoy such covert allusions. After several hundred years of Latin literature, the language was developed into a tissue of implicit allusion, glancing references to metaphors and quotation from elsewhere in the canon, and similar plays on words. Renaissance humanists recognized quite early that this was a game the Romans had played—a game fostered by the habit of comparing Latin works with their Greek prototypes. The problem was to find a way of teaching the rules to students who could not immerse themselves in the classics as Petrarch might have done. (Grafton and Jardine, 11–12)

Finally, the teacher turns to the result of the fourth reading, what Erasmus calls "philosophy," which is presented somewhat misleadingly as merely the final step of the process. But it is possible to argue that this is the most important one; after all, Erasmus

31

had begun *De Ratione Studii* valorizing things over words—"in principle, knowledge as a whole seems to be of two kinds, of things and of words. Knowledge of words comes earlier, but that of things is the more important" (666)—and even though his famous work on richness of style (which, we should remember, is titled *De duplici copia verborum ac rerum commentarii duo*) is most famous for its scores of variations on the sentences "Your letter pleased me mightily" and "Always, as long as I live, I shall remember you," the longest section in the whole work, by far, is the one devoted to the use of examples, likenesses, and so forth for the purpose of expanding matter (605–35). Here he considers the use of commonplaces, examples, parallels, likenesses, maxims, fables, dreams, fictional narratives, and scriptural allegories.

For Erasmus, the moral implications of a text—or more precisely, of the passages and examples suitable for collection in a commonplace book—can be variously conceived. In the section of *De Copia* which treats the use of examples, he first distinguishes between historical and fictional examples—the former actually occurred, while the latter have been feigned by poets to make a particular point—and then complicates (one hesitates to say deconstructs) the distinction. Real examples— "We include under 'examples' stories, fables, proverbs, opinions, parallels or comparisons, similitudes, analogies, and everything else of the same sort" (607)—wear their meanings on their sleeves. Fictional examples, however, require interpretation:

> Although the principle of the allegory or hidden meaning is not equally obvious in every case, experts in antiquity are agreed that under all the inventions of the ancient poets there does lie a hidden meaning, whether historical, as in the story of Hercules fighting the twin-horned Archelous; or theological, as in that of Proteus turning into all kinds of shapes or of Pallas springing from the head of Jove; or physical, as in the story of Phaeton; or moral, as in the case of the men whom Circe turned into brute beasts with her cup and wand. Quite often there is a mixture of more than one type of allegory. (611)

32

After explaining the significance of various Homeric stories, he defers to Eustathius, for "any number of interpretations of this sort can be found" there (612–13). (For similar interpretations, though of "facts" from natural history and adages from the classics, one might turn to Erasmus's own *Parabolae*.[13])

Complicating the distinction between the fictional and the factual is the habit cultivated by the poets of including factual material in their fictions—"Certainly there is no doubt that a good many incidents in Virgil and particularly in Lucan are real historical events" (613) and although much of what is presented as fact, especially by Herodotus and Xenophon, is fiction, "poetry provides a lot of material which is to be taken as genuine historical fact, dealing for example with Scipio, Hannibal, Augustus, Pompey, or Julius Caesar" (614). More tellingly, fictions specifically created by poets to function as examples have the same force as factual examples:

> again, poetry also offers passages which no one would deny are fictional, but since it is generally accepted that they were invented precisely for the purpose of functioning as examples, and what is more were invented by great writers, they have all the weight of examples; I mean things like the goddess Envy, Rumor, Discord . . . and also characters in dramatic or mixed poetry, especially comedy. (614)

The most important consideration, as we should expect, is finally rhetorical, based on what an audience will accept: discussing Herodotus and the *Cyropaedia* (which he considers "more a manifesto on the training of the young than as a genuine historical record") he argues that "If the audience take these as true, they will be effective because people believe them; if they take them as inventions, since they are the productions of wise and revered authors, they will be effective for the very reason that they were put out by men whose authority gave what they wrote the force of precept" (614). History is persuasive because it actually happened; fiction is persuasive because it mimics history, because people recognize its intent to mimic history, or because it can be given an allegorical interpretation.

This emphasis on the effect of the passage on the reader is closely related to—and in a sense justified by—the practice of compiling commonplace books, a topic to which Erasmus devotes a good deal of attention in *De Copia*. The student provides himself with a list of subject headings which "will consist partly of the main types and subdivisions of vice and virtue, partly of the things of most prominence in human affairs which frequently occur when we have a case to put forward" (637). In the latter category are examples ("things like: remarkable longevity, vigorous old age, old head on young shoulders, remarkable happiness") and commonplaces, here conceived of as aphorisms ("It is very important what interests you develop as a boy; It matters what company you keep; . . . He gives twice who gives readily") or stock comparisons ("Is the married or unmarried state happier? public or private life?" [637]).

Educational theorists of the time differ among themselves about the details of what should go into the commonplace books. For Vives, for instance, they begin with the class notes the student takes:

> In a separate division, let him make history notes; in another,
> notes of anecdotes; in another, clever expressions and weighty
> judgments; in another, witty and acute sayings; in another, prov-
> erbs; in other divisions, names of well-known men of high birth,
> famous towns, animals, plants and strange stones. In another
> part, explanations of difficult passages in the author. In another,
> doubtful passages, which are still unsolved. These beginnings
> seem simple and bare, but later he will clothe and ornament
> them. The boy should also have a larger book in which he can put
> all the notes expounded and developed at length by the teacher,
> also what he reads for himself in the best writers, or the sayings he
> observes used by others; and just as he has certain divisions and
> heads in his note-books, so let him make indexes of these places

for himself and distinguish them by headings in order to know
what he shall enter in each division. (108)

Ascham is less encyclopedic and more systematic in his advice:
"Books of commonplaces be very necessary to induce a man into
orderly general knowledge, how to refer orderly all that he readeth
ad certa rerum capita and not wander in study" (107), but his terse
methodicalness reflects a point of greatest importance for the
study of reading and interpretation in this period: reading occurs
against a background always already known; the fundamental interpretive question to be asked of any passage is not "what does it
mean?" or "what is it?" but rather "what is it an example of?" Even
Erasmus, who allows more individual latitude than most of the
others ("But each person should draw up a list of vices and virtues
to suit himself" [*De Copia,* 636]) goes on to indicate how circum-
scribed this apparent freedom actually is: "I would not have him
putting into his lists every small hair-splitting division of a topic,
but only those that look as if they will be of use in speaking. This
can be discovered by looking at the topics that occur in various
types of speech" (636). The students learn to look for and value
what has been used in the past; reading is continual recovery
rather than discovery:

> So prepare for yourself a sufficient number of headings, and ar-
> range them into the appropriate sections, and under each section
> add your commonplaces and maxims; and then whatever you
> come across in any author, particularly if it is rather striking, you
> will be able to note down immediately in the proper places, be it
> an anecdote or a fable or an illustrative example or a strange inci-
> dent or a proverb or a metaphor or a simile. (638)

There is no hint that an incident could be so strange as not to fit
into—or be fitted into—the sufficient number of headings.

If the theorists differ about the details of the construction of
commonplace books, they agree on their utility. As we have seen,

35

Ascham stresses the role of preset topics in focussing attention. Erasmus and Vives agree that writing aids memory; as Vives puts it, "It is a very useful practice to write down what we want to remember, for it is not less impressed on the mind than on the paper by the pen, and indeed the attention is kept fixed longer by the fact that we are writing it down" (109–10). Finally, though this is a point only Erasmus raises, compilation of such a commonplace book gets "you in the habit of using the riches supplied by your reading" and it provides the materials for future speeches "whatever the occasion demands" (*De Copia*, 638).

That the theorists were generally unaware of how much the practice of compiling a commonplace book affected reading (undoubtedly because they considered it preparation for writing rather than a constituent of reading) is indicated by John Brinsley, writing early in the seventeenth century after commercially produced commonplace books had become familiar. In his view, individually compiled books were

> a great help where the scholars have the leisure and judgment to gather them; I mean, to glean out all the choice sentences and matter in the most Authors. Or, because that is an over-great toil, and requires more judgment than can be looked for in so young years; if they had but only books of References, it would be exceedingly profitable: to wit, such Common-place books as did but contain the general heads of the matter, and then the Quotations of three or four of the chief Authors; as, *Reusner, Erasmus Adages, Tullies* sentences, or some other; setting down the book and the page, where to turn of a sudden to any such matter in them. This would ease them of much searching, and make the scholars to do the exercises [themes] much sooner.[14]

Here commonplace books are seen simply as repositories of matter for themes, their earlier function of guiding reading—articulated most clearly by Ascham—completely forgotten.

The theorists were also indifferent to a possibility that strikes modern readers, who are used to being hurled into whatever *abyme* is handy: it is relatively easy to see how compiling a commonplace book could lead to a nascent recognition of the contingency of interpretation. Erasmus acknowledges that "some material can serve not only diverse but contrary uses, and for that reason must be recorded in different places" (639). The death of Socrates, for example, "can be used to show that death holds no fear for a good man, since he drank the hemlock so cheerfully; but also to show that virtue is prey to ill will and far from safe amidst a swarm of evils; or again that the study of philosophy is useless or even harmful unless you conform to the general pattern of behaviour. This same incident can be turned to Socrates' praise or blame" (639). That is, the "philosophy" or "moral implications" of a passage are not always straightforward, may in fact even be contradictory, and the existence of a commonplace book, with its myriad pigeonholes to be filled, could have encouraged an alert reader to use each passage for as many entries as possible. But for Erasmus, this is not a matter of great—or even minor—concern: the value of the story inheres not in the lasting verities it illustrates but in the ways it can be deployed, and an example that can be used in many different ways may well be more valuable, because more useful, than one that is more limited. Or, as Erasmus goes on to exclaim, "If you look at this example of Socrates and determine its successive scenes, how many subject headings will you thus elicit!" (639).

The existence—or preexistence—of the commonplace book thus severely constrains the teacher's explanation of the moral implications of a passage, the third step in Erasmus's method. The student is constructing a commonplace book, but the teacher has already compiled his own, and so in interpreting a passage and uncovering its moral implications the question is not so much "What could it mean?" as "Which of these preexisting possibilities is it an example of?" The idea of the commonplace book, with its topics set before reading begins, defines the possibilities for interpretation.

Throughout the pedagogical instructions in *De Ratione,* the emphasis is on utility: the teacher has stressed the benefits of the form or genre in his introduction to the text, and individual passages are considered as material for later use ("any etymology, derivation, or composition *worth knowing*"). Erasmus identifies the aims of his education (which is, after all, primary) as judgment and eloquence (689–91), so it is no surprise that he stresses whatever leads to one or the other when he turns to discuss in more detail the best way to teach tragedy and comedy:

> In tragedy, [the teacher] will point out that particular attention should be paid to the emotions aroused, and especially, indeed, to the more profound. He will show briefly how these effects are achieved. Then he will deal with the arguments of the speakers as if they were set pieces of rhetoric. Finally, he should deal with the representation of place, time, and sometimes action, and the occurrence of heated exchanges, which may be worked out in couplets, single lines, or half-lines. In comedy, he should show in particular that decorum and the portrayal of our common life must be observed, and that the emotions are more subdued: that is, engaging, rather than passionate. He should show that decorum especially is studied, not only in its universal aspect, I mean that youths should fall in love, that pimps should perjure themselves, that prostitutes should allure, the old man scold, the slave deceive, the soldier boast, and so on, but also in the delineation of different characters as developed by the poet. (687)

The eloquence of the student is developed by studying examples of rhetorical efficacy. Instead of using the Aristotelian categories we would find more congenial, Erasmus treats tragedies as examples of successful rhetoric in which the profound emotions are aroused, in part by the heated exchanges that are especially to be noted. How these emotions are aroused is an extremely important rhetorical question, so the means to those effects will be studied by themselves, and presumably also in the treatment of the speaker's arguments as rhetorical set pieces. (In *De Copia*, "vividness" is identified as "especially remarkable in messengers' speeches in tragedy" [578].) Rather than a passing glance at the classical dramatic unities, the reference to time, place, and action is related to a rhetorical concern with amplification or decoration by means of descriptions of times or places, as discussed in the sections on "Description of Places" and "Description of Times" in *De Copia* (587–89). Similarly, his emphasis on the decorum of character types in comedy is less related to dramatic criticism than to the fact that these types are useful in making a speech vivid and forceful: the section of *De Copia* devoted to using "descriptions of persons" as a means of achieving vividness discusses "characterization"—the use of types—and specifically mentions that "the comic poets especially seem to have aimed at a variety in characters belonging to the same general type" (584).

Having studied the means by which the passage achieves eloquence, the teacher turns to judgment: "he will not shirk from pointing out the merits or even the faults of particular authors in particular passages, in order that the young may become accustomed, even at so early an age, to employing what is, in everything, of paramount importance—judgment" (*De Ratione*, 689). Again the emphasis is on the judgment of "particular passages": young readers must learn to judge what is good in order to know what is worthy of emulation. And the judgment to be developed is related to a particular end: rhetorical efficacy. "Relevant to this [apparently the whole process of interpreting authors] is the theory underlying the literary form: why, for example, did Cicero feign fear in his defence of Milo; and what lies behind Virgil's eulogistic portrayal of Turnus, the enemy of Aeneas?" (690). "The theory underlying the literary form" is the theory of practical effects: the student must learn to judge the means employed to achieve certain ends so he can adapt them to his own purposes.

A student educated in accordance with this Erasmian ideal would thus have learned to read in a particular way. First, the reading itself would have been subordinated to a larger aim: that of gaining judgment and eloquence which would later be exhibited in the student's own conversation and composition. Second, the reading would occur in the context of fairly precise expectations about the benefits to be derived from specific genres. Third, reading would be of passages rather than of works: after a brief introduction to the beauties of the form and the author's background, the teacher would proceed through the work section by section, commenting on each one. There is never any suggestion that a work will be read as some sort of unified whole. Fourth, each passage would be read four times, the first two concentrating on various aspects of its presentation or style, and considering first grammar and then rhetoric. Next, each passage would be seen as the nexus of a rich intertextuality, echoing earlier works in various ways. In the final reading, the philosophy or moral implications of the passage, conceived in terms of the set topics of a commonplace book, are emphasized.

Of these characteristics, two—one the product of pedagogical necessity, the other of choice—are the most important. The first is the habit of considering passages rather than texts. On the one hand, this can lead to intellectual and moral benefits: in discussing the teaching of Terence, Joel B. Altman observes that the extraction of "moral precepts . . . from the plays without regard to their dramatic relevance" is "a striking instance of that search for general principles in the particular which we have observed elsewhere," "a source of *moral* instruction."[15] On the other is a perhaps less lofty consequence: students continually subjected to discussions of snippets will eventually focus on snippets. Although there is a problem of cause and effect, it is not impossible to see the period's fascination with witty sayings, apophthegms, sententiae, epigrams, proverbs, and so forth as directly related to this aspect of education.

This is not to suggest that the theorists or students of the age were ignorant of larger structures, such as the organization of a letter, oration, or theme. Indeed, the production of written documents is the basic aim of the educational system. But these larger structures were discussed by the theorists (and presumably taught by the teachers) in relation to writing rather than reading. Erasmus, for instance, suggests a series of writing exercises:

At one time [the teacher] should set out the subject-matter of a short but expressive letter in the vernacular which has to be construed in Latin or Greek or both. On another occasion he should set a fable; on another a short but meaningful narrative; on another an aphorism composed of four parts, with comparison between each of the two parts or with an accompanying reason attached to each. At one time the adducing of proofs should be dealt with in five parts; at another, the dilemma in two; at another what is called *expolitio* or refinement should be developed in its seven parts. (*De Ratione*, 678–79)

In Erasmus's presentation, subjects for translation into Greek or Latin lead naturally into the simpler forms of structure, and as the students become more adept at writing longer and longer exercises, these develop into the more elaborate structures of orations (or themes) and letters:

[The teacher] will regularly set out the argument of the persuasive, dissuasive, exhortatory, dehortatory, narrative, congratulatory, expostulatory, commendatory, and consolatory letter. He will point out the nature of each type, some features and set-phrases they have in common, and, once the argument has been set out, their peculiarities as well. . . . Furthermore he will show the order of the propositions and how one follows from another. Next, the number of reasons by which each proposition should be supported and the number of proofs of each reason. Then he will indicate sources for the circumstances and grounds of proof. . . . He should of course set out the principles governing connection and what form the best transition would take: from the opening section to the main outline; from the main outline to the division; from the division to the proofs; from proposition to proposition; from reason to reason; from the proofs to the epilogue or peroration. . . . Finally he should, if it is possible, point out some passages in authors where they [the students] may be able to take something for imitation because of its relevance to the task in hand. (680–81)

41

Drilled as they constantly were in the forms and parts of letters and themes or orations, it is unlikely that students could have escaped the grammar school without having internalized some feeling for larger forms. And this feeling would be of two kinds: one, the standard forms and parts of letters and orations, the exordium, narration, confirmation, confutation, and conclusion (see Brinsley, 172–73, 179). Second, the organization (or method) of argumentation, which Erasmus mentions here in terms of propositions with their proofs and transitions between the separate parts of the argument, and which properly is the province of dialectic. Here, for instance, is William Kempe, writing toward the end of the century:

> And by this time he must observe in authors all the use of the
> Arts, as not only the words and phrases, not only the examples of
> the arguments; but also the axiom, wherein every argument is dis-
> posed; the syllogism, whereby it is concluded; the method of the
> whole treatise, and the passages whereby the parts are joined
> together.[16]

In his recommendation of dialectic and rhetoric for advanced (fifth-form) students, Kempe is suggesting the kind of analysis one finds in William Temple's minute consideration of Sidney's *Apology*[17] and in other books of logic, such as Abraham Fraunce's analysis of Virgil's second eclogue in *The Lawiers Logicke*[18] or Dudley Fenner's of various Biblical texts in *The Artes of Logicke and Rhetorike*.[19] Temple, for instance, examines each argument separately and in painstaking detail, and the relation between adjacent arguments is explained. At the end there is a consideration of the "method" or organization of the whole work, but it is relatively short and thus seems to correspond to Erasmus's "gist of the plot," which the teacher should explain to his students before he begins detailed treatment of any specific passage. That is, while the teacher may outline the overall structure of the work, it is the individual segments which get detailed attention. Students will thus learn a method of reading that nods at larger structures while concentrating on the individual passages which comprise it.

The second important characteristic of the educational system is the habit of constructing commonplace books as a preparation for future writing or speaking, in particular, as Altman has reminded us, in preparation for arguments "*in utramque partem—* on both sides of the question" (3). This provided a concrete teleology for reading: students never "just read"; they were always reading, as Ascham recommended, with their attention directed to the collection of commonplaces of various kinds. All of the mechanisms of reading are subordinated to a goal that is not any part of the process, but rather its product. These mechanisms thus become psychologically and pedagogically opaque, presupposed rather than predicated, just as the presuppositions of a sentence must be assumed to be valid for the truth value of the sentence to be questioned. To return to my earlier comparison, they are like the operations of addition and subtraction, which we unthinkingly internalize because we are interested more in the answer than in how we arrive at the answer. For Tudor grammar-school readers, close attention to the language, construction, and antecedents of short passages became the normal way to read at least partially because it was never presented as a method of reading that might be contrasted to other methods of reading; instead, it is the always already assumed way to prepare for the reuse of what is read. It is never, as it is today, a goal in itself that might be interrogated for utility or efficacy.

But the commonplace books served another function as well: they validated interpretation. One of the primary problems in any discussion of interpretation is the justification of interpretations, of what kind of evidence can be brought forth in favor of one or another competing interpretation. For Tudor readers, the commonplace book provided the yardstick: a passage was understood "correctly" or "sufficiently" when it could be located within a commonplace book, when it was understood as an example of one of the topics previously specified. And even though Erasmus realized that one example might illustrate more than one common-place, and so potentially allowed the possibility of multiple inter-pretations, his advice is concerned primarily with the use one makes of the commonplaces once they have been compiled: the same example may be used to develop two quite different argu-ments. There is never any suggestion that readers should actively try to relate passages to more than one commonplace, that is, should cultivate multiplicity of interpretation.

Once ensconced in a commonplace book, an example is natu-rally seen as closely related to the other selections gathered under the same heading; in fact, as more closely related to them than to other passages in the work it came from. The juxtaposition of one passage with others illustrating the same place encourages an awareness of intertextuality and thus validates the emphasis on intertextuality in teaching: since different versions of stories, fa-bles, examples, and so forth by different authors will illustrate the same point, teachers (who have constructed their own ency-clopedic commonplace books before beginning their pedagogical duties) will find in their commonplace books the necessary re-sources for the comparative study of texts. And once they have presented the comparisons to the students, the two passages will presumably appear side by side in the students' own commonplace books, where they will provide the context for each other.

The conception of knowledge that underlies these characteris-tics of reading, and indeed, the entire educational system, is radi-cally static; after more than 1,400 pages of attention to the gram-mar school alone, Baldwin concluded, "Whatever the sixteenth century was, intentionally original it never was. Its avowed philos-ophy and conscious practice was through imitation so to analyze the old that by imitative synthesis the old might be reincarnated in the new" (II, 677).

What is lacking in this whole process, from our point of view, is any conception of reading as an end in itself, as a pleasurable aesthetic experience valuable in its own right. Corresponding to this is a lack of our reverence for the integrity of the work: in Erasmus's presentation the text is, to use a favorite Tudor metaphor, a garden from which the reader gathers blooms for his own nosegay. It is not so much that there is a different concept of authorship and creativity in operation here as that there is a strikingly different conception of the purpose of reading. Authors may be appreciated—even perhaps venerated—but it is because they have produced something that the reader can use and not simply contemplate and enjoy; it was expected that the words of a dead man would be modified in the guts of the living. Finally, there is a remarkable lack of surprise or novelty: "the moral implications of the poets' stories," like the characteristics of the genres (in tragedy, "attention should be paid to the emotions aroused," while in comedy, "decorum especially is studied"), seem as precisely defined as the rhetorical figures or meters the student will learn to identify. While allowance must be made for the fact that Erasmus is writing an educational tract, and an elementary one at that, still it is hard not to notice the extent to which reading is expected to confirm rather than to challenge previous knowledge.

Grafton and Jardine have reminded us that there is a considerable gulf between pedagogical theory and what the student actually derives from a lesson ("the printed texts [here of Ramus's commentary on Cicero] capture to the letter the experience of the controversial teacher at work; what they do not capture is the student's vain attempts to follow the teacher in action" [166; cf. 87, 89]). There is thus no guarantee that students in grammar school in Tudor England necessarily adopted the kind of reading I have been describing. However, two kinds of information provide evidence that the basic characteristics of reading I have established above would be widespread. First, if this method is what schoolboys would have learned from "the best masters," it is possible to infer from criticisms of contemporary methods of teaching what other boys, less fortunate in their teachers, would have learned. John Palsgrave, whose textbook translation of Fullonius's *Acolastus* we consider below, complained about those who "for to seem therein more diligent, than the common sort, spend in manner whole forenoons and afternoons, in the declaring of a few lines of such latin authors, as they for the season have in hand."[20] In this criticism he was echoing Erasmus, who had earlier warned his prospective teacher against contemporary practices: "Now in reading authors I should not like you to follow the practice of today's common run of teachers who, through some perverse ambition, attempt to treat every passage as a text for exhaustive disquisition, but would like you to confine yourself to those points alone which are relevant to the interpretation of the passage under consideration—unless the occasional digression seems appropriate to enhance their enjoyment" (*De Ratione,* 682). And Gabriel Harvey, in *Ciceronianus,* an oration he delivered to the students of Cambridge in 1576, complained about professors who devote too much time to digressions:

> Again they like to discuss for a few hours—nay, not such a mere trifle as hours, but several weeks or months—matters which could be very easily explained in a half-hour or two, such as the state of the circumstances, the type of case, the thesis and the hypothesis. . . . They like to declaim by the clock on eloquence, perorate on glory, and speechify on nobility. They like to digress from the case into commonplaces and stray off to some popular and splendiferous topic or other.[21]

But there were voices on the other side also—Vives, we remember, had warned against the "Stoic" method of providing only minimal commentary—and the safest conclusion is that only the most disciplined teacher could constantly resist the temptation to display his learning before his scholars. Unfortunately, this learning was not always the kind most useful to the scholars. Harvey identifies the further problem that professors too often focus exclusively on expression to the detriment of content:

> Merely pointing out, as some have done, the ornaments of tropes and the embellishments of figures, without indicating the stores of arguments, the quantities of proofs, and the structural framework, seems to me tantamount to displaying a body that is surpassingly beautiful and lovely but deprived of sense and life. . . .

among so many interpreters of Cicero's orations and such illustrious university professors, how many are there to be found . . .
from whom you could expect anything but that hackneyed tune
of theirs: "This is a notable repetition; this is an elegant agnom-
ination; this is an appropriate transfer; this is an illustrious and
splendid translation, like an exceedingly bright star shedding
abundant light upon the oration." (87)

You will find these same men, in their interpretations of single
words, wherein there lurks nothing obscure, nothing involved in
any difficulty, considerably more loquacious than grackles, but
when it comes to explaining the subject matter itself, . . . or to expounding the usages of the Roman state and the statutes important for the commonweal and the preservation of the republic, or
to elucidating the whole sweep of ancient civilization—in fact, all
questions of politics, history, and thought you will find them
dumber than the very fish. (89)

Harvey must be taken with a grain of salt, of course, since he was
recommending his own Ramistic approach to Cicero's orations
and thus stressing the necessity of teaching dialectic and history,
but even so his criticism alerts us to the propensity of teachers
(even university professors) to dilate on what they know about and
ignore what they are ignorant of. Those who had mastered only
the necessary philology or rhetoric would expatiate on that, while
those who had worked up some background information about a
case treated in one of Cicero's orations would spend as much time
as possible on that, before the inevitable digression on eloquence,
glory, or nobility distracted them from the text for the rest of the
day. The danger here is the one Erasmus foresaw when he warned
that a great deal of background knowledge is necessary for teaching ("I shall not be content with the usual ten or twelve authors
but will demand the proverbial 'encyclopedia', so that even someone who is preparing to teach a very little is very widely read," [*De
Ratione*, 672]): those who lack the requisite knowledge must make
do with what they have, and that leads to hours (forenoons, weeks,
months) devoted to the teacher's hobbyhorse.

Boys who had been exposed to the "common run of teachers"—those who could not distinguish between appropriate and inappropriate digressions, or who agreed with Vives that a more compendious commentary was actually better for the students, or who rode their own hobbyhorses roughshod over the class—would be even more likely to consider a text as a series of unconnected passages to be studied independently. And when they considered a passage, they would be more likely to focus on its expression than on its content. They would be—to use a favorite metaphor of the period—collecting the flowers of previous authors, but their interest lay more in their own bouquets than in the ancient gardens they ransacked. Palsgrave provides a stereotypical example of the trope when he explains that he chose *Acolastus* as the subject for his ecphrasis because it was "a very curious and artificial compacted nosegay, gathered out of the much excellent and odoriferous sweet smelling gardens of the most pure latin authors" (55), but Harvey indicates how that metaphor should be modified into good practice: "from [Cicero's] pleasant gardens I began to pluck the fruits of reason as well as the flowers of oratory" (79).

Harvey alerts us to another distortion of the Erasmian approach that would affect those students who were exposed to the common run of teachers:

> There are some men, not ineloquent in my opinion and exceedingly eloquent in their own, who think that everything depends on their jotting down in a diary proper words, figurative words, synonyms, phrases, epithets, differences, contraries, similes, and a few notable maxims; after gleaning these from everywhere, they compile them into commonplace books. (91)

This obvious echo of Ascham indicates how the practice of compiling commonplace books could be perverted. Ascham had suggested compiling just such a notebook, but his advice was meant for beginners first learning Latin (18–19). His comments on the utility of a commonplace book "to induce a man into an orderly general knowledge, how to refer orderly all that he readeth *ad certa rerum capita* and not wander in study" (107) comes much later in his educational scheme as an example of *Epitome,* one of the methods he considers "fitter for the master than the scholar, for men than for children, for the university rather than for the grammar schools" (83).

As Harvey presents it, commonplace books too often contained primarily linguistic material, grammatical and rhetorical aids in the process of imitation. Presumably the teachers who could be more loquacious than grackles in their explanation of unproblematic words would be the ones to encourage this approach to the commonplace books, and their students would be limited to the purely verbal level in their reading, the benefits that compiling a commonplace book might confer in intertextuality or confirming of interpretations lost to them. In fact, his presentation of what he considers a rather innovative approach to Cicero suggests how far the educational system might have declined from the Erasmian ideal:

> Suppose that in reading Cicero one encounters any matter that is especially worthy of remark, such as a matter of grammar, rhetoric, dialectic, or (to carry the principle further) ethics, politics, physics, or even geography, or whatever has any other special virtue to commend it and has some fame and renown. If anything of that sort is encountered which has its own obvious importance, I should like to have it very plainly indicated by the teacher and very thoroughly understood by the pupil. (97)

This is almost precisely the Erasmian formula for good teaching, and the fact that Harvey presents it as innovative some sixty-five years after the first publication of *De Ratione Studii* suggests that many teachers in the meantime had concentrated their efforts on grammatical and rhetorical matters worthy of remark and had ignored, to a greater or lesser extent, content.

The second kind of evidence for the spread of the kind of reading I have outlined derives from educational materials. Like many educational programs, Erasmus's is idealistic; he himself admits that "someone will criticize all this [his whole method of teaching] as involving too much hard work" (*De Ratione Studii*, 690). Is there any evidence that it was actually put into practice? Baldwin argues that "the curricula of English grammar schools are founded squarely upon the authors designated by Erasmus, and the methods pursued in teaching them are those suggested by him" (130), but his accounts of the schools, detailed as they are about what the students read and wrote, do not provide much actual evidence about how the teachers presented the reading materials to the boys, and thus are less useful in our inquiry. Instead, we must turn to other sources. One of the best of these, both for criticizing what other teachers do and for providing a clear example of what he does, is John Palsgrave's *Acolastus*. Palsgrave intends his "ecphrasis" or explanation of Fullonius's Latin play to complement the Latin grammar (known, not entirely accurately, as Lily's[22]) that Henry had approved for use throughout England: just as the universal use of that grammar "intended, that every school of your Grace's realm, should begin to wax one self school," Palsgrave wanted to provide a means for "one steady and uniform manner of interpretation [i.e., translation] of the latin authors into our tongue" (4). His title page indicates what he feels is necessary: first, a translation, "after such manner as children are taught in the grammar school, first word for word, as the latin lieth, and afterward according to the sense and meaning of the latin sentences" (sig. B). This first stage provides the students with not only the English translation, but also information about the difference between Latin and English style, and is intended to prevent the scholars from becoming competent in Latin while remaining unable to express themselves acceptably in English. (In this Palsgrave differed from contemporary schoolmasters; Baldwin notes that "most schoolmasters were intensely interested in preventing their students from using English at all, rather than teaching them to use it well" [182].) Second, some indication is necessary of "Adages, metaphors, sentences, or other figures poetical or rhetorical" (sig. B) which are identified in the margins throughout. Third, he recommends an introduction to meter: "afore the second scene of the first act, is a brief introductory to have some general knowledge of the divers sorts of meters used of our author in this comedy. And afore Acolastus' ballad is showed of what kinds of meters his ballad is made of" (sig. B). Finally, there is some consideration of rhetorical composition: "afore the sixth scene of the fourth act, is a monition of the Rhetorical composition used in that scene, and certain other after it ensuing" (sig. B).

Bearing in mind that no book can reproduce all that a teacher can do in the classroom—Palsgrave thought his book would ease the masters and students of "three parts of their pains" so "the masters have both time and better occasion, to open their farther learning, and to show unto their scholars the great artifice used of the authors, in the composition of their works, which aforetime they had no such opportunity to do" (11)—it is instructive to see how much of Erasmus's approach is reproduced in the book. Palsgrave does not supply the kind of introduction Erasmus suggests, probably because Fullonius is a contemporary, and since *Acolastus* was specifically composed as a text, its benefit is relatively clear. The text (the story is the Prodigal Son) offers a "variety of interpretations," but Palsgrave leaves them to the teacher to explain, just as he leaves it to the teacher to "mention how much enjoyment and instruction may be had from reading comedy" (*De Ratione*, 683). The gist of the plot is supplied by Fullonius's own "Argument," but Palsgrave supplements this with "A declaration what the names used by the author in this Comedy, do signify" (13), explaining, for instance, that the name of Acolastus's father, Pelargus Ciconia, signifies a stork, and then citing Pliny to establish the relevance of that fact. Following Erasmus's advice, Palsgrave devotes considerable attention to meter: the meter of each scene is identified, and the introduction to the topic promised on the title page is reasonably detailed, explaining various kinds of lines, feet, and scansion (including ellipsis and synaloepha), and providing sample scansions of two lines (41–44).

Erasmus next suggests that the teacher should treat various aspects of the language and style of the passage, emphasizing the cultivation of a correct and eloquent Latin style. It is here that the difference between Erasmus's project and Palsgrave's becomes apparent. Though Palsgrave regularly (if marginally) identifies Latin idioms, and less regularly points out Graecisms, elegances, and rhetorical devices (he says he is trying "to show the phrases, Adages, sentences notable, metaphors, elegances, or the eloquent words used of the author" [145], but he is not uniformly successful), his primary emphasis is on translating the Latin text into "the purest English" and on explaining the differences between English and Latin (6). Erasmus identified his aim as eloquence and judgment in Latin. Palsgrave, on the other hand, emphasized the ability to express oneself equally in English and Latin: a major failure of the current educational system, he argued, was that although many had become relatively expert in Latin, "they be not able to express their conceit in their vulgar tongue, nor be not sufficient, perfectly to open the diversities of phrases between our tongue and the latin" (6). The first benefit of his system, were it to be adopted across the country, would be that

> the English tongue, which under your Grace's prosperous reign is come to the highest perfection that ever hitherto it was, should by this occasion remain more steady and permanent in his endurance, not only by the well keeping of his perfection already obtained, but also have a great occasion to come to his most highest estate, and there, by that means long to be preserved. (10)

For Erasmus, words were a prelude to things—"Knowledge of words comes earlier, but that of things is the more important" (667). For Palsgrave, dealing exclusively with the more elementary levels of instruction, most (but as we shall see, not all) of the emphasis is on Latin words and phrases and their English counterparts (*not* equivalents). So although he identifies phrases in Latin, rather than assaying their purity as Latin, he stresses what he considers the purest English translation.

But almost as an illustration of what Erasmus would have wanted, Palsgrave does provide an "Observation of the Rhetorical composition used by the author in this scene next ensuing" before the sixth scene of the fourth act (145). Here he identifies (instead of the adages, etc., usually noted) "what schemes or exornations rhetorical the author useth . . . and what authors, as Terence, Plautus, Vergil, Seneca in his tragedies, he doth in these three scenes follow and imitate, and . . . show what kinds of arguments he useth" (146). In this introduction (and in the margins of the scene) he identifies the exornations—"anexis, exclamation, dubitation, collation of contraries, simulations, precision, correction, exaggeration, argumentation, epiphonomona"—and the "schemes rhetorical, as dissolution, interpretation, complexion *ex repetitionibus*, subjection, and conduplication" (146). Here he clearly follows Erasmus's advice to "compare parallel passages in authors"—he identifies "the evident imitation of the authors above rehearsed" (146)—without, however, "bringing out differences and similarities"(*De Ratione*, 683).

Finally, he regularly supplements his ecphrasis with a consideration of what Erasmus calls "the moral implications of the poets' stories" (683). As an example of his general practice, consider his treatment of two lines from act 4, scene 6:

> *O coelum, o terra. Iupiter*
> *Aspicis haec, & patere? quem dicunt hospiti*
> *Dare iura.* (4.6.2–4)

Marginally he notes the echoes of Terence and Virgil, the auxesis of "O coelum, o terra. Iupiter" (he ignores the period), and the exclamatio. His ecphrasis is as follows:

> O heaven, o earth, o helping father, beholdest thou these things, and sufferest them? whom they say to give laws to an host .i. [i. e.] whiche as men reporte hast appointed laws, how an host should treat his guest .i. since that thou amongst thy other titles, art called Ζευς ξεννιος .i. *Iupiter hospitalis,* and diddest so sore punish Lycaon for his cruelty showed upon his guest, that thou diddest not only burn his house with lightning, but also diddest turn him into a wolf, wilt thou see me suffer this wrong done to me, by mine host, and by his consent, and leave it unpunished?

(for the host should not consent to have any wrong or violence
done to his guest in his house). (146–47)

Palsgrave first translates the lines more or less "as the latin lieth,"
ignoring the full stop after *terra* and supplying the understood
object for *patere,* but retaining the infinitive of *dare,* and then goes
on to suggest the moral implications of the exclamation by intro-
ducing the story of Lycaon as a moral pattern for edification. This
is a somewhat fuller consideration of moral implications than he
usually supplies, but it illustrates nicely how a passage may provide
a point of departure for the commentary of an industrious schoolmaster: Lycaon is never mentioned in the text. Even Palsgrave,
who had earlier fulminated against the overzealous schoolmasters
who could not confine their attention to the text being considered,
finds it difficult to focus on a passage when its significance derives
not from its relation to the rest of the text of which it is a part, but
rather from its other affiliations.

Baldwin says that Palsgrave's book "gives a very full and complete idea of how about 1540 a piece of literature would be taught
by the best masters in grammar school" (183), but also notes
that "apparently his contemporaries were not enthusiastic, for no
method was prescribed and no other edition of the book was
called for" (182). This is perhaps explained by Palsgrave's unchar-
acteristic enthusiasm for inculcating a good English prose style in
his students. But allowing for that difference, it is fairly clear that
Palsgrave does provide a concrete application of Erasmian principles, and it is also fairly clear that students educated in accordance
with those principles would agree with John Crowe Ransom that
"a poem is much more like a Christmas tree than an organism,"[23]
if only they were acquainted with modern Christmas trees.

Having considered what Erasmus's method would have been
like in practice, it is easier to hear echoes of it in the school
curricula Baldwin provides. The curriculum from Eton about
1560, for instance, indicates that from nine until ten in the morning the master read various authors to the fourth, fifth, and sixth
forms, "from which lectures the boys excerpt flowers, phrases,

or locutions of speaking; likewise antithets, epithets, synonyms, proverbs, similitudes, comparisons, histories, descriptions of time, place, persons, fables, merry jests, schemes, and apothegms" (Baldwin, 355). A later description of Westminster, incorrectly attributed to Archbishop Laud, says that "betwixt one to 3 that lesson which out of some author appointed for that day, had been by the Master expounded unto them (out of Cicero, Virgil, Homer, Euripides, Isocrates, Livy, Sallust, etc.) was to be exactly gone through by construing and other grammatical ways, examining all the rhetorical figures and translating it out of verse into prose, out of Greek into latin or out of latin into Greek" (360). William Kempe, presenting in 1588 his methods in *The Education of Children*, suggests that the most advanced students, those who have mastered grammar, rhetoric, and logic, should "observe in authors all the use of the Arts, as not only the words and phrases, not only the examples of the arguments; but also the axiom, wherein every argument is disposed; the syllogism, whereby it is concluded; the method of the whole treatise, and the passages, whereby the parts are joined together. Again, he shall observe not only every trope, every figure, as well of words as of sentences; but also the Rhetorical pronounciation and gesture fit for every word, sentence, and affection" (446).

And indeed, when Charles Hoole wrote *A New Discovery of the Old Art of Teaching Schoole* (1660) nearly a century later, he repeated largely the same method.[24] Hoole states his aim as "*facilitating the good old way of teaching by Grammar, Authors, and exercises*" (169), deriving his method directly from Erasmus. Ovid's *Metamorphosis* is one of the books he recommends for the fourth form; he suggests that the students memorize four or five verses, construe them ("minding the propriety of the words, and the elegancy of every phrase"), parse them, identify "the Tropes and Figures, the Derivations and Differences of some words, and relate such histories as the proper names will hint at," scan and prove every verse, "note more difficult quantities of some syllables," and finally "Turn the Fable into English prose, and to adorn it with fit Epithets, choice Phrases, acute Sentences, witty Apophthegms, lively similitudes, pat examples, and Proverbial Speeches" (161–

62). (If Palsgrave's students would not think of a poem as a modern Christmas tree, Hoole's certainly would. But it must be remembered that the ornaments to be used are the product and the purpose of earlier reading.) The English is then translated again into Latin, and then into English verses. The advice for the fifth form reading Virgil is almost exactly the same. Beginning with the *Eclogues,* the students first memorize ten or twelve verses, "2. Construe and parse, and scan and prove exactly," "3. Give the tropes and Figures with their definitions," "4. Note out the Phrases and Epithets, and other Elegancies," and "5. Give the Histories or descriptions belonging to the proper Names, and their *Etymologies*" (179). Hoole's prescriptions for two consecutive years provide especially clear evidence that although the selection of authors may have varied from year to year, the method of studying them remained constant.

And it has been my argument that students who learned to read in Tudor grammar schools would have been exposed to this method of "interpreting" a text so insistently that—like modern students learning elementary arithmetic—they could not conceive of any alternative. That method emphasized the utility rather than the pleasure of the text (though of course everybody, including Sidney, mentioned pleasure as an incitement to learning), and more especially, the utility of separable parts of the text. This tendency to consider texts as collections of separate passages is illustrated and to some extent motivated by the habit of compiling commonplace books. Students learned to think of these chunks as the locus of interpretation, which at best consisted of extremely close analysis of the language of the text and its literary affiliations and, at something less than best, of the digressions Erasmus and Palsgrave deplored, connected only tenuously to the passages which served as their excuse. There was little or no sense of overall structure divorced from the forms sanctioned by classical examples; the "judgment" Erasmus extols is confined to segments of the text rather than to whole texts.

Finally, and most importantly, the basic purpose of reading was to prepare for future persuasion, whether written or spoken. After outlining a number of written exercises, Erasmus advises that "the reading of good authors should always be constantly interspersed with those exercises so that the pupils always have material for imitation" (679). This admonition seems specifically designed for the schoolroom until one hears Thomas Blundeville echoing it for an adult audience in quite different circumstances: "And though we seek by reading Histories, to make our selves more wise, as well to direct our own actions, as also to counsel others, to stir them to virtue, and to withdraw them from vice, and to beautify our own speech with grave examples, when we discourse of any matters, that thereby it may have the more authority, weight, and credit."[25] To put this point more positively, what for us is a private experience was for those in Tudor England part of a social practice. Mortimer Adler explains the rewards of reading good books in terms of individual enhancement: "there is the improvement in your reading skills. . . . You become wiser . . . in the sense that you are more deeply aware of the great and enduring truths of human life."[26] The construction of Blundeville's sentence demonstrates quite clearly that for those educated in Tudor grammar schools this kind of private edification was only a prelude to social action.

CHAPTER 3
TUDOR READERS
READING

For evidence about actual Tudor reading, one could hardly do better than to turn to Gabriel Harvey, who in his copious marginal annotations provides the fullest record of reading we have from the period. Before we turn to the annotations, however, it is useful to consider in more detail his *Ciceronianus,* the lecture he addressed to his Cambridge students, presumably at the beginning of the Easter term in 1576, as an introduction to his topics for the coming term. To prepare the students for the Ramistic approach he will be taking, emphasizing content as much as eloquence, strictly distinguishing between rhetoric, grammar, and dialectic, and treating the appropriate topics under each heading, he provides an autobiographical account of his own conversion from being a "great and simonpure Ciceronian" (63) who considered it "a wicked offense to touch Erasmus" (61) into "not a make-believe, but a most perfect and pure Ciceronian, such a man as Ludovicus would perhaps call 'Ciceronianissimus'" (83) who is "willing to recognize the eloquence of Ramus, Erasmus, Sturmius, Fregius, Smith, and Cheke, and even prefer it to that of the Italians" (81), and whose mind now "not merely expects but promises something greater than Cicero in Cicero himself. For he has surpassed himself, the new Cicero has surpassed the old, in every point of praise" (59). What has occasioned this wonderful change is his acquaintance with Ramus and his insistence on considering content as well as expression:

Do you wish, then, to be honored with the glorious and magnifi-
cent appellation of "Ciceronian"? . . . Consider not merely the
flowering verdure of style, but much rather the ripe fruitage of
reason and thought. . . . Remember that words are called by Homer πτεροεντα, that is, winged, since they easily fly away, unless
they are kept in equilibrium by the weightiness of the subject
matter. Unite dialectic and knowledge with rhetoric, thought
with language. Learn from Erasmus to conjoin an abundance of
matter with an abundance of words. (83)

As a self-confessed Ramist, Harvey was propounding a new, "modern" way to read Cicero and the other classics, and even at Cambridge, where the Ramistic influence was strongest (19), his enthusiastic support of Ramus stirred up controversy: when he was
denied grace for his M.A. degree in 1573, one of the reasons was his
support of Ramus.[1] When in the *Ciceronianus,* then, Harvey explains what he has come to see as the shortcomings of his previous
approach to Cicero—his simon-pure approach—we may assume
that he is describing the way the great majority of educated readers
(who had not been illuminated by Ramism) still approached Cicero as late as the 1570s.

In the opening section of the oration, Harvey recounts his experiences while at his "Tusculan villa," reading Cicero, Caesar, Virgil, and other Latin writers: he lived

so familiarly and assiduously . . . that now your friend Tully in-
vited me to breakfast, now Julius Caesar himself to lunch, now
Virgil to dinner, now the others to their desserts, which were delightful for a change. . . . All the others uttered conversation that I
thought delightful, and indeed nothing less than pure delight; but
Cicero alone (my heart leaps at the recollection) had the sweetest
voice to invite me, the clearest to entertain me, and far the pleas-
antest to dismiss me. (47)

What Harvey chooses to emphasize in his account is the language
of the writers: after comparing his reading to a banquet, he focus-

ses on "the words of my hosts, which were the equivalent of the sweetest condiments" (47). As we shall see, this is not an entirely fortuitous choice, since diction was the focus of much commentary on ancient writers. In Cicero is found all the felicity of speech: "His speech flowed, not sweeter than honey, as did Nestor's in Homer, but more splendid and better than nectar, than ambrosia, than all the feasts of the poets" (47). Approaching Cicero in what Harvey has come to see as the old-fashioned way what one notices is rhetoric:

> I recognize, unless I am mistaken, the emphases, amplifications, and hyperboles of oratory; I have observed the choices and the most spirited formulas of exaggeration; I know what are the sinews in tropes, what the muscles and tendons in figures; I have even noted some unique matters. With all of these Marcus Tully so fortified himself that not even these same devices, distinguished as they are, can suffice to proclaim his excellent glory. (53)

But one is also limited to rhetoric, and the most daring one can be—especially for a simon-pure Ciceronian—is to compare the uses of rhetoric in more than one author, in itself anathema to strict Ciceronians who would read no one but Cicero:

> This is the thought, then, of my entire discourse: that we should not refrain from reading occasionally other writers who are excellent in their kind, nor fail to return always to Cicero as the eldest son and indeed heir of Eloquence. (57)

Reading other authors is profitable because it enables one to recognize and appreciate more fully both the limited excellences of other authors and the true excellence of Cicero: "The fact is that when I proceeded rather casually to compare Cicero with the others, I derived from my comparison such intense and pure pleasure, and perhaps profit as well, as I really had never experienced before in my life" (55). Thus one can see "the difference between the redundancy of Osorius and the copiousness

60

of Cicero" even while admitting that both possess "fluent diction" (57).

The goal of this kind of reading is imitation, and in recounting what he imitated from Cicero, Harvey identifies what most struck him in his reading:

> Why should I tell how great and simon-pure a Ciceronian I was at that time in the choice of every single word, in the composition and structure of sentences, in the discriminating use of cases and tenses, in the symmetry of cut-and-dried phrases, in the shaping of sentence-divisions and clauses, in the rhythmical measuring of periods, in the variety and smoothness of clausulae, in the careful and elaborate multiplication of all sorts of refinements. . . . Now if necessity imposed upon me some dialectical disputation, from which during just about all of this period I was wont to shrink, . . . you would have heard a man more careful than Perionus himself in the choice of words, a man often barely satisfied, or not even barely, with the vocabulary of Sturmius, . . . a man having Marcus Tully's *Topica* constantly in his mind and very often on his lips and in his writings; a man captiously criticizing the reasoning of his opponents and polishing his own. (63, 65)

Words, phrases, clauses, balance: these were what attracted the attention of the pure Ciceronian, and it was only the chance reading of Sambucus's *Ciceronianus,* which led him to Ramus's work of the same title, that enabled him to realize that he

> valued words more than content, language more than thought, the one art of speaking more than the thousand subjects of knowledge; [he] preferred the mere style of Marcus Tully to all the postulates of the philosophers and mathematicians; [he] believed that the bone and sinew of imitation lay in [his] ability to choose as many brilliant and elegant words as possible, to reduce them into order, and to connect them together in a rhythmical period. In [his] judgment—or perhaps [he] should say opinion rather than judgment—that was what it meant to be a Ciceronian. (69)

But for the strict Ciceronian it is difficult to shift to any other method of reading. After reading Sambucus and Ramus, Harvey's conception of what it means to be a true Ciceronian changes, but at first the change is limited to linguistic matters:

> I saw that I must return to the old masters . . . Terence, Virgil, Plautus, Caesar, Varro, Sallust, Livy, and Pliny. . . . I also saw that from them I must borrow, with due regard to the purity of Latin style, whatever was Ciceronian in them; and Ramus interprets Ciceronian to mean excellent and in conformity with the most careful usage of speech and thought. (71)

In these authors he finds many qualities "worthy of being imitated by us and all posterity" (71)—a revelation for the strict Ciceronian—but they are still qualities of expression: "in Terence . . . appropriateness of diction and easiness of style; in Virgil majesty of both words and verse; in Plautus a sort of gaiety and copiousness" (71).

Significantly, this is his reaction even after reading what he presents on the next page as "the thing in the beginning of [Ramus's] book that particularly delighted me . . . that fundamental principle, both Brutine and Tullian . . . of tracing causes and not merely effects" (70). It is this principle which will alter his reading, but in his presentation his initial reaction to Ramus is that he must reconsider the language of other ancient writers to learn what he can from them as well as from Tully; attention to language has for so long shaped his reading practice that he cannot easily escape it. Thus his exclusive attention, in the early part of his oration, to the condiments of the authors he was reading in his "Tusculan villa." Before his Ramistic conversion he was able to taste and appreciate only the condiments; it is only afterward that he understands that "in seeking magnificence and splendor of oratorical feasts what we need is not so much the condiments of the Italians. . . . Rather we need the omnifarious viands and victuals, as they call them, of the Germans, French, and British" (81), and he invites his students to emulate his own conversion and "serve [him] at the feast not only condiments, as formerly, but somewhat more substantial food, as you have recently begun to do" (81).

One hesitates to accept this as a frank autobiographical account: there is, after all, a well-known tradition of Pauline conversions, Harvey was familiar with a number of contemporary examples of academic autobiography (Wilson, 16–17), the text is (as befits a master of imitation) a tissue of allusions (see the notes by Harold S. Wilson), and he is consciously trying to induce his students to adopt the Ramistic method he goes on to outline in the second half of his lecture. Nonetheless, it is hard not to see in the account of the simon-pure Ciceronian the effects of the grammar-school educational system. Writers were valued because they provided material for the students' own imitations, and Harvey provides eloquent testimony about the kind of material students were most likely to adopt. Even an enlightened Ciceronian, one who read other authors, concentrated on their disposition of language rather than content, on the one art of speaking instead of the thousand subjects of knowledge. And while it is unlikely that most of the students educated at grammar schools were Ciceronians, either strict or enlightened, it is not difficult to see how the whole educational system to which they were exposed would orient them toward concentration on the language of the texts they read.

It is in his marginalia, however, that Harvey provides the fullest evidence of the period of how an extremely well-educated reader would read, or at least annotate, his books. Harvey's marginalia abound; the most recent full-length study[2] estimates that there are at least 180 of his books extant (Stern, 140) out of a library that may have been as large as 3,500 volumes, though perhaps 1,300 is nearer the actual number (250)—this at a time when the University Library at Cambridge contained fewer than five hundred books and manuscripts (194). The marginalia range from identifying marks and single words to more elaborate disquisitions only tangentially connected with the text they annotate. They seem to record Harvey's reminders and notes to himself, but it is difficult in reading through them not to get the impression that Harvey was engaged in a rather elaborate performance, a way of presenting himself to the many friends to whom he loaned his books. In a number of his books, the autograph is not the usual "Gabriel Harvey" (or one of a number of Latin variations on it), but "Gabrielis Harveij, et amicorum" (see Stern's annotation to Alciato's *De verborum significatione libri quatuor*, 199, and other examples on 199, 204, 208, 211, 214, 216, etc.). In his Letter Book[3] there is a letter to Arthur Capel while Harvey is still at Pembroke Hall (the letter comes between two in which Harvey indicated he was writing from Pembroke (167, 169), and thus dating from the period before he became a fellow of Trinity Hall in December 1578 (Stern, 48). The reason for the letter is to request the return of one of his books, but to mitigate this presumption, he pretends to be inquiring about the progress of Capel's reading:

> M. Capel, I dout not I, but you have ere this sufficiently perusid or rather, thurroughly red over thos tragical pamflets of the Quen of Scots, as you did not long ago that pretti elegant treatis of M. Chek against sedition: and verry lately good part of the Mirrur for Magistrates, thre books iwis in mi judgment wurth the reading over and over, both for the style and the matter. Now, if your leisure will serve you (for truly I praesume of your good wil) to run thurrough ani part of M. Ascham (for I suppose you have canvassid him reasnably wel alreddi), or to hear the report of the furious outragies of Fraunc in Inglish, or read over the Courtier in Lattin (whitch I would wish, and wil you to do for sundri causes) or to peruse ani pes of Osorius, Sturmius, or Ramus, or to se ani other book, ether Inglish or Lattin, that I have, and mai stand you in stead, do but cum your self, or send on for it, and make your ful account not to fail of it. (167)

Although he had presumably loaned Capel the books he mentions here, Harvey is aware of the peculiarity of his writing a letter to make such an offer, and he feels some need to justify the missive:

> Perhaps you wil marvel at the sudden proffer. In good sooth mi purpose is nothing els but this: I would have gentlemen to be

conversant and occupied in thos books especially, whereof thai
mai have most use and practis, ether for writing or speaking, elo-
quently or wittily, now or hereafter. (167–68)

At the end of the letter, almost as an afterthought, comes the
request that is the real reason for the letter:

There is a frend of mine that spake unto me yesterniht for mi
book of ye Queen of Scots. If you have dun withal, I prai you
send me it presently, otherwise he shal for me tarri your leisure; or
if you send it now, assure your self to have it again at your pleasure. (168)

If Harvey was in the habit of loaning his books, or even pressing
them on friends, especially influential friends such as Capel, there
is some reason to suspect that the annotations he made in the
books were not entirely unself-conscious. But even if they were
part of his continual campaign to convince the political world that
he deserved a place in it, they attest to his conception of what a
learned reader should say about a text. And of course, many of his
annotations, particularly the ones that encourage good habits, do
seem to be more personal.

The marginalia themselves reflect to a large extent the characteristics of reading I outline as Erasmian in the first chapter. Even
the relatively superficial advice Erasmus provides about using a variety of distinguishing marks for annotation is interestingly illustrated in the exuberant variety of letters and astrological symbols
Harvey used. Harold S. Wilson explains most of the signs used "as
an index of subject-matter" (354): *J. C.* referred to legal matters, as
did *L. L.;* the astrological sign for Mercury "commonly stands for
eloquence," while that for Mars indicates anything related to war-
fare.[4] A star or asterisk is used to indicate astronomical matters; the
sun, for matters related to emperors, kings, and lords; the sign for
earth for natural history. A square seems "to distinguish writers in
the humanities" (358). There are a few signs that Wilson does not
explain that seem designed to call attention to a passage:

He placed crosses before the names of a large proportion of the
authors listed, and for the titles underscored he placed additional
crosses in the margins and above keywords of titles in the text
itself . . . as well as other signs, like the horizontal check-mark, the
double comma, the double *s,* and the curved bracket. . . . These
markings appear to be arbitrary symbols of emphasis, to draw attention to anything Harvey wished to note or which he admired.
(354)

In addition to these symbols, Harvey regularly inscribed single
words or short phrases as summaries of the material in the text. In
his copy of Thomas Blundeville's *The four chiefest Offices belonging
to Horsemanship,* for instance, he wrote "How the Rider ought to
sitt in his Saddle" at the top of one page, and "Semeiotice" (diag-
nosis) at the beginning of a chapter on the colors of horses (Stern,
141). Erasmus had written that "not only must a variety of marks
be employed, but appropriate ones at that, so that they will immediately indicate their purpose" (*De Ratione,* 670), and Harvey
seems to have concurred.

Two of the most important characteristics of Erasmian reading
are its focus on passages or selections rather than entire works and
its radical intertextuality, and Harvey's marginalia provide evidence for both of these. It is in the nature of reading, of course,
that it proceed by segments (though not necessarily words), just as
it is in the nature of marginalia that they must be localized and
thus seem to reflect attention to segments rather than works, so the
fact that annotations exist is not ipso facto evidence of reading
sections. However, the general character of these annotations illuminates the kind of reading they reflect. We may distinguish
between internal and external notations—those that refer to other
places in the same text, and those that refer to something outside
the text at hand. Modern annotations, especially those of teachers
preparing texts for class presentation, are likely to contain both
kinds: internally, what the author says in one place is compared to
what is said in another, one scene recalls a similar one, recurrent

66

images are noted; externally, references are made to other writers or to other circumstances occurring to the reader. Internal annotation reflects a reader's perception that different parts of a text are related to each other and part of a larger whole; external annotations reflect the place of a passage in the reader's mental life. Now the striking thing about Harvey's marginalia is that they are free of internal annotation: virtually all of his notes lead away from the text at hand. This is only circumstantial evidence, to be sure, but it suggests what we should expect from the educational system: that readers read sections of text and considered them independently.

Another characteristic of Harvey's marginal annotations corroborates this point: the elaborateness of many of the annotations—both in their length (many are over a hundred words long) and in the intricacy of the penmanship itself—implies a substantial shift of attention from reading to writing. To produce these annotations at all, Harvey must have read a section of the text and then stopped reading, first to consider the passage and what it reminded him of, and then to record that consideration. Indeed, many of the annotations are short essays, like the following from Quintilian's *Institutes,* and thus reflect the habit of reading sections and then shifting attention elsewhere.

> Demosthenes Jestes, cam hardly and harshly from him: not with any naturall facility, but artificially enforcid, as it were shorne against the wooll. He had no maner of grace or fylicity this way. Tully as pleasurable, and as full of his conceytid jestes and merriments, when he floorished—as owr S[r] Thomas More of late memory. Theire speciall grace, and fylicity this way. Both to be reckonid in the number of those, whome we terme very good at a Kutt; & of whome we may say: They were borne with a iest jn their mowth.[5]

If the various signs Harvey used were intended to recall his attention in rereading his books, these mini-essays (whatever their effect in his self-presentation) indicate the extent to which his reading was interrupted rather than consecutive. Thus the very existence of extended annotation suggests the continuing habit of reading, and pondering, sections of a text independently.

The second characteristic of Erasmian reading, its radically intertextual nature, is everywhere evident in the marginalia. The quotation above suggests how easily Harvey referred to other authors, and later in the Quintilian there is an even more explicit example:

> De jocis, et facetijs, conferendi Lib: 2. de Oratore: jl secondo libro del Cortegiano del Conte Castiglione: Jouiani Pontani de Sermone urbano, et faceto libri sex: præsertim tertius: M. Secretary Wylsons Rhetoric: of delighting the Hearers, and stirring them to Lawghter: The diuision of pleasaunt behauiour: pleasaunt sport made by delightfull, and liuely rehearsing of A whole matter: Sport moouid by telling owld merry Tales, or straunge Historyes. fol. 69. 70, 71. 72. 73 &c. Jocorum, ueterum, ac recentium libri tres Adriani Barlandi. (114; cf. the list of historians, 194–95)

In their 1990 article on Harvey's reading of Livy, Anthony Grafton and Lisa Jardine suggest that Harvey used a book wheel—a mechanical device upon which many books could be placed and then rotated so that a number of volumes could be easily compared—to facilitate this intertextuality, and it may well have been so.[6] If he did use such a device, that would of course be further evidence for the focus on passages fostered in the grammar schools, since the whole purpose of the wheel is to allow the reader to read one passage and then move quickly to another passage to compare them. One who reads books through from beginning to end has little need of such a device.

But before we assume from the existence of such a tool that Harvey actually used one, we should remember that Harvey's ideal of reading requires digesting a book so thoroughly that a book wheel would be unnecessary. Toward the beginning of his edition of Ramus's οικονομια (one of his most heavily annotated volumes) he inscribed the following advice:

This whole booke, written & printed, of continual & perpetual use: & therefore continually, and perpetually to be meditated, practised, and incorporated into my boddy, & sowle.

In A serious, & practicable Studdy, better any on chapter, perfectly, & thorowghly digested, for praesent practis, as occasion shall requier: then A whole volume, greedily deuowrid, & rawly concoctid: to no actual purpose, or effect of valu.

No sufficient, or hable furniture, gotten by unperfect posting, or superficial ouerrunning: or halfelearning: but by perpetual meditations, repetitions, recognitions, recapitulations, reiterations, and ostentations of most practicable points, sounde and deepe imprinting as well in ye memory, as in the understanding: for praegnant & curious reddines, at euery lest occasion. Every Rule of valu, and euery poynt of vse, woold be continually recognised, and perpetually eternised in yor witt, & memory.

Omnia, quae curant, etiam senes meminerunt. (146–47)

How many books Harvey thoroughly digested in this manner is open to question, but a number of marginalia stress the necessity of having information readily available ("Legem pone, Legem pone: Erubesce sine Lege loqui: Vt Ludovicus protonotarius, qui memoriter quamque Legem citabat; tanquam de Libro pronuncians," 146; see other examples on 112, 200, 208), and entries in his commonplace book suggest that such complete mastery of texts was only part of his ambitious educational program:

The L. Cromwell, by ye only promptnes of his wit, facility of speach, & A pragmatical dexterity to all purposes, ouershadowed & obscured, euen our greatist clarkes. My L. Treasurer, alyke singular by semblable meanes, with sum lytle more lerning, & lyke politique Method. Any Art, or science, liberal, or mechanical may summarily be lernid for ordinary talke, in *three dayes;* for vse, practis, & profession, in *six:* a language, to vnderstande, in *six:* to speake, & write, in *twelue.* . . . Many such pragmatical feates, praesently gotten. (91)

Reade, & repeate for lyfe, with as much liuely conference, as

possibly you may: & euermore post on to practis: wch only work-
ith praesent masteryes. Auoyde all writing, but necessary: wch con-
sumith unreasonable much tyme, before you ar aware: you haue
alreddy plaguid yourselfe this way: Two arts lernid, while two
sheetes in writing. (89)

Reading, repetition, lively conference, all leading to complete digestion: these were the keys for proper mastery of texts. If an art or
science could be mastered in six days, or a language in twelve,
there is no reason to suppose that books could not be similarly
digested, especially with perpetual meditation, repetition, recognition, and so forth. And Harvey was apparently prepared to
meditate upon his books almost continuously: among the charges
brought against him when the grace for his M.A. was denied in
1573 was that he "did disdain everi mans cumpani" (*Letter-Book*, 4)
and that he "wuld needs in al hast be a studdiing in Christmas,
when other were a plaiing, and was then whottist at [his] book
when the rest were hardist at their cards" (14; see the entire letter to
John Young in *Letter-Book*, 1–20, and Stern, 17–25).

Whether or not Harvey used a reading wheel, his reading was
radically intertextual: thorough digestion requires conference. In
the schoolroom, these comparisons would result in entries in a
commonplace book, as similar passages, or passages on the same
subject, were grouped together under their own heading. Although Harvey did compile a commonplace book (and perhaps
two, though only fragments of the second remain: see Moore
Smith, 79), it seems that he used the margins and blank pages in
his books for the same purpose. Among the number of scholars
who have remarked that his marginalia are reminiscent of a commonplace book, Wilson is the most straightforward: "It is obvious
that Harvey used his system of symbolic reference in lieu of a
commonplace book" (359). Others are more tentative: Eleanor
Relle says that "One has the impression that Harvey designed his
marginalia as a kind of commonplace-book, a source of raw materials for the books he never wrote,"[7] and Caroline Ruutz-Rees
suggests that "Perhaps they were intended as guides in the com-

70

pilation of a commonplace book."[8] For our purposes it is unnecessary to decide whether the marginalia do in fact represent a substitute for a commonplace book; what is important is that they reveal the same approach to reading, in which comparison of texts—lively conference—both focusses attention and guides the course of reading. Unlike the checks or lines we are accustomed to use to indicate something noteworthy, the full panoply of Harvey's marks (to say nothing of his extended essays) indicates the set of expectations within which reading occurred.

The longer annotations provide evidence for another characteristic of the kind of Erasmian reading fostered in the schools: reading was typically seen as a preparation for some other activity. Within the confines of the schoolroom, this other activity was writing, but the broader concept was that reading prepared one to participate in the life of the commonweal. Perhaps the most characteristic note in Harvey's marginalia is the exhortation to prepare for future action of some kind. Grafton and Jardine stress this preparation: the title of their piece is " 'Studied for Action': How Gabriel Harvey Read His Livy," and near the beginning of the article they indicate that

> we intend to take that notion of *activity* in a strong sense: not just the energy which must be acknowledged as accompanying the intervention of the scholar/reader with the text, nor the cerebral effort involved in making the text the reader's own, but reading as intended to *give rise to something else*. We argue that scholarly reading (the kind of reading we are concerned with here) was always goal-orientated. . . . Above all, . . . this "activity of reading" characteristically envisaged some other outcome of reading beyond accumulation of information; and that envisaged outcome then shaped the relationship between reader and text. (30–31)

In the course of their article, Grafton and Jardine show that Harvey read Livy at least four times, with slightly different purposes in mind, and that these different readings led to different outcomes. What they have in common, as Grafton and Jardine argue at the

end of the article, is that Harvey's Livy shows "a coherent pro-
gramme to master the whole world of learning and make it readily
usable in political action" (75), certainly an illustration of the way
reading was seen as preparative to something else.

But the emphasis on political action is at least partially determined by the subject matter of Livy and by the circumstances in
which Harvey read it. Other marginalia, produced in other circumstances, indicate a somewhat wider range of possible outcomes of reading. On the simplest level, what he read continually
led Harvey away from the text into his own life. So, for instance,
references to Dr. Wath, "unhappy Philip" (Moore Smith thinks
this is the earl of Surrey who pursued Harvey's sister Mercy [265]),
Cartwright, Dr. Perne, Tom Turner, Sir Thomas Smith, Mrs.
Strachie, and Dr. Fulk—with the exception of Cartwright, all from
Saffron Waldon or Cambridge—appear in the marginalia to Erasmus's *Parabolae*, which Harvey acquired in January of 1566 and
reread in September of 1577 (136–41).

Closely related to these autobiographical references are those
annotations that have to do with either self-improvement or with
Harvey's dreams of future accomplishment. The typical note is
struck in the epigram he supplies for Ramus's οικονομια, which
he acquired in 1574: "Il pensare non importa, ma jl fare," followed
by "Etiam exquisitissima sapientia mera Vanitas est, nisi priuatam,
publiceque exerceatur, et jn mundo proficiat" (141). But another
typical note is struck by the use of the same saying on page 3 of
Foorth's *Synopsis Politica* (thus Moore Smith; Stern claims that it is
on the title page, 154), where it is followed by "resolutely for jntent;
lustily for act; mightily for effect. resolute lusty, & mighty Indus-
try" (193). This repetition serves as a warning that we must be wary
of concluding too rashly that Harvey's marginalia directly reflect
his reading; instead, the margins of his books may at times simply
provide the opportunity for him to retail his own opinions. Title
pages and flyleaves provide especially good examples of this, since
they contain little or no text to respond to. So the advice on diet
and general moderation found on the flyleaves of Hopperus's *In*

veram Iurisprudentiam Isagoge reflects a bee in Harvey's bonnet rather than anything instigated by his reading of Hopper:

> We schollers make an Asse of owr bodye, & witt. what foolishnes, & maddnes, to studdy after meate? being so extremely pernicious not only to ye stomok, & nutrition: but to ye brayne, witt, & memory? Lancton
> Smell ye saver of Musk, Camamell, Redd roses: drink wyne measurabely: eate sage, but not too much: keepe ye hed warme: wash your hands often: walk measurabely: sleep measurabely: heere lytle noyse of Musique, or singars: eate Mustard, or pepper: wash ye Temples with rose water
> Good for ye brayne. (177)

This small selection of much longer comments should serve as sufficient warning that the relation between the text and the marginal annotation is not always unproblematical, especially when the annotation has to do with personal matters (and with Harvey, practically everything is personal), and also illustrates how similar to a commonplace book the marginalia may become.

One topic to which Harvey returned frequently was the relation between reading and writing. We have already seen his hyperbolic exclamation that two arts could be learned in the time it would take to write two sheets, and that only echoes an annotation from his copy of Xenophon, dated 1570 on the title page and 1576 on the last page just after a longish annotation containing the following advice:

> Lege quotidie, quantum potes, alacerrime: viuida analysi penitus excutito singula: sed heus Socratico more, mente, non penna: desine scripturire, et serio cogita quod res est, scriptitandi istud vulgare cacöethes, ipsum esse pretiosi temporis prodigum filium. (125)

In the margin of the index to Ramus's οικονομια he inscribed "Abijce pennam, et Linguam acue. Linguam acue, et insuda vehementi perpetuaeque Exercitationi," and later on the same page,

Lyttle or no writing will now serue, but only upon praesent necessary occasions, otherwise not dispatchable. All writing layd abedd,
as taedious, & needles. All is now, jn bowld Courtly speaking, and
bowld Industrious dooing. Actiuity, praesent bowld Actiuity.
(144–45)

Later in the volume,

Diuine Apollonius.
    Apollonius being asked why he writ nothing, being so excel-
lently hable: answered, It was not his dessigne, To sitt still. And
surely it is not my platform, to ly by-it.
    The Hed: The fountain of Witt, & fine conceits; must euer be
kept cleare, pure, neat, & sweet. Apollonius diet, Bred, & frute.
(153)

It is impossible to date these remarks with any precision, but the
two dates recorded in the Xenophon (1570 and 1576) make it one
of the earliest annotated books extant. Ramus's οικονομια has
dates of 1574 and 1580 on the title page, while the commonplace
book is undated and presumably compiled over a number of years.
These comments about writing, themselves composed over a period of ten or twenty years, suggest to me that Harvey felt some
continual anxiety about his lack of writing, almost as if (as a
justification) it was necessary for him to remind himself that the
natural connection between reading and writing that had been
forged in school was now no longer profitable. Another annotation in the Ramus sheds some light on this:

Common Lerning, & yᵉ name of a good schollar, was neuer so
much contemn'd, & abiected of princes, Pragmaticals, & common Gallants, as nowadayes; jnsomuch that it necessarily concer-
nith, & importith ye lernid ether præsently to hate yʳ books; or
actually to insinuate, & enforce themselues, by uery special, &
singular propertyes of emploiable, & necessary vse, in all affaires,

74

as well priuate, as publique, amounting to any commodity, ether æconomical, or politique. (151)

Stern suggests that this annotation was the result of Harvey's dismissal as Leicester's secretary in 1580 (46–47), and it may well be, since a number of entries in Harvey's commonplace book suggest admiration for the very pragmatical approach he now appears to be condemning:

> The right pragmaticall karrieth euermore liuely and quyck spir-ites, and takith continually the nymbliest, and speediest way. for the dispatch of his busines:wch he neuer attemptith withowt cause, nor euer slackith, or forslowith withowt effect. (87)

Whatever happened to change Harvey's attitude about the value of "right pragmaticals" and also about the value of education and learning, the upshot apparently was to encourage him to insinuate and force himself by his properties of employable and necessary use: "who would not rather be on of ye Nine Worthyes: then on of ye Seauen Wise masters?" (151).

One way to retain the fruits of learning and indeed make them useful was to stress oratory rather than writing, and it is presumably no accident that the Ramus volume has several comments (similar to the one already cited suggesting "bowld Courtly speaking, and bowld Industrious dooing") recommending the utility of oratory:

> A gentleman, without Eloquence, & fortitude: is lyke A cock of ye game, without voyce [?], & spurres. (143)

> Sir Roger Williams Rede: As he that doth most, so he that saieth most, is most to be commendid: So it be to purpose, & with Rea-son. (157)

> He that woold be thowght A Man, or seeme anything worth; must be A great Dooer, or A Great Speaker: He is a Cipher, & but a

peakegoose, that is nether of both: He is ye Right man, that is
Both: He that cannot be Both, lett him be On at least, if he meane
to be accounted any boddy: or farewell all hope of valu. (157)

The link between reading and speaking was of course also stressed
in the schools, and it may be that Harvey fell back on this after he
failed to win recognition by his writing. Whatever the precise
reason, these marginalia provide convincing evidence that Harvey
continued to see reading not as an end in itself, but as preparation
for something else, whether that something else be writing, advis-
ing, speaking, or what he would much have preferred but seldom
got the chance to do, "Actiuity, praesent bowld Actiuity."

Toward the end of their article, Grafton and Jardine summarize
Harvey's method of reading:

Thus critical reading, skilful annotation and active appropriation
emerge as the central skills, not just of the student of history, but
of the intellectual *tout court*. Reading always led to action—but
only proper reading, methodical reading—reading in the manner
of a Gabriel Harvey. (76)

Reading in the manner of a Gabriel Harvey was not something
Harvey himself invented; it was, simply, the kind of reading
taught in the grammar schools of the time. That reading would
have been seen as preparative for some other activity; it would
have been radically intertextual; and it would have encouraged
detailed consideration of relatively small sections of text rather
than entire works. It was in Grafton and Jardine's terms *active;* it
required what Harvey calls conference and meditation for thorough digestion. And the fruits of that conference and meditation,
lest they be lost, were recorded, in school in a commonplace book;
in Harvey's later custom, in the margins of the books he read. In
Harvey's practice we may see the quintessence of Tudor reading,
for he was able to maintain the extreme earnestness of the schoolboy well into his later life.

If Harvey's marginalia represent an uneasy compromise between genuine private reaction to reading and public self-presentation, E. K.'s introductions and notes to *The Shepheardes Calendar* are clearly public and exemplary. E. K.'s identity has ceased to exert the fascination over critics that it once did, but his function in the work is still contested. A recent commentator on the poem, Lynn Staley Johnson, suggests that E. K. is one of three Spenserian voices in the poem, the others being Immerito and Colin.[9] For our inquiry, the identity of E. K. is not particularly important; whether he is actually Edward Kirke, Edmund Spenser, or even Gabriel Harvey, his voice is an educated one, and the kind of commentary he provides is a revealing example of how an educated reader would approach a poem like *The Shepheardes Calendar*. In considering his dedicatory epistle to Harvey, the "Generall Argument," and the arguments and glosses to the separate poems, one is struck by the extent to which E. K. substantially recreates or perhaps parodies the method Erasmus had outlined in his advice about presenting authors to students.

Erasmus's first step, it will be remembered, was to "give a brief appreciation of the writer" (*De Ratione,* 682), and this is precisely what E. K. does (after flogging the phrase "uncouth unkiste" for longer than actually necessary):

> No lesse I thinke, deserueth his wittiness in deuising, his pithiness in vttering, his complaints of loue so louely, his discourses of pleasure so pleasantly, his pastorall rudeness, his morall witnesse, his dewe obseruing of Decorum euery where, in personages, in seasons, in matter, in speach, and generally in al seemely simplicitie of handeling his matter, and framing his words.[10]

Erasmus suggests that the teacher provide the appreciation of the writer to win over the audience, and this is E. K.'s explicit justification: he is trying to argue that "so soone as his name shall come into the knowledg of men, and his worthines be sounded in the tromp of fame, . . . he shall not onely kiste, but also beloued of all, embraced of the most, and wondred at of the best" (7).

The next steps in Erasmus's presentation deal with the argument: the teacher should first "point out the pleasure and profit to be derived from his argument" (682). That E. K. recognizes this as one of the expected components of an introduction is underlined by his pointed refusal to provide it:

> Now as touching the generall dryft and purpose of his AEglogues, I mind not to say much, him self laboring to conceale it. Onely this appeareth, that his unstayed yougth had long wandered in the common Labyrinth of Loue, in which time to mitigate and al-lay the heate of his passion, or els to warne (as he sayeth) the young shepherds .s. his equalls and companions of his unfortu-nate folly, he compiled these xij AEglogues. (10)

But of course E. K. cannot completely refrain from speculation and explanation, and so he goes on in the "Letter Dedicatory" to justify his "Glosse or scholion for thexposition of old words and harder phrases":

> which maner of glosing and commenting, well I wote wil seeme straunge and rare in our tongue: yet for somuch as I knew many excellent and proper deuises both in wordes and matter would passe in the speedy course of reading, either as unknowen, or as not marked, and in that kind, that we might be equal to the learned of other nations, I thought good to take the paines vpon me, the rather for that by meanes of some familiar acquaintaunce I was made priuie to his counsell and secret meaning in them. (10–11)

In its mixture of assumptions and justifications, this passage sheds a good bit of light upon E. K.'s approach to reading. First, he reflects an educated familiarity with glosses and commentaries; what is strange about his is simply that he is providing them for a vernacular text. He assumes that readers will be interested in the "excellent and proper deuises both in words and matter," but that inattentive reading might render them unnoticeable: readers lack-ing the focussing constraints provided by a commonplace book or by the marginal notations Harvey habitually wrote might overlook some of the "excellent and proper deuises" of the text, and E. K. wants to prevent this oversight. These inattentive readers are not pursuing a different kind of reading; they are simply practicing a debased form of the proper kind of reading, missing much of what they should notice, and E. K.'s glosses serve both to remind them of this fact and to provide some of the requisite focus. The second justification is the familiar appeal to national honor, which echoes E. K.'s earlier remarks on the glories of the Saxon heritage. The third continues the project of tantalizing the reader: E. K. has already declined to explain the "generall dryft and purpose" of the individual poems on the grounds that the author has himself attempted to conceal them, and he now continues to suggest that he in fact does know a good deal more about the argument and its possible applications than he is willing to divulge.

The third step of an Erasmian presentation is an explanation of "how much enjoyment and instruction may be had from reading [a particular genre]; next, the significance of that form of litera-ture, its origins, the number and types of [the genre] and its laws" (683; Erasmus is here using Terence as an example, so I have substituted "genre" for his "comedy"). Again, this is precisely what E. K. provides (in his oblique manner) in "The generall argument of the whole booke," where he is pedantically at pains to explain the origin of the genre and its utility. Although he begins paralep-tically by pretending that the discussion is unnecessary ("Little I hope, needeth me at large to discourse the first Originall of Aeglogues, hauing alreadie touched the same," 12), he cannot re-frain from displaying his knowledge. As opposed to "the best learned (as they think)," who derive 'eclogue' from "eclogai, as they would say, extraordinary discourses of vnnecessary matter," he prefers the Petrarchan derivation from "AEglogaj . . . that is Goteheards tales" (12), citing the seminal influence of Theocritus, who (unlike Virgil and even Spenser) does have goatherds as speakers. What is curious about E. K.'s discussion of the whole matter is how academic (in the worst sense, of parading learning with little or no relevance to the matter at hand) it is: the derivation, as he admits, does not describe Spenser's poems, since they are spoken by shepherds rather than goatherds. Even more important, he never indicates how his proposed derivation would affect the reader's understanding of the individual poems. We are left—perhaps purposely—with a definition to the wrong derivation: "extraordinary discourses of vnnecessary matter."

This is presumably part of his effort to suggest throughout, without actually stating it, that there is more to these poems than meets the eye. Earlier in the "Dedicatory Epistle" he had defended Spenser's use of the term by the fact that other poets had produced eclogues as their virgin efforts—Virgil, Mantuan, Petrarch, Boccaccio, Marot, Sanazarro (10), but this justification is only the third offered. The first is couched in a deliberately confusing syntax: "And also appeareth by the baseness of the name [Colin], wherein, it seemeth, he chose rather to vnfold great matter of argument couertly, then professing it, not suffice thereto accordingly. which moved him rather in AEglogues" (10). The phrase "not suffice thereto accordingly" is not clearly related to anything else in the sentence, and the punctuation of the original, with a period after the phrase, confuses the issue even more. "Wherein" at first leads the reader into believing that the "great matter of argument" is somehow contained in the name itself, and only later to realize that the poet, in the name of Colin, is unfolding "great matter." The "great matter of argument," which is unfolded covertly rather than openly, is echoed by the later incorrect derivation of "eclogue" ("extraordinary discourses of unnecessary matter") in a tantalizing way, as E. K. turns Erasmus's advice about profitable presentation into a maze of mirrors: the genre is identified, but the only utility explained is one attached to the wrong derivation, so it doesn't apply to the poems in question, and this is then contrasted with a correct definition, given earlier, which characterizes the poems but is unrelated to the genre. One wonders whether E. K. is here purposely presenting material from a student's point of view, since the confusions and difficulties recall so obviously the characterization Grafton and Jardine provide (87, 166).

The confusion is heightened when E. K. suggests a further generic classification for the eclogues:

> These xij. Aeglogues euery where answering to the seasons of the twelue monthes may be well deuided into three formes or ranckes. For eyther they be Plaintive, as the first, the sixt, the ele-uenth, and the twelfth, or recreatiue, such as those be, which con-ceiue matter of loue, or commendation of special personages, or Moral; which for the most part be mixed with some Satyrical bit-ternesse, namely the second of reuerence dewe to old age, the fift of coloured deceipt, the seuenth and ninth of dissolute shep-herdes and pastours, the tenth of contempt of Poetrie and pleas-aunt wits. And to this diuision may euery thing herein be reasonably applyed: a few onely except, whose speciall purpose and meaning I am not priuie to. (12)

As Johnson points out, " 'moral', 'plaintive', and 'recreative' are in no dictionary of rhetorical terms, no handbook of poetic forms. . . . Used as terms of literary criticism, Moral, Plaintive, and Recreative sound logical, but they exist only within the closed world and language of *The Shepheardes Calender*" (38). Even without the hint of mystery at the end of his passage, E. K.'s generic identifications further tantalize the reader by appearing to promise some insight without really providing it. Apparently firm generic identifications turn out to be simply labels to attach to the poems they apply to.

The next step in an Erasmian presentation is for the teacher to "explain as clearly and concisely as possible the gist of the plot" (683), an obligation which E. K. both does and does not fulfil. The arguments prefixed to the individual eclogues do provide the gist of each plot, and so E. K. has prepared the student-reader to understand what is going on. However, the introduction in "The Generall Argument" at first appears to be providing the gist of the entire plot and then fails to. His characterization of the individual poems as fitting the twelve months of the year—"These xij. AEclogues euery where answering to the seasons of the twelue monthes," (12)—echoes the advertisement on the title page that the twelve eclogues are "proportionable to the twelve monethes" and anticipates his remarks in the argument to December, in which Colin "proportioneth his life to the foure seasons of the year" (113). And indeed E. K. in his arguments and glosses frequently refers to the months or seasons, for example in his explanations of the astrological identifications of the months (including the obviously incorrect one for the present "November"; see 243, 405). However, this is all he does with the year as a unifying principle; on the rare occasions where his arguments or glosses refer the reader to other eclogues, it is almost always because a character has been repeated (see, e.g., his comparison of Colin's posie in June to the one from January [65], the gloss wondering whether the Cuddie in October is the same as the one in August [99], and the reference back to the first eclogue in the argument to "December"). When E. K. again refers to the year as an organizing principle, it is in reference to the comparison between life and the year, a commonplace that structures the December eclogue (113).

We should be hesitant, then—especially remembering the general Tudor reluctance, discussed in Chapter 1, to deal in any detail with larger structures—to ascribe to E. K. too firm a feeling for overall structure, as Johnson does: "he elaborates on the calendrical structure of *The Shepheardes Calendar,* suggesting that we consider the twelve eclogues as units in one work whose proportions reflect those of a natural year. By relating each of the eclogues to a grander pattern, E. K. prevents us from taking them separately and directs us to all twelve, to a work Spenser clearly conceived as a single poem" (37). It would be more in keeping with the general Tudor approach to structure to say that the twelve months of the year guarantee that there is some overall structuring principle, just as the general expectations about what constituted a comedy or a tragedy did, but that there is no expressed interest (either in the introductory material or in the individual arguments and glosses E. K. supplies) in how that structuring principle actually worked within the text to relate different parts of it to each other.

In his glosses, E. K. provides just the kind of close commentary

on language Erasmus had recommended: "draw . . . attention to
any purple passage, archaism, neologism, Graecism, any obscure
or verbose expression, any abrupt or confused order, any etymology, derivation, or composition worth knowing, any point of
orthography, figure of speech, or rhetorical passages, or embellishment or corruption" (*De Ratione*, 683). As E. K. makes clear in the
dedicatory epistle, he is especially interested in the poet's labor "to
restore, as to theyr rightfull heritage such good and natural English
words, as haue ben long time out of vse and almost cleane dis-
herited" (8), and throughout his glosses he provides explanations
of such words. Sometimes he adds an etymology, as when he
explains that "couthe" "commeth of the verb Conne, that is, to
know or to haue skill" (18) or relates "a loorde" in July to "lur-
danes" (73). Rhetorical figures are infrequently identified, as in the
gloss to January when he calls attention to "a pretty Epanothorsis
in these two verses, and withall a Paranomasia or playing with the
word" (18).

In the glosses themselves he pays little attention to syntax (Erasmus's "any obscure or verbose expression, any abrupt or confused
order"), but in the dedicatory epistle he had treated composition
immediately after diction:

> Now for the knitting of sentences, whych they call the ioynts and
> members thereof, and for all the compasse of the speach, it is
> round without roughnesse, and learned without hardnes, such in-
> deede as may be perceiued of the leaste, vnderstoode of the moste,
> but iudged onely of the learned. For what is in most English wry-
> ters vseth to be loose, and as it were vngyrt, in this Authour is well
> grounded, finely framed, and strongly trussed up. (9)

Erasmus next deals with imitation: "Next he should compare
parallel passages in authors, bringing out differences and similarities" (683), and E. K. provides a sketchy version of this comparison by identifying words other authors had used: "gride" is "an
olde word much vsed of Lidgate, but not found (that I know of) in
Chaucer" (26), or "Cheuisaunce": "sometime of Chaucer vsed for

gaine; sometime of other for spoyle, or bootie, or enterprise, and sometime for chiefdome" (56). He frequently identifies brief imitations of earlier poets, usually Virgil (e.g., in the glosses to January [37], Februarie [33], March [40]), and more infrequently, longer imitations of stories: "This tale of the Oake and the Bryere, he telleth as learned of Chaucer, but it is cleane in another kind, and rather like to AEsopes fables" (27). The antecedents of the names in the poem (Colin, Rosalinde, Hobbinol [17–18], even "the Widowes daughter of the glenne" [42]) are explained. He sometimes identifies entire eclogues as imitations (see the gloss to March [33] and the argument to August [76]). Only once does he devote much time to considering the imitation, when in glossing May (69) he identifies the source as "the Epitaphe of the ryotous king Sardanapalus" written in Greek, provides Cicero's translation and an English version, and then compares the epitaph of "a good olde Erle of Deuonshire" (56).

In the second chapter I explain that Erasmus skipped over the part of a teacher's presentation which dealt with identifying references in a text (except for what was considered the application of the arguments), perhaps because he was too aware of the opportunities for abuse it afforded, and quoted Vives on its necessity. This is a lesson E. K. has learned well, and most of the space in his glosses is devoted to explaining classical references and providing the necessary stories: Boreas (28), Flora (33), Lethe (34), Thetis dipping Achilles in the river Styx (34), Helicon, Syrinx (42), and so forth. He identifies the names of the speakers in the poems and is especially interested in contemporary allegorical references: Colin Cloute "is a name not greatly vsed, and yet I haue sene a Poesie of M. Skelton's vnder that title. But indeede the word Colin is Frenche, and vsed of the French Poete Marot. . . . Vnder which name this Poete secretely shadoweth himself, as sometime did Virgil vnder the name Tityrus" (17–18); Hobbinol "is a fained country name, whereby, it being so commune and vsuall, seemeth to be hidden the person of some his very speciall and most familiar freend, whom he entirely and extraordinarily beloued, as peradventure shall be more largely declared hereafter" (18); Rosalinde "is also a feigned name, which being wel ordered, wil bewray the very name of his loue and mistresse, whom by that name he coloureth. So as Ouide shadoweth hys loue vnder the name of Corynna" (18). Later in the poem, Syrinx is identified and her story recounted, and then she and Pan are related to Elizabeth and Henry VIII (43).

This kind of commentary shades almost imperceptibly into the final stage of Erasmus's presentation of the text, when the teacher "should turn to philosophy and skillfully bring out the moral implications of the poets' stories, or employ them as patterns" (683). This too E. K. is eager to do; in his gloss to March, for instance, he identifies and allegorizes Cupid ("a naked swayne"):

> a boye: For so is he described of the Poetes, to be a boye .s. always freshe and lustie: blindfolded, because he maketh no difference of Personages: with diuers coloured wings, .s. ful of flying fancies: with bowe and arrow, that is with glaunce of beautye, which pryk-eth as a forked arrowe. He is sayd also to haue shafts, some leaden, some golden: that is, both pleasure for the gracious and loued, and sorow for the louer that is disdayned or forsaken. (34)

And his explanation of the emblems for the same month seem to supply the very kind of moral commentary teachers were supposed to provide for their charges:

> Hereby is meant, that all the delights of Loue, wherein wanton youth walloweth, be but follye mixt with bitternesse, and sorow sawced with repentaunce. For besides that the very affection of Loue it selfe tormenteth the mynde, and vexeth the body many wayes, with vnrestfulnesse all night, and wearines all day, seeking for that we can not haue, and fynding that we would not haue: euen the selfe things which best before vs lyked, in course of time and chaung of ryper yeares, whiche also therewithall chaungeth our wonted lyking and former fantasies, will then seeme lothsome and breede vs annoyaunce, when yougthes flowre is withered, and we fynde our bodyes and wits answere not to suche vayne iollitie and lustful pleasaunce. (35)

85

In his prefaces, arguments, and glosses, E. K. thus provides exactly the kind of introduction to a literary text Erasmus had recommended, with one exception: he never treats the meter. Whether this is due to Spenser and Harvey's affection for classical meters is unclear, but it does not seem to be an especially important omission. What is equally illuminating in illustrating how the Erasmian approach to literature structures an educated reader's attention is to consider how much material in the apparatus E. K. provides for the poem does not derive from Erasmus. All of the material in the arguments and glosses reflects Erasmian influence, and in the "dedicatory epistle," only the extended opening play on "uncouth unkist," the lengthy defense of the vernacular, the excoriation of "the rakehelly route of our ragged rymers" (9), the references to Spenser's other works, and the dedicatory material directed at Harvey depart from a strict Erasmian skeleton. In the "Generall Argument," the discussion of the proper beginning for the calendrical year seems, from a strict Erasmian point of view, unnecessary, and in fact almost one of the unnecessary digressions Erasmus deplores, especially the section about the Egyptian calendar.

What should be clear from this brief consideration is how thoroughly the Erasmian approach to literary texts provides a model for E. K.'s commentary. This is the approach that E. K.—whoever he was—would have learned at school, and the approach he continued to consider the appropriate one for literary commentary, even commentary intended for adults. One explanation for this, of course, is that E. K. is Spenser's creation, a pompous schoolmaster in the tradition of Sidney's Rombus or Shakespeare's Holofernes, an identification Johnson hints at by relating "the droller aspects of E. K.'s two prefaces" to bombastic literature Spenser knew, including Sidney's Rombus (28), and by later comparing the sort of commentary E. K. provides to what a teacher would: "Fittingly, and like the schoolmaster he at times resembles, E. K. begins with eloquence" (32); "Like a schoolman, E. K. begins with the obvious" (49). Alternatively, E. K. could be a parody of a schoolmaster created by somebody else, perhaps Edward Kirke.

86

I would like to suggest that E. K.'s voice and method of presentation recall the practice of the schoolroom because that was the only model available for the sort of commentary (reading, interpretation) he provides. Unlike the parodied schoolmasters, his language is not especially pompous, nor is it unnecessarily interlarded with learned Latin tags; there is no chopping of logic. He may well be a consciously comic figure, but that is because of what he says (or doesn't say) and not because of the kinds of things he says. And it is the kinds of things—the topics suitable for literary commentary—that derive from the classroom. Whether E. K. is finally a person or a persona is less important for our inquiry than the evidence he provides, whatever he was, that educated Tudors had only one way to talk about a literary text, and that way was the Erasmian approach they had learned in the grammar school.

From E. K., caught—at least for us—in the never-never land between person and persona, we turn to one of the most vivid personalities of the period, Sir John Harington, for a final example of reading in the period. As penance for having translated the indecent tale of Gioconda from the twenty-seventh canto of Ariosto's *Orlando Furioso* and circulated it around the court, "the Queen's saucy godson" was banished from court until he should produce a translation of the entire poem.[11] To this project he devoted years, finally publishing an extremely lavish translation, complete with an engraved title page and illustrations at the beginning of each canto, a dedication to the queen, a critical preface and an "Advertisement to the Reader Before He reads in this Poem, of some Things to be Observed," and marginal notes and commentary at the end of each canto (which he referred to as a book) about the moral, historical, and allegorical significance of the tales therein, together with a section identifying the various allusions in the text. After the poem itself, he added "A Briefe and Summarie Allegorie of Orlando Furioso, Not Unpleasant nor Unprofitable for those that Have Read the Former Poeme," a brief life of Ariosto, "An Exact and Necessarie Table in Order of Alphabet, wherein You May Readilie Finde the Names of the principall

Persons treated in this worke, with the chiefe matters that concerne them," and a listing of "The Principal Tales in Orlando Furioso that may be read by themselves" (McNulty, xlvii–xlix). The elaborateness of this edition, which imitates earlier Italian editions (McNulty, xli–xliv), reflects the high contemporary estimation of Ariosto, but is also, perhaps (at least partially) another extended witticism by the queen's saucy godson: if the translation is a penance for translating a bawdy tale, he will compound it by turning it into one of the most lavish books published in England until that time (McNulty, xlvii). And despite the fact that most of the apparatus was plagiarized from various Italian sources, what Harington chose to include reflects his conception of what a proper edition of a venerated author comprises, and provides evidence for the way he expected his translation to be read.

It should come as no surprise that most of the apparatus Harington supplies fulfills one or another of Erasmus's suggestions for presenting authors to schoolboys. The brief appreciation of the author is supplied primarily by the life of Ariosto following the translation but also by material in the preface. The pleasure and benefit of the argument are treated at length in the preface, while the various applications and moral implications of the tales are explained in the notes to the cantos and in the "Briefe and Summary Allegorie" at the end. Harington shows a good deal more concern about the gist of the plot than most other authors of the period in the list of principal tales he provides at the end, in the table of main characters, and in the marginal notes which indicate where an interrupted tale is continued. Marginally and in his notes he indicates Ariosto's similarity to other authors (without, it is true, discussing them in any detail), and in the preface he justifies Ariosto's poem by comparing it to the *Aeneid*. He consistently identifies similes, sentences, and proverbs in the marginal notes (in case any reader needs guidance in compiling a commonplace book?), and even the meter is considered when Harington justifies his retention of polysyllabic rhyme (15). He explains references in the text either marginally or in the "Exact and Necessarie Table" containing all the names in the poem (mythological, fictional, historical, and geographical) and provides the historical background for each canto in the section on "Historie" following it. In short, with the exception of a close consideration of the language of the text, which would be impossible in a translation, the material Harington provides for his edition reflects what he would have learned about a famous author at school.

Two characteristics of Harington's translation provide additional perspective on matters which we have touched on only slightly until now: his attention to the plot, and his emphasis on allegorical interpretation. There is general agreement in the period that narratives or stories are immediately appealing; we remember that one of Sidney's arguments for the superiority of poetry over philosophy is that, unlike the crabbed definitions of philosophy, poetry provides "a tale which holdeth children from play, and old men from the chimney corner,"[12] a sentiment Harington liked so much that he incorporated it into his own "Briefe Apologie" (8). And as I discussed in chapter 1, Erasmus considered historical examples or feigned examples equally effective in teaching, partially because both compel the same kind of attention. But the emphasis on reading sections rather than works militates against following a lengthy story, especially when the story is consistently interrupted by others, as is typical in Ariosto. Harington recognized the problem: one of the objections to the *Orlando* he considers in his "Preface" is that Ariosto "breaks off narrations verie abruptly so as indeed a loose unattentive reader will hardly carrie away any part of the storie." His answer stresses both utility and authority: "but this doubtlesse is a point of great art, to draw a man with a continuall thirst to reade out the whole worke and toward the end of the booke to close up the diverse matters briefly and cleanly. If S. Philip Sidney had counted this a fault, he would not have done himself in his Arcadia" (13). Whatever the theoretical justification, however, he attempted to solve the practical problem by providing a table of principal tales at the end of the volume, which gives the beginning of two dozen tales, and by the "Exact and Necessarie Table," which lists alphabetically the "names of characters, beasts, weapons, places, and classical figures alluded to, usually a brief phrase or sentence of identification—'*Agramant* Emperour of the Turkes, sonne of *Trajano, alias* the Southerne king'—and a detailed list of the places the entry appears in the poem" (McNulty, xlix). Equally importantly, whenever a tale is interrupted, he indicates in the margin where it is continued:

> Further, where divers stories in this worke seene in many places abruptly broken off I have set directions in the margent where to find the continuance of every such storie, though I would not wish any to reade them in that order at the first reading, but if any thinke them worthie the twise reading, then he may the second time not unconveniently use it if the meane matter betweene the so devided stories (upon which commonly they depend) be not quite out of his memorie. (16)

Guidance in reconstructing the tales is provided, not for the casual reader who would read the poem only once, but for the more thoughtful reader who is willing to reread it. And it is precisely this kind of reader who would derive the most benefit from the allegorical meanings of the tales Harington is so much at pains to explain in his "Briefe and Summary Allegorie" at the end of the book. By his notes at the end of each canto, Harington ensures that reading canto by canto in the normal way is edifying; but to appreciate the fullest significance of the stories, one must be able to follow them through the maze of Ariosto's narrative. The tale of Isabella, for instance, which Harington thought Ariosto had devised "to lay before all chast and vertuous matrones an example how the troubles that happen to their husbands must be a meane to set forth their prayse the more," and which elicited from him the exclamation "Oh worthy *Isabella* that deservest to be painted in Tables and set foorth in clothes of Arres for an example to all young Ladyes of constant chastity" (565), begins at the end of canto twelve with her discovery by Orlando in a cave, continues through the thirteenth canto, then breaks off until the twenty-third canto, where she is reunited with her husband Zerbino. She remains with him until he is killed in the twenty-fourth canto,

90

whereupon she becomes a Christian and disappears with a godly hermit until she is rediscovered by Rodomont at the end of the twenty-eighth canto, and, to preserve her chastity, manages to trick him into killing her in the twenty-ninth canto. To derive the full moral value of her story, the reader must be able to follow its intermittent appearance over the course of some seventeen cantos, and Harington's apparatus makes this possible.

The second characteristic of Tudor reading that Harington provides especially good evidence for is the habit of reading allegorically. In justifying poetry generally in his "Preface," Harington defends a basically medieval approach to reading:

> The ancient Poets have indeed wrapped as it were in their writings divers and sundry meanings which they call the sences or mysteries thereof. First of all for the literall sence (as it were the utmost bark or rine) they set down, in manner of an historie, the acts and notable exploits of some persons worthy memory; then, in the same fiction, as a second rine and somewhat more fine as it were nearer to the pith and marrow, they place the Morall sense, profitable for the active life of man, approving vertuous actions and condemning the contrarie. Many times also under the self-same words they comprehend some true understanding of Naturall Philosophie or politike government and now and then of divinitie, and these same senses that comprehend so excellent knowledge we cal the Allegorie which *Plutarch* defineth to be when one thing is told and by that another is understood. (5)

This may not be an especially sophisticated understanding of allegory (indeed, in comparison to Harington's source in *La spositione di M. Simon Fornari da Rheggio sopra l'Orlando Furioso di M. Ludovico Ariosto* it is quite pedestrian; see McNulty, xxxvii–viii), but is serviceable, and Harington is able to use it to provide in the notes at the end of each canto a consideration of the historical, moral, and allegorical senses of the material covered. Erasmus, we will remember, had suggested that some works required allegorical interpretation but supplied no guidance in determining which ones; Harington assumes that all (or almost all, since he does not supply any allegorical commentary for eleven cantos; he does, however, provide a "Morall" commentary for every book) of *Orlando Furioso* will repay an allegorical approach.

The central problem with allegorical readings, of course, is to determine what kind of allegory is present. As we see in the next chapter, this was a problem the religious writers found a principled solution to. Harington's formulation—that some true understanding of natural philosophy, politic government, or divinity may be suggested—reflects a reading process in which the text is scrutinized for its relevance to a short list of important topics; the possible types of allegory suggest an abbreviated version of a commonplace book. The problem is its generality, in two senses: first, the terms natural philosophy, politic government, and divinity are so broad that they cover practically any conceivable reading. Second, it is a very general solution which does not provide specific guidance in the reading situation; in the terms I use in the appendix, it is teleological rather than operational, identifying the goal rather than the means of attaining it. As I discuss in the second chapter, identification of the goal—say as a topic in a commonplace book—can provide a means of validating an interpretation, since any example of the goal will automatically be acceptable, but Harington's terms are so broad that they validate almost all readings and thus suggest no way to choose between competing interpretations. For instance, in the twenty-third canto, Astolfo gives Bradamante his winged horse, corslet, and spear in preparation for his journey around the world: "All these he left behind to make him light / Before that he begins to take his flight" (23.9, p. 251). Fornari's explanation of the episode relates Astolfo to the poet:

In Astolfo who gives to Bradamente the horse and all his arms to make himself lighter for making his journey through the air is demonstrated figuratively the poet, who desiring to acquire knowledge of the various things and see diverse countries and make himself master of custom, puts aside in parting all impedi-

92

ments which could either deter him or retard his voyage. (McNulty, xxviii)

Harington changes the significance to emphasize its relation to divinity:

In Astolfo that put of his armor and gave away his spare horse, and all his superfluous weapons when he was to take the Griffith horse and fly about the world may be gathered a good allegoricall sence or rather it may be called Theologicall, namely that he that will betake him selfe to so high a profession as to teach and studie the high mysteries of Christen religion and live in contemplation of heavenly things should cast away the burdenous clog of all worldly incumbrances and, to use the phrase of our Saviour him-self (leave father wife and children) and what soever else may be a hinderance to our proceedings in this kind. (McNulty, xxviii; 263)

McNulty's comment, "Actually Astolfo, here and elsewhere in the *Orlando,* shows little to make him the type either of a poet or of a theologue except a passing acquaintance with the decidedly un-Pegasian flying horse" (xxviii), is not entirely accurate. It is Astolfo, after all, who ascends to Paradise to learn from St. John how to recover Orlando's wits. Before his ascent, however, he bathes in a crystal stream to remove the smoke he had encountered in his descent into hell and the dirt and dust he got on himself when stopping up the cave that is the mouth to hell (34, 47–49). Har-ington curiously has nothing to say about the descent into hell, but he does pick up on the crystal stream:

First, whereas *Astolfo* washeth himselfe in a Christall well of cleare water before he can fly up to Paradise, it signifieth that after a man shall by remorse and devout consideration weigh and behold the filthiness of his sinne he must then wash himselfe with the clear spring water of prayer and repentance, and then and not be-fore, he may mount to Paradise, which may here be understood the comfortable peace of conscience, the only true Paradise of this world. (398–99)

Harington's allegorical interpretation here seems more obviously justified than his earlier one, partially because of the temporal contiguity between the preparation of bathing in the stream and the action of ascending into paradise, and a long tradition associating bathing of various kinds with purification. But does Astolfo's ascent in the thirty-fourth book justify the allegorical reading Harington provides for disburdening himself in the twenty-third book? Presumably Harington is anticipating the later ascent when he provides the earlier reading, but between the two incidents come Astolfo's tour of the world and further adventures in Senapo, so if the action in the twenty-third canto is a preparation for the ascent in the thirty-fourth, it is curiously anticipatory. Whether the later events justify Harington's earlier reading or not, they do emphasize the necessity of following the gist of the plot: unless Astolfo's widely separated actions can be related to each other, there is no basis at all for Harington's reading of the earlier scene.

Nor is there any justification, either in the twenty-third book or later, for seeing Astolfo as a type of the poet, as does Fornari. These two allegorical readings of Astolfo pose a problem which I intend not to solve but merely to underline: without some guiding conception of what constitutes an acceptable allegory, readers have no way to decide what their readings should be or to choose between two that are presented to them, and the guidelines Harington supplies in the list of goals for allegorical reading are so general that they provide little guidance in themselves. As Harington explains in "A Briefe and Summarie Allegorie" following his translation, he is determined to find an allegorical reading wherever possible:

> because I know in mine own conscience that all the verses in this worke be not so full weight but, if they shalbe tryed in so severe a ballance, some will be found many graines to light, I would endevour all I might to supply that defect with the more weightie

and sober consideration of the Allegorie which, as I have partly touched in every severall booke, so now I entend to present for your consideration, the whole body of the same. (558)

At the beginning of the "Briefe and Summarie Allegorie," he recounts that he was impelled to write it by reading in Robert Parsons' *Resolution,* or *The First Booke of the Christian Exercise Appertayning to Resolution* (or perhaps Edmund Bunny's revised version of it; see McNulty, xxx) that

> *the glory of St. Paul is encreased dayly in heaven and shall be to the worlds end by reason of them that dayly do profite by his writing and rare exemplar life upon earth, as also on the contrarie part that the torments of* Arrius Sabellius *and other wicked heretikes are continually augmented by the numbers of them who from time to time are corrupted with their seditious and pestilent writings. . . . The like they hold of dissolute Poets and other loose writers who have left behind them lascivious, wanton, and carnall devices.* (558)

The "Briefe and Summarie Allegorie" was written after the translation was completed, as were at least some of the commentaries at the end of the cantos (in the notes to canto 43, for instance, he refers to his dog Bungy, "whose picture you may see in the first page of the book," indicating that he knew what the title page would look like when he composed the note [xlv], and the notes are generally lacking from the Bodleian manuscript of the first twenty-four books in Harington's own hand [xliv, xlvii–viii]). Thus it is not impossible to see in at least some of the allegorical interpretations an afterthought to the translation, probably instigated by his reading of Parsons/Bunny and by his consequent desire to "justify his translation to enemies of poetry, the Reformers."[13]

For Harington himself, then, the predetermining desire to find moral allegories wherever possible provides the necessary criterion of acceptability. And his advice at the end of "A Briefe and Summarie Allegorie" commends the same kind of ruminative approach to the reader: "Thus much I thought good to note of the

generall Allegorie of the whole work to give you occasion to rumi-
nate, as it were, and better to digest that which you before in
reading did perhaps swallow down whole without chewing" (568).

Two additional factors may have influenced the content and
length of these allegorical annotations. Simon Cauchi has shown
that Harington's imitation of his Italian sources in including annotations after each canto served not only an apologetic end but
also an aesthetic one: "we can be sure that Harington, as a rule,
liked his annotations to finish neatly at the foot of the page," and
that he tailored his comments to fit the available space.[14] Ideally,
the annotations would end at the bottom of a recto, so the plate for
the next book would appear on the following verso, facing the
argument to the canto Harington had claimed would help the
reader "to understand the picture the perfecter" (Harington, 17).
This ideal was not always achieved, but in most cases, the annotations did in fact end at the bottom of the page (Cauchi, 160), an
outcome Harington helped ensure with notes to the printer like
the one at the end of book 29: "Yf thear bee roome enowgh in the
page print the verses at length yf not then print them as they are
heer written [two lines of verse per line of script], and yf need be
leave out the latten verse quyte" (Cauchi, 161). The annotations at
the end of each book, then, with their moral, historical, allegorical, and intertextual (as we may call what Harington refers to as
"Allusion") sections, are constrained by their contribution to "the
silent poetry of book design" (Cauchi, 166).

This presumably helps to explain what Townsend Rich had
long ago called a "certain spasmodic quality" in the notes, "some of
them being extremely long and some extremely short" (149). His
only explanation was to suggest that "Sir John was not particularly,
or at least consistently, interested in the allegory" (149), but with
Cauchi's research, we may conclude that Harington *was* interested
in the allegory—why else include the "Briefe and Summary Allegorie" at the end at all, or the allegorical notes to the separate
cantos, which are absent from the Italian editions (McNulty, xlvii;
Cauchi, 159)—but considered the allegorical notes to each canto

less crucial to his overall purpose than an impressive bibliograph-
ical design. Additional support for this explanation comes from
T. G. A. Nelson's contention that Harington's book indicates "a
growing awareness of the limitations of the allegorical method as a
way of interpreting, and justifying, poetry."[15] Harington himself
indicates some doubts about the allegorical method even while
purveying it:

> If at times he advanced interpretations of which he himself enter-
> tained some doubts, he more than once went out of his way to
> warn his reader that they might be spurious. He never grappled
> with the problem of intentionality. At one moment he expresses
> nervousness about searching for an allegory where none was in-
> tended by the author himself, while at the next we find him sug-
> gesting that an allegory "may not unfitly be gathered" from the
> passage whether the author intended it or not. (Nelson, 378)

But he continued in his allegorical presentation because "he feared
that the poem would not otherwise pass muster among his own
friends and contemporaries" (378–79).

Fortunately, for our purposes it is unnecessary to decide whether
Harington entertained doubts about the allegorical method; probably the safest conclusion is the one Nelson eventually reaches: "on
the whole, then, it seems likely that Harington himself reserved his
judgment" (378). Whatever Harington's private position on the
question—whether he believed allegorical interpretations justified
all or part of the time, or simply included them because he thought
that his readers expected them—the presence of the allegorical
apparatus in his edition of the *Furioso* testifies to the continued
influence of the allegorical method of reading.

In these three writers, we see the ways in which the effects of
classroom presentation of authors persisted; it provided the basic
model for critical commentary, the topics to be covered, and the
methods to be used. Nor is this particularly strange: readers, then
as now, read the way they were taught to read, and the method of

reading taught in the grammar schools was derived from Erasmus. But the grammar schools educated only a very small minority of the population; where did readers who learned to read elsewhere find their models for reading? That is the topic of the next two chapters.

CHAPTER 4

READING IN
A RELIGIOUS
SETTING

From those who were highly educated we turn to those who were not. My argument until now has been that those who attended grammar schools were exposed to a method of reading so monolithic that they would carry this method with them for the rest of their lives. But what about those who had not attended grammar schools: where would they find their models for reading? An obvious place to look is into their initial instruction, whether provided in the petty schools or dame schools, or by neighborhood women who taught them. T. W. Baldwin summarizes the goal of the petty school as follows: "It aimed to teach to read and write always, and to cast accounts frequently. Its chief texts for reading are the *ABC, Catechism,* and *Primer.*"[1] As is apparent from the texts cited, "[p]etty school was predominantly religious" (Baldwin, 85) and the texts aim primarily at providing children with the fundamental theory and practice of their religion. The catechism, at least in the form in which it appeared in the 1549 *Book of Common Prayer,* supplied the Creed, the Ten Commandments, the Paternoster, and general paraphrases of them.[2] The primer was essentially a fuller version of the catechism (Baldwin, 50–51). *King Henry's Primer* of 1545, for instance, provided what the catechism had, plus "The Calendar, . . . The Matins, The Evensong, The Complene, The Seven Psalms, The Litany, The Dirige, The Commendations, The Psalms of the Passion, The Passion of our Lord, [and] Certain godly prayers for sundry purposes."[3] The aim of these books was to provide first, the basic instruction in the fundamentals of religion, and second, proper forms in which to pray; as King Henry put it in his preface to the primer, the goal was "that men may know both what they pray, and also with what words, lest things special good and principal, being inwrapped in ignorance of the words, should not perfectly come to the mind and to the intelligence of men; or else things being nothing to the purpose, nor very meet to be offered unto God, should have the less effect with God" (440). These books provide simply the material to be memorized, rather than explanations of it, and so, unfortunately, provide few models of reading.

The religious instruction that began in petty school continued in church, at which attendance was required: an order from 1553 states that "all and every person, and persons, inhabiting within this realm . . . shall diligently and faithfully (having no lawful or reasonable excuse to be absent) endeavour themselves to resort to their Parish Church, or Chapel accustomed . . . upon every Sunday, and other days, ordained, and used to be kept as holy days, and then, and there to abide, orderly and soberly, during the time of the common prayer, preachings, or other service of God" (Baldwin, 52), and an act of Parliament reaffirmed the statute under Elizabeth.[4] Even those who had little formal schooling would have experienced every week in church examples of reading and explication in the form of sermons and homilies, catechisms, and instruction in the Creed, the Paternoster, the Ten Commandments, and other prayers.

As we survey the kinds of instruction, formal and informal, provided in church, we must be mindful of several limitations. First, there is on the face of it no guarantee that anybody would transfer the kind of reading and interpreting done in church to the secular sphere. But there are two reasons to think that this kind of reading might in fact be generalized. The first is that much of the reading done by the relatively uneducated would be religious in any case; living when evangelical fervor is widespread, we might be somewhat less surprised by this than was Louis B. Wright over fifty years ago, but his account puts the case nicely:

> No phase of Elizabethan literary interest seems stranger today than the inordinate appetite of that age for "good books." The zest for collections of pious aphorisms, books of prayers and religious guidance, printed sermons, adaptations of the Psalms, and moralized allegories was limited only by the ability of the printers to pour out such works.[5]

The second is that people who have few models of reading may not have the choice of what to transfer: if the kind of reading they were exposed to in church provided the only model available, the question for them would not be whether to read in the religious fashion exemplified in church or in a secular fashion learned somewhere else, but simply whether to read or not. The kind of reading they would have learned is perhaps a little overzealously explained by Thomas Lever in his preface to John Bradford's exposition of the commandments, the Lord's Prayer, and the Creed, but only a little:

> For when as we recite, reade, take, or heare any portion of Gods worde, without any desire, meditation, or consideration of the meaning thereof to enter into our mindes, then doe we abuse the letter which killeth, refusing or neglecting the spirit which quickeneth. . . . And it can be nothing els but a grievous sinne and a plague, so to be delighted and deluded with the vaine sound, number, and order of wordes, that a man can not, or will not tast of the most comfortable matter and meaning conteyned in the same words. . . . But here note, that when there is any desire and diligence to have the mind moved and edified by the meaning of good wordes: that is profitable to man, and acceptable to God.[6]

The kind of reading Lever recommends, meditative and preparative, is obviously related to the kinds we have already seen in Erasmus and more especially in Harvey, with his Ramistic emphasis on matter as much as expression.

101

It may well be an oversimplification of the actual situation to assume that many readers derived their sole models of reading from religious sources, but for us to understand the reading practices of an earlier age we must somehow escape our own assumption that they will be basically the same as ours; assuming that differences will exist makes it easier to recognize them. It requires an act of the imagination for us to conceive of a society in which there are only one or two models available. And we should be reassured when we find Lever so zealously promulgating one of the characteristics of reading we have already identified: that it is always preparation for some other activity. In any case, whatever model it is possible to reconstruct from the religious material to be examined here will be *a* model for reading, even if not the exclusive pattern.

Third, a limitation that applies as well to the instruction in schools: the teacher, had he read Erasmus or other educational theorists, might have had a reasonably explicit model in mind for the interpretation and presentation of authors. In the terminology of Bourdieu discussed in the appendix, he had not only individual paths to follow, but also some conception of the whole map his paths traversed. The students, on the other hand, lacked the theoretical background: they had only examples of the teacher's presentation of authors from which to derive their own models of interpretation. They may very well have had paths without being aware of the larger landscape. The same thing is true to an even greater extent of what parishioners learned in church: while the examples of the *artes praedicandi* to be discussed below indicate that preachers, even those with no Latin, had access to explicit instruction for the interpretation of Scripture, the parishioners heard only the results of the preacher's interpretation, and the models for reading derived from those interpretations were thus largely implicit.

A final, and major, difference is that in an era of religious controversy, different interpretations of important texts abounded. In the self-congratulatory preface to *A necessary Doctrine and Erudition for any Christian Man* (1543; known as *The King's Book* because of its preface by Henry VIII), Henry rejoices that his efforts "to purge and cleanse our realm from the apparent enormities of [hypocrisy and superstition] . . . by opening of God's truth, with setting forth of the scriptures" "have not been void and frustrate," but he laments the appearance of a new danger: "we find entered into some of our people's hearts an inclination to sinister understanding of scripture, presumption, arrogancy, carnal liberty, and contention."[7] *The King's Book* was an attempt "to set forth, with the advice of our clergy, such a doctrine and declaration of the true knowledge of God and his word, with the principal articles of our religion, as whereby all men may uniformly be led and taught the true understanding of that which is necessary for every Christian man to know" (3–4). The same desire for uniformity of understanding occasioned *The Primer* two years later, in 1545: Henry "set forth this Primer, or book of prayers in English, to be frequented and used in and throughout all places of our said realms and dominions, as well of the elder people, as also of the youth, for their common and ordinary prayers" "for the avoiding of the adversity of primer books that are now abroad, whereof there are almost innumerable sorts, which minister occasion of contentions and vain disputations rather than edify; and to have one uniform order of all such books throughout all our dominions, both to be taught unto children, and also to be used for ordinary prayers of all our people not learned in the Latin tongue" (457–58). Even more specific in its reference to multiplicity of interpretation is the Bishop of Rochester's justification for expounding the relevant Scriptures in "An Instruction of the Manner in Hearing of The Mass" contained in his *Primer,* issued at the behest of Cromwell in 1539:

And first shall I rehearse the Scriptures which the sacramentaries go about to enstablish their heretical opinion, as concerning the body of Christ, presence of the same sacrament, declaring such places of Scripture, that they have chosen, in their own native sense, that thereby may appear both that they distort the scripture for their singular opinion, and also that their opinion is no less

103

than an heresy, and therefore utterly to be forsaken of every true Christian. Secondly, I will infer the Scriptures with the consent of a few sentences of the most ancient doctors, to the confirmation of the upright and infallible truth and verity.[8]

The authorized homilies, *CERTAYNE SERMONS OR HOME-LIES, Appoynted by the Kynges Majestie to Be Declared and Redde by All Persones, Vicars, or Curates, Every Sondaye in Their Churches Where They Have Cure* (1547), were issued under Edward to combat the same kind of heretical multiplicity of interpretation:

The Kynges most excellent Majestie . . . considerynge the manifolde enormities whiche heretofore have crept into hys Graces realme . . . callynge to remembraunce that the next and moste readie way to expell and avoide, aswell all corrupte, vicious and ungodly livynge, as also erronious doctrine tending to supersticion and idolatrie, and clerely to put away all contencion which hath heretofore rysen through diversitie of preachynge, is the true settyng furthe and pure declarynge of Gods Woorde . . . hath caused a booke of homelies to bee made.[9]

Elizabeth reissued the collection in 1559, with a new preface again citing the desire "to avoyde the manyfolde enormities which heretofore by false doctrine have crept into the church of God" (57), and she continued throughout her reign to have faith in their efficacy: "For Elizabeth, then, a minister who did not deviate from the text of the homilies was a minister who could not lapse into theological error and would not provoke controversy" (Bond, 10).

These references to contention, disputation, sinister understanding, and the enormities of erronious understanding provide eloquent testimony that both prayer and interpretation of the Scriptures were sites of contestation. We can assume that schoolboys, who would have had one master throughout their grammar school educations (unless, of course, they changed schools or the schoolmaster was replaced), were exposed to a uniform method of interpretation, and that, more particularly, the individual texts they studied received univocal readings. Neither of these assumptions can be made about religious instruction. Different preachers, especially if they represented different religious factions, might well provide different explanations of Scripture; as late as 1583 Elizabeth complained to Archbishop Whitgift, "I have heard there be six preachers in one diocese the which do preach in six sundry ways" (Bond, 10). Since going to sermons was a major form of entertainment, those people who were most interested and thus also the most likely to derive their own reading practices from what they heard were also the ones most likely to hear a variety of approaches. So while schoolboys would have learned *one* way of reading, churchgoers may have been exposed to several different ones, each claiming to be *the correct* one—the one revealing the native sense of the passage—the others being wrong and heretical. In such a circumstance, it makes especially good sense to enquire into the underlying interpretive strategies to see what they have in common.

Finally, we must be aware that not everything churchgoers heard in church could have provided a model for reading. In fact, very little did, just as today, very little of what elementary students hear in school relates to addition and subtraction. But for people with few other examples of interpretation to base their own models of reading on, that little may have been decisive.

As early as 1536 a royal injunction specified that "parsons, vicars, and other curates aforesaid shall diligently admonish the fathers and mothers, masters and governors of youth, being under their care, to teach their children and servants, even from their infancy, the Pater Noster, the Articles of our Faith, and the Ten Commandments in their mother tongue."[10] The curates were encouraged to "deliberately and plainly recite of the said Pater Noster, the Articles of our Faith and the ten Commandments, one clause or article one day, and another another day, till the whole be taught and learned by little, and shall deliver the same in writing or show where printed books containing the same be to be sold, to them that can read or will desire the same" (Wood, 139). As a royal order of 1538 makes clear, there were two goals of this instruction. First, rote memorization: "Ye shall every Sunday and Holy day through the year, openly and plainly recite to your parishioners twice or thrice together, or oftener if need require, one particle or sentence of the Pater Noster or Creed in English, to the intent that they may learn the same by heart." Second, some level of comprehension: "And as they may be taught every sentence of the same by rote, ye shall expound and declare the understanding of the same unto them" (Wood, 140). This basic instruction provided for parishioners is a kind of adult education version of what the primer and catechism supplied for those who attended petty schools.

Following, but not entirely as a result of, these injunctions, a number of expositions of the specified texts appeared. *The King's Book,* with its royal imprimatur, was one of the most influential of these. It was published in 1543 with the twin purposes of correcting error and instructing the people in the right. Correction was necessary, as we have already seen, because there "entered into some of our people's hearts an inclination to sinister understanding of scripture, presumption, arrogancy, carnal liberty, and contention" (3), but instruction, especially of the new dispensation—"a doctrine and declaration of the true knowledge of God and his word, with all the principle articles of our religion, as whereby all men may uniformly be led and taught the true understanding of that which is necessary for every Christian man to know" (4)—was equally important. The book contains expositions of faith, the Creed, the seven sacraments, the Ten Commandments, the Lord's Prayer, the Ave Maria, articles on free will, justification, good works, and a discussion of the efficacy of praying for the dead. Although the preface addresses all the king's loyal subjects—"we heartily exhort our people of all degrees willingly and earnestly both to read and print in their hearts the doctrine of this book" (5)—it continues on to distinguish between the teachers who must read the Scriptures themselves and the taught, for whom "the reading of the Old and New Testament is not so necessary for all those folks" (6), and we may extend this distinction to the literate clergy and others who would actually read the book and would thus derive one model of reading, and those who would hear some version of its "necessary doctrine and erudition" explained to them, just as they heard the Bible explained to them, and would derive a quite different model. In this latter group we would expect to find not only the illiterates, but also those marginally literate who had no desire to enquire more closely than necessary into spiritual matters.

One aspect of the kind of reading modelled by *The King's Book* is apparent in the first section, treating the meaning of the word *faith,* since without some understanding of what faith is, the "common people" would have little idea of how to have faith in the articles of belief—"to the intent that it may be known what is meant properly by the word *faith,* as it is appertaining to a Christian man" (9). Two senses of the word are distinguished: first, "a several gift of God by itself, distinct from hope and charity; and so taken, it signifieth a persuasion and belief wrought by God in man's heart, whereby he assenteth, granteth, and taketh for true, not only that God is, . . . but also that all the words and sayings of God which be revealed and opened in the scripture, be of most certain truth and infallible verity" (9). Second, "faith . . . is considered as it hath hope and charity annexed and joined unto it: and faith so taken, signifieth not only the belief and persuasion before mentioned in the first acception, but also a pure confidence and hope to attain whatsoever God hath promised for Christ's sake, and an hearty love to God, and obedience to his commandments. And this faith is a lively faith, and worketh in man a ready submission of his will to God's will" (10). Those reading or hearing this explanation would be alerted to the multiple significance of words, and might even be encouraged to seek multiple senses in the words they read.

Indeed, emphasis on the (multiple) meanings of words is one of the characteristics of *The King's Book*. The explanation of the Creed proceeds article by article, sometimes providing the necessary scriptural and historical background, sometimes considering the meanings of the various words. The discussion of the first article ("I believe in God the Father Almighty, Maker of heaven and earth") begins "For the plain understanding hereof, every material word of this article shall be declared hereafter" (15), and then continues to explicate "God," "God the Father," "almighty," "maker of heaven and earth," and finally, "believe." Later in the treatise, in the treatment of the Ten Commandments, there are explanations of what "have" (in "Thou shalt have none other gods but me") means (84), how "father," "mother," and "honour" are to be taken (it takes no great imagination to predict that "in this commandment, by these words *father and mother* is understand not only the natural father and mother which did carnally beget us, and brought us up, but also princes and all other governors, rulers, and pastors, under whom we be nourished and brought up, ordered and guided" [99], or that "honour" includes "a prompt and ready obedience to their lawful commandments" and that "this is the very honour and duty which not only the children do owe unto their parents, but also all subjects and inferiors to their heads and rulers" [99–100]), and how "murder," "adultery," "theft or stealing," and "false witness" are to be understood (very broadly). The section on the Paternoster proceeds similarly, with explanations of all the key terms and their implications; by "bread" (in "Give us this day our daily bread"), for instance, we are to understand not "superfluous riches or great substance, or abundance of things above our estate and condition, but such things only as be necessary and sufficient for every man in his degree. . . . meat, and drink, and clothes" (130). But since it is "our bread," the petition is also a reprehension of "persons which eat not their own bread, and devour other men's bread" (131). The bread may also signify the Eucharist, and finally, "the true doctrine of the word of God, which is the spiritual bread that feedeth the soul" (133).

To see how this polysemy is achieved, it is useful to look more closely at the explanations in *The King's Book* of the Ten Commandments. The general pattern of exposition of each commandment utilizes three slightly different means of broadening the significance of words. Typically, after the statement of the commandment (e.g., "Thou shalt not steal"), there is a paragraph explaining the meaning of what is proscribed:

108

> Under the name of *theft* or *stealing,* in this commandment, is un-
> derstand all manner of unlawful taking away, occupying, or keep-
> ing of another man's goods, whether it be by force, extortion,
> oppression, bribery, usury, simony, unlawful chevisance or shifts,
> or else by false buying and selling, either by false weights, or by
> false measures, or by selling of a thing counterfeit for a true, as gilt
> copper for true gold, or glass for precious stones; and generally all
> manner of fraud and deceit. (114)

In this paragraph (and similar ones for the other commandments),
the generalization of the key term is primarily semantic, indexed
by the word "generally," which appears in the discussion of other
commandments as well. Linguistically, the operations used are a
combination of generalization and specification; here, *theft* is immediately generalized to "all manner of unlawful taking away,
occupying, or keeping," and this unlawful activity is then specified
in a number of examples. At the end, these examples provide the
basis for the further generalization to "all manner of fraud and
deceit." That this generalization is part of a conscious pattern is
indicated by a summary discussion of the last commandment:

> Furthermore, like as in the fifth commandment, under the name
> of *father* and *mother,* is understand all superiors; and in the sixth
> commandment, under the name of *killing,* is understand all wrath
> and revenging; and in the seventh commandment, under the
> name of *adultery,* is understand all unchaste living; and in the
> eighth commandment, under the name of *theft,* is understand all
> deceitful dealing with our neighbors; and in the ninth command-
> ment, under the name of *false witness,* is understand all misreport
> and untrue use of our tongue; so in this last commandment, un-
> der the name of *desiring of another man's wife and goods,* is under-
> stand all manner of evil and unlawful desire of any thing. (120)

This form of generalization is especially rampant in the discussion of the Ten Commandments, since they provide an oppor-

tunity for the authorities to define proper behavior, religious and civil, and it is related to the other two methods of generalizing the meaning of words in these explanations. First, and most obviously, understanding of the commandments is intended to lead to various kinds of behaviors—reading is prologue to practical action of some kind—and so it seems only fitting that the discussion of each commandment contains several sections explaining what kind of behavior satisfies the commandment. The explanation of the eighth commandment provides a good example: separate paragraphs (of which I give only the first few clauses) detail the various ways one might break the injunction not to steal:

> Against this commandment offend all they which by craft or violence, upon the sea or land, spoil, rob, or take away any other man's servant or child, land or inheritance, horse, sheep, or cattle, fish, fowl, conies or deer. . . .

> Likewise offend all they against this commandment which have goods given to an use, and put them not to the same use, but keep them to their own advantage, as masters of hospitals and false executors, which convert the goods given to the sustention of poor folks, and to other good and charitable uses, unto their own profit. . . .

> And so all they which take wages or fee, pretending to deserve it, and yet do not indeed, as labourers and hired servants, which loiter, and do not do their business. . . .

> Also all idle vagabonds and sturdy beggars. . . .

> Moreover all they transgress this commandment which buy any stolen goods, knowing they be stolen, or that buy things or them that have none authority to sell them, or alienate them, if they know the same. . . .

> They also which defraud their hired servants of their due wages, and they that borrow any thing, or retain any thing delivered to them upon trust, and will not restore the same again. . . .

And they that engross and buy up any kind of wares wholly into their own hands, to the intent that they may make a scarceness thereof in other man's hands, and sell it again as they list.

And generally all covetous men, which by any means unlawfully get or unmercifully keep their goods from them that have need, be transgressors and breakers of this commandment. (115–16)

This exposition is more extended than the others, presumably because it offers the opportunity to redress so many civil disorders, but even so, it is only slightly more extended: the discussion of the first commandment contains nine paragraphs detailing how one may offend against it, of the third commandment, eight, of the fourth and sixth, six, of the second, the seventh, and the ninth, four, and of the tenth, two; the fifth commandment, of which the discussion is the longest, is the only one which departs from this customary pattern.

Complementing the discussion of how one may offend against a commandment is an explanation of how one may fulfil its intent, the third method of generalizing meaning. This expansion by contrarieties is a standard part of the explanations. To take the eighth commandment again, immediately following the initial paragraph explaining the various meanings of theft is one expanding its opposite:

And like as the vices before rehearsed be forbidden by this precept, even so sundry virtues, contrary to the said vices, be commanded by the same; as, to deal truly and plainly with our neighbors in all things, to get our own goods truly, to spend them liberally upon them that have need, to feed the hungry, to give drink to the thirsty, to clothe the naked, to harborough the harbourless, to comfort the sick, to visit the prisoners; and finally, to help our neighbors with our learning, good counsel, and exhortation, and by all other good mean that we can. (114–15)

The exposition of some of the commandments begins with this kind of expansion by contraries, for example the third—"In this

111

commandment God requireth of us to use his name with all honour and reverence" (90), which leads to five paragraphs of explanation of the proper ways to use God's name before any consideration of the ways it is possible to take His name in vain—but
all the explanations contain a mixture of the positive and the
contrary.

Polysemy is nothing new to *The King's Book,* nor are the methods used to achieve it: Luther's *Small Catechism* divides the discussion of three petitions of the Lord's Prayer into semantic and
behavioral realms by asking of each both "What does this mean?"
and "How is this done?"[11] and those familiar with rhetoric would
recognize the operations of generalization and distinction. But this
kind of extended consideration of individual words would have
been new to nascent readers. The first insight about reading they
would have derived from the discussions in *The King's Book,* then,
is that words have many significations, allegorical as well as literal,
and that reading could require a consideration of all of them:
bread is not only what the baker prepares, it is also everything
necessary for life without being excessive or superfluous, it is the
Eucharist, it is true doctrine. If so straightforward a word, tied so
closely to such a common substance, could be understood in so
many different ways, what was the limit for more complicated
words? These more complicated words—theft, adultery, murder—
have almost limitless implications, each of which has ramifications
for behavior, for what should be performed or avoided. Reading
would have to move beyond the obvious literal referents of words
to consider what else they could mean, and these meanings might
suggest practical responses. And there are no guidelines about
when to stop the movement.

The second relevant aspect of the kind of reading modelled by
The King's Book is a very strong emphasis on analysis. Everything is
broken down into its constituents, and each constituent is considered separately. The Creed contains twelve articles, the Paternoster
is divided into seven petitions, the Ten Commandments (obviously) are ten. Although there are sometimes cross-references from

one article or commandment to another, each is usually treated in isolation. And the priest who treated one article or commandment each Sunday, as the royal injunctions suggested, would separate them even more decisively from each other: it would take several months to treat the twelve articles of the Creed or the Ten Commandments; even the Lord's Prayer, divided into seven petitions, would require almost two months. The effect of this is twofold: first, to emphasize the constituent structure of the prayer or Creed, and second, to concentrate attention on the separate constituents. Each petition or article or commandment becomes the focus of attention, just as within the articles, petitions, or commandments each word becomes the focus of attention.

The third characteristic of reading modelled in *The King's Book* is the religious counterpart of intertextuality: intratextuality, the heaping up of references to other parts of the Bible. Though there are references to the Scriptures in all the articles of *The King's Book,* they are again concentrated in the expositions of the Ten Commandments. The explanation of the fifth commandment (the longest exposition) refers to thirty scriptural texts, many introduced by a formula locating the citation: "In the Proverbs it is written. . . . In the Book of Deuteronomy it is also written. . . . And in the Book of Leviticus it is said. . . . And in the Book of Exodus it is also written" (100). The words of Christ are identified but not always specifically located by book ("Christ saith in the gospel" [106]), and the same is true of Paul's pronouncements: "And St. Paul saith" (106). The density of allusion is much lower in the explanations of the other commandments (none of which has more than eight) and in the other sections of *The King's Book,* but even so, a fledgling reader who heard the commandments or the Creed explained in the manner of *The King's Book* in church would be likely to conclude that reading required some kind of allusion, some kind of gathering of texts to attest that the point being made was one made elsewhere in the Bible. As we shall see in the discussion of the *artes praedicandi,* this gathering of testimony from elsewhere in the Scriptures served a purpose very similar to that of the commonplace book in the secular sphere: it validated the interpretation of the text under consideration by proving that the point was one made elsewhere—that is, was a *common*place.

Whether the members of the congregation would have derived this model of reading from what they heard in church is less clear, for throughout the period there are complaints about lack of attention in church: even if the minister preached what the royal injunctions required, there was no way to ensure that inattentive members of the congregation would profit from it. This very situation prompted one J. F. (perhaps John Foxe) to prepare a brief pamphlet, descriptively titled *A most breefe manner of Instruction, to the principles of Christian Religion* (1550?).[12] He is prompted to his work by "the short memories and dull wits, of many to conceive & remember, the most briefe & short sum of Christian Religion" (sig. A.ii.r). The reasons for this are two: "the Parents slacknesse in sending [the youth] to the Ministers; and theyr carelessnesse when they doo come, and heedlesse hearts in hearing and regarding; and theyr mindlessnesse when the ministers endeuour is in the best and plainest manner bestowed among them" (sig. A.ii.v). His solution is to provide "a few questions, with Aunsweres annexed and ajoined, verie fitte for the simpler sorte, both of youth and age" (sig. A.ii.r). The pamphlet (fourteen pages of large print) has the same general aim as the royal injunctions discussed earlier: to make the populace aware of the basic tenets of Christianity; it differs in being explicitly aimed at those who had not been reached through the church.

As one might expect, the doctrine is essentially similar; what is more important for our inquiry is that the approach—even when it is addressed to "the simpler sort"—is also similar. The Ten Commandments are given (in a fuller form than in *The King's Book*) and then divided into two books, one containing the first four, the other, the second six. More important than this traditional distinction, which J. F. here reproduces without building upon, is the one between the positive and negative commandments: there are only two positive commandments ("Remember thou keep holy the Sabbath day" and "Honour thy Father and thy Mother"); the rest are negative. The point J. F. is anticipating is that very little positive action is actually required of us, and even so we don't succeed; to underscore this, he renumbers the commandments to group the negative ones together. The first three commandments are negative (the first was typically considered to be "Thou shalt have none other Gods but me"), and so retain their normal numbers, but the final five, being also negative, are assigned double numbers, "Do no murder," for instance being 4. 6.: the fourth negative commandment and the sixth commandment in the biblical order (sig. A.v). Though little is made of this renumbering (aside from the fact that the Ten Commandments require very little positive action on our part), the analytical impulse discussed above is again apparent: the Ten Commandments need not be considered in their biblical order; they can be treated separately or rearranged at will. This enacts a contemporary principle of biblical interpretation—that to understand a given passage it must be compared with other similar passages—but J. F. has no time for justification or explanation; he merely rearranges, and thus provides a model for others to follow.

The analytical impulse is again apparent in his treatment of the Creed and the Paternoster. The twelve articles of the Creed are divided into three general parts treating God the Father and Creation, God the Son and redemption, and God the Holy Ghost, sanctification, and regeneration; and then two special parts, one treating the Holy Catholic Church and the communion of saints, the other, "three Articles, specially to be noted, as the sum, comfort, and effect of all our faith," that is, the forgiveness of sins, the resurrection of the body, and the life everlasting (sig. A.vii). Similarly, the Paternoster is divided into a preface, six numbered petitions, and a conclusion. The first three petitions deal with the glory of God, the second three (provided with double numbers like the commandments) with the necessities of men (sig. A.viii).

What ideas about reading would the simpler sort derive from a pamphlet like this? First, that analysis is necessary: texts must be segmented into their constituent parts, and these constituents may be provided with names (article, petition, preface, conclusion, etc.). Second, that these constituents may be rearranged into a more logical order: all the positive commandments together, all the negative ones, all the petitions dealing with the glory of God, then all those dealing with the necessities of men. Third—though this is less apparent, because J. F. devotes little time to explaining what the various articles, commandments, and petitions mean— that each component can be understood by itself. The other characteristics of reading modelled in *The King's Book*—intratextuality and polysemy—are not much in evidence in this pamphlet, but the assumption that reading is prologue to action informs it from the beginning: one of the three things learned from God's law is that "I learne thereby, both what God's will is I should doo, and what I ought to doo. And what God's will is I should not doo, and so, what I ought not to doo" (sig. A.iii.v). Indeed, it is this emphasis on correct action that justifies the analysis: short statements of what to do or avoid will be more effective for the simpler sort than longer and more complicated expositions. And this may be the justification for avoiding polysemy and intratextuality as well, since the possible confusion arising from them would compromise a clear call to action.

That this emphasis on analysis is not accidental is suggested by Thomas Lever's advice on how to read Bradford's meditations:

> And my advise is, that when thou commeth to the perusing of Bradfordes Meditations, that thou provide thee a quiet mind, time and place, rather perusing one commaundement, article, or petition advisedly and well, then many with much haste and little consideration. So shalt thou find most sweetenes in that thou readest, and best print and keepe the effect and somme of it in thy memorie, reading and considering one thing after an other, as thou findest to thy time and capacitie, may best agree. (sig. A.iv–v)

The second basic type of evidence about religious models of reading derives from homilies and sermons rather than from specially prepared educational materials. There are two ways to proceed to examine this material. The first is the more straightfor-

116

ward: it is simply the examination of a mass of sermons, especially those which reached a large audience, to see what kind of models for reading they provide. These would include the sermons at Paul's Cross at which "the audiences are estimated to have been as large as six thousand" (Herr, 24), and popular sermons frequently reprinted, such as those by Arthur Dent, Edward Dering, Henry Smith, and William Perkins (Herr, 119–69). The drawback of this obvious method is that these sermons would most likely be heard, and read, by the relatively sophisticated, who had derived their models of reading from previous education. Dering, for instance, preached while he was Divinity reader at St. Paul's, and Perkins was a fellow of Christ's College, Cambridge.[13] The scholars and preachers we are most likely to esteem today—Colet, Hooker, and later, Donne and Andrewes—addressed themselves to the well educated. Even the large crowds at the Paul's Cross sermons were likely to be much more cosmopolitan than the simpler sort for whom J. F. prepared his explanations; grammar school students were expected to attend sermons and return with notes (for the younger) or complete copies (for the older ones),[14] a practice that many retained in adulthood, to judge from the sermons reproduced in John Manningham's diary.[15] The information to be derived from these sermons, then, would provide another perspective on the reading of those who had completed some formal education and had thus already learned a method of reading.

To discover what the simpler sort would have learned from the sermons they heard, we must adopt a different approach. First, we examine the manuals or guides to preaching that prepared the less learned preachers for their parish duties, to see what they, perhaps not much better educated than those they preached to, would have learned to pass on to their congregations. Then we look at the authorized homilies, which were read in churches when the preacher prepared no sermon.

The most important of these *artes praedicandi* was William Perkins's *The Arte of Prophecying* (1592),[16] which W. Fraser Mitchell calls "an outstanding example" of "the older type of English preaching-manual. . . . Its influence and vogue were enormous, owing to the extraordinary contemporary reputation of its author" (99), but the advice given in the other two available in English— Neils Hemmingsen's *The Preacher,* translated by John Horsfall (1574),[17] and Andreas (Gerhardt) Hyperius's *The Practice of Preaching,* Englished by John Ludham (1577)[18]—is essentially the same.

For the preachers, these *artes praedicandi* prescribe a complex and sometimes confused method of interpretation. All three follow Luther and other Reformers in proclaiming the self-sufficiency of the Bible: "the supreame and absolute meane of interpretation is the Scripture it selfe" (Perkins, 737), but the Scripture itself can only be understood by somebody who has undergone the requisite preparation in divinity. This involves memorizing "the substance of Divinitie described, with definitions, divisions, and explications of the properties," analyzing the Scriptures "using a grammatical, rhetoricall, and logicall analysis, and the help of the rest of the arts" to read the books of the Bible in a certain order, consulting the church fathers, and compiling a commonplace book consisting of "commonplace heads of every point of divinitie" (736–37).

When Perkins writes that "the supreme and absolute mean of interpretation is the Scripture itself," then, he realizes that this is a more complicated concept than it at first appears: Scripture has a determinate meaning only for those who have properly prepared themselves to receive it, and even they must use three "means subordinated to the Scripture" for complete understanding. First, and most important, "the analogy of faith," which is "a certain abridgment and sum of the Scriptures, collected out of most manifest & familiar places"—the Ten Commandments and the Apostles' Creed (737). Second, "the circumstances of the place propounded," which are *"Who? to whom? upon what occasion? at what time? in what place? for what end? what goeth before? what followeth?"* (737–38). Finally, "the collation or comparing of places together, . . . whereby places are set parallels one beside another, that the meaning of them may more evidently appear" (738).

Perkins explains the use of these three means in the next section of the treatise, which treats "the ways of expounding." Here he distinguishes between places which are either "analogical and plain, or Cryptical and dark" (740). The former "have an apparent meaning agreeable to the analogie of faith, and that at first view" (740); for them there is a straightforward rule for interpretation: "*If the naturall signification of the wordes of the place propounded doe agree with the circumstances of the same place, it is the proper meaning of the place*" (740). For the "crypticall or hidden places . . . which are difficult & darke" the following rule is applicable: "*If the native (or naturall) signification of the wordes doe manifestly disagree with either the analogy of faith, or very perspicuous places of the Scripture: then the other meaning, which is given of the place propounded, is naturall and proper if it agree with contrarie and like places, with the circumstances & wordes of the place, & with the nature of that thing, which is intreated of*" (740).

In these prescriptions, Perkins assumes that the literal meaning—the "natural signification"—is always available, but since he is addressing preachers who have already prepared themselves in accordance with his introduction to divinity, we should perhaps read these references to "natural signification" as "natural to those properly prepared to receive them." In any case, the literal meaning of the text is first grasped and then compared with the other three means of interpretation: first, and most importantly, the analogy of faith: when the literal meaning is agreeable to the analogy of faith, one proceeds to check the circumstances. When the literal sense disagrees with the analogy of faith or other clear statements of the Bible, then one is dealing with a dark place and must understand it in another sense, which Perkins assumes is always available. Here the three means of interpretation are more important, as the proposed interpretation is tested against each of them before it is accepted. In Perkins's view, then, expounding is a conscious procedure: every text has a literal meaning which the expounder must compare to the analogy of faith, the circumstances, and other clear places in the Scriptures. Where there is agreement, the literal meaning is the correct one; where there is not, some other meaning is "natural & proper."

The alternatives to a literal reading become available through the application of a series of rules or "consectaries" Perkins provides for interpreting texts. Ellipses may be expanded (741), passages may be understood as tropes in ten different ways (742–44), and these figurative meanings themselves may have the effect of emphasis (744–46), apparently contradictory places may be reconciled in various ways (746–49), and the analogy of faith, consideration of the circumstances, and comparison of like places elsewhere in the Bible guide one in determining the proper meaning of polysemic words (749–50). For instance, the fourth consectary (*"If the Opposition of unlike palaces shal be taught to be, either not of the same matter, but of name onely, or not according to the same part, or not in the same respect, or not in the same manner, or not at the same time, a reconciliation or agreement is made"* [746]) allows two apparently contradictory statements about the place of faith and works in salvation ("Judge me, O Lord, according to my righteousnesse" [Psalms 7.3]; "We have all been as an uncleane thing, and all our righteousness is as filthie clouts" [Isaiah 64.6]) to be reconciled:

> It appeareth by the scope and circumstances of both the places, that this contradiction is not in the same respect. Distinguish therefore. There is one righteousnes of the cause or action; and an other of the person: the first place speaketh of the former: and the second of the latter. (746)

The application of these various consectaries allows one to derive alternatives to the literal meaning of dark passages, and the tests by the analogy of faith, the circumstances, and the agreement of other passages in Scripture (what he calls reconciliation) lead to a satisfactory understanding of them.

This process is analogous to the deriving of allegorical readings in secular education. In discussing allegorical interpretations in the third chapter, I noted that the basic problems were a fundamental lack of control over the proliferation of meanings and a corresponding lack of any method of testing the viability of any proposed reading. In the religious context, Perkins's three means of interpreting Scriptures supplies precisely such a limit and test. Interpretations (we shall see below that they are not to be considered allegorical) are valid so long as they agree with the analogy of faith, the circumstances, and other places in the Scriptures; otherwise, they are unjustified. In practice this test for acceptable readings may have been less restrictive than one would expect, but that (as we shall see) was because the strict interpretation of Scripture tended to shade off into its application, which was governed by much more general rules.

But this is only the first step in preparing a sermon; the second is what Perkins calls "the *right cutting,* or the *right deviding*" of the word, "whereby the word is made fit to edify the people of God" (750). Hemmingsen and Hyperius provide somewhat fuller discussions than Perkins of this part of preparing a sermon, and so it is to them that we now turn. The preacher's own understanding of a scriptural passage is the first step in preparing a sermon; to edify his congregation, he must both explain and apply it. This is accomplished through what Hyperius calls a commonplace; the point, topic, or theme of a scriptural text, something that can serve as the "state" of a sermon. His discussion makes it clear how naturally the kind of strict interpretation described by Perkins modulates into application:

> If thou takest in hand any parte of the sacred Scripture to expounde, it is verilye thy dutye, to bestowe somtime in readinge and perusing it ouer oftner then once or twice, attentively weighing and considering euerye part and parsell thereof, with all the causes and circumstances of the same. Then thou shalt diligently recount and gather with thy selfe, what the authors meaninge in the whole, and so far forth as may be, thou shalt in a briefe sentence comprise the effect and summe thereof. This sentence shalbe the state of the whole sermon. (51r)

The initial weighing and considering of the Scripture would be what Perkins calls interpretation, but when the expounder begins to comprise the effect and sum of the reading, a different process is taking place. It may be difficult to reduce an entire book of the Bible to one commonplace, but it is sometimes possible: "the state of the booke which is entituled *Ecclesiastes,* is: that the sovereigne felicitie is the coniunction with God, and the perpetuall fruition of the dietie" (51v). In reducing shorter segments of the Scriptures to commonplaces, the preacher must analyze the text according to both theological and philosophical places. To the former belong the five kinds of instruction that distinguish the major types of sermon: didascalic, which promulgates true doctrine; redargution, which refutes false; institution, inciting hearers to good actions; correction, reproving hearers for bad actions; and consolation (51–54). The preacher reads the Scripture for examples of one of these theological commonplaces:

> we should diligently enserche, whether in the wordes of Scripture which we have in hand, anything be either openly affirmed or covertly signifyed that ought to be referred to some article . . . of fayth, or to a principle of christian religion.
>
> For it cannot be, but that, when we have some space together stirred by the powers of our minde in musing and considering of things, some such matter will come to remembraunce, if in the meane tyme we beare about fixed in our memory all the articles of faith, or the principall poynts and commonplaces of christian doctrine. (55)

This extended musing and considering against the background of a memory filled with the principles of Christian religion is an intermediate step between the strict interpretation of Scripture and its applications; it retains the comparison essential to interpretation, but its goal is to relate the reading to something else. From the philosophical places, "we easely learne, what euerything is, howe many partes or formes be thereof, what the causes, what the effects or duties, what thinges be of alyaunce, what Contrary thereunto" (58r). This philosophical or logical analysis consists of the application of twenty-eight logical places, which Hyperius lists without explaining (curious readers are referred to "masters & teachers of Logicke" [58]). He is clearly more interested in the following twenty-two theological places which he lists and provides examples of. Since they form one of the most comprehensive and explicit sets of rules for interpreting, it is worth reproducing them in full, without the accompanying examples. Each place allows either generalization from a scriptural passage or the movement from one thing to another.

1. Of the usurpation of the voyce of any man in the sacred Scriptures [i.e., the application of a speech to different circumstances].

2. Of the certaine forme of speakinge, or of the phrase of holy Scripture [i.e., the implications of what is said].

3. Of the signification of the wordes to the sentence or meaninge of the speaker.

4. Of wordes goinge afore and comminge after.

5. Of a generall sentence in Divinitie.

6. Of the thinges attributed to God.

7. Of the signe to the thinge signified.

8. Of one tyme to an other, or of the tyme of the lawe to the tyme of the Gospell.

9. Of one tyme to all tymes.

10. Of the head to the members.

11. Of the members to the head.

12. Of a thinge corporall to a thinge spirituall.

13. Of a thinge spirituall to a thinge corporall.

14. Of a thinge earthly to a thing heavenly.

15. Of the threatening of God to the effect thereof.

16. Of the promise of God to the effect thereof.

17. Of a prophesy or propheticall prediction.

18. Of the truth of a divine or propheticall determination.

19. Of the person of one good man to the person of all the godly.

20. Of the person of one ungodly man, to all.

21. Of a type or figure to the trueth ment thereby.

22. Of an allegory to the thing signifyed. (59–62)

Taken together, these twenty-two places allow the generalization and application of biblical passages to the lives of the congregation; the just provide examples for the godly, the unjust, of what should be avoided. Spiritual and corporal, heavenly and earthly seem to metamorphose precariously, but it should be remembered that these are applications of the Scripture, not interpretations of it, used for the purpose of amending the lives of the congregation, not for establishing dogma. And everything is tested by the proportion of faith, which provides at least a modest brake on the proliferation of readings.

Although Hemmingsen is less compendious than Hyperius in his instructions for deriving commonplaces, his rules are even more explicit and detailed:

> First of al therefore when any text is read, & understanded, the occasion, the briefe summe, & comprehension, and the ende, and the use of the texte must be sought out, which thinge, how and in what order it oughte to be done, in the Logitian his kinde of interpreting before is declared. Secondlye the partes, or the propositions of the text must be sought out. And last of al out of these according to the rules following, common places must be drawne, which seeme to conduce to the ende of that matter which we haue compounded. (37r–37v [for 36r–36v])

The eight rules following are methods to ensure wider applicability of any text read. The first, for instance, allows generalizations from the subjects of propositions: "If the subiecte of the proposition be a singuler bonde, or ende, in steede thereof put by degree and in order his superiours, that is to saye the forme in the first place. Secondly the kind next. Thirdly if you so thincke good, the superiour and higher kind" (37v [for 36v]). Thus, if something is predicated of David, the interpreter may produce commonplaces by predicating the same of all kings, all magistrates, and all men. The third rule is the most general: "If in steede of the subiecte and predicate, thou substitute by order formes and kinds: plenty of common propositions will growe thereof" (37v). From the fact that David was banished from his kingdom for committing adultery, for instance, we can generalize from David to all men, from committing adultery to being generally wicked, and from being banished to being punished, to conclude that "wicked men at one time or other shalbe punished" (37v). Other rules suggest consideration of the antecedents and consequences of actions and states, their causes and effects, and even what Hemmingsen calls "the contrary sense": "It is good sometimes by the contrary sense, to frame a place when the termes or bondes be equall, as for example. The iust man liueth by fayth, ergo, hee that is not iust liueth not by faythe. Thereof it followeth that neither righteousnes nor life, is of woorkes" (42r).

These rules for deriving commonplaces define the process by which narratives (or less pretentiously, anecdotes or stories) become examples for others. In the second chapter I noted that narratives were considered inherently attractive and examined Erasmus's emphasis on the use of examples, both historical and fictional. But in the secular sphere there is no attempt to explain or justify the process whereby a story about one specific historical or fictional character becomes generally applicable to others; the transfer is simply assumed. In these *artes praedicandi* there is a nascent attempt to formalize this process by showing the steps by which a story about David, for example, may become a universal guide to behavior. A major part of the reason for this explicitness is the Protestant desire to avoid the kind of fourfold allegory typical of the Roman Catholic Church:

> The Church of rome maketh 4. senses of Scriptures, the literall, allegoricall, tropologicall and anagogicall. . . . *There is one onely sense and the same is the literall.* An allegorie is onely a certaine manner of uttering the same sense. The Anagoge and Tropologie are waies, whereby the sense may be applied. (Perkins, 737)

In common with the reformers, and particularly Luther, the authors of these *artes praedicandi* reject what Farrar calls "the dreary fiction of the fourfold sense" of Scriptures.[19] They retained allegory and some typology (the last two of Hyperius's refer to types and allegories, and Perkins advises that "Allegories are to be propounded according to the scope or intent of the place" [747]), for how else could the Song of Solomon or the parables of Jesus be understood? But tropology and anagogy were both discarded as applications of the literal meaning, and the commonplaces allowed a sharp distinction between that literal meaning and its applications: in the stories of David, the Bible does not say that all wicked men will be punished; that is something the preacher derives from the story and uses for the edification of his congregation.

In rejecting the fourfold sense of the Scripture, in retaining localized allegory, and in distinguishing between the meaning of the text and the various applications of it, the authors of the *artes praedicandi* were echoing what Tyndale had written so perspicuously over half a century earlier in *The Obedience of a Christian Man:*

> Thou shalt understand, therefore, that the scripture hath but one sense, which is the literal sense. And that literal sense is the root and ground of all. . . . Neverthelater, the scripture useth proverbs, similitudes, riddles, or allegories, as all other speeches do; but that which the proverb, similitude, riddle, or allegory signifieth, is ever the literal sense, which thou must seek diligently: as in the English we borrow words and sentences of one thing, and apply them to another, and give them new significations. . . .
>
> Beyond all this, when we have found out the literal sense of the scripture by the process of the text, or by a like text of another place, then go we, and as the scripture borroweth similitudes of worldly things, even so we again borrow similitudes or allegories of the scripture, and apply them to our purposes; which allegories are no sense of the scripture, but free things beside the scripture, and altogether at the liberty of the Spirit. Which allegories I may not make at all the wild adventures; but must keep me within the compass of the faith, and ever apply mine allegory to Christ, and unto the faith.[20]

Here the relation between the various kinds of meaning is most clearly expressed, the necessity for interpretation of allegories and similitudes is linked to natural language processes, and the applications or accommodations of the Scripture to the purposes of the congregation both endorsed and controlled by what Tyndale calls the compass (instead of analogy or proportion) of faith. Altogether, it is perfect summary of the kind of Biblical interpretation the *artes praedicandi* recommended.

These rules for interpreting Scripture and deriving commonplaces (or understanding the full significance of sentences) are strategies for reading, and very permissive strategies at that. Clearly the analogy of faith is the operative constraint here, for these rules allow a wide variety of what today would be considered illicit logical conclusions. Another way to make the same point is to say that for us, the test of whether an interpretation is warranted is based on some (perhaps mistaken, or partially understood) conception of logic or probability within a general set of expectations, while for Hemmingsen the test is faith, whether the interpretation provides guides for godly behavior. And not for Hemmingsen only: in his introductory epistle, Horsfall explains that he translated the book, which he considers a "*Christiana Rhetorica,* that is to say, an arte out of the whiche the true and faithfull Ministers of Christe, may learne playnely, and orderly, to brake and distribute the worde of God vnto the people," at the instigation of "divers others of [his] brethren, godly and zealous Ministers of this citi of London . . . [for] the great profite that hereby might come, firste vnto the Churche of Christe, and nexte vnto themselves, and to all their other brethren and fellow Ministers throughout this little realm of Englande" (n.p.). Although it is hard to know how many preachers Horsfall's translation reached (it went through a second edition), we may still see in this treatise an example of the way some ministers read the Scriptures, and the way that they exemplified for the simpler sort of their parishioners in their sermons.

The advice considered so far deals with the preacher's breaking of the word of God; equally important is the way he distributes it to his parishioners. Hyperius insists more than the others on the proper observation of generic distinctions in sermons: as we have seen, he distinguishes five different kinds, and argues that "unlesse [the preacher] be assured at the beginning touching the kynde of his sermon, he shall never atteyne to an apt and perfect order of invention and disposition of his argument, but of necessitye they will appere confused, inconvenient, unordered" (51r). But all agree that the explications must appear straightforward (Hyperius specifies "nothing hard, wrested, or farre fet" [119r]) and applicable to the auditors. Perkins concludes his work with four rules summarizing "the order and summe of the sacred and onely methode of preaching":

1. To read the Text distinctly out of the Canonicall Scriptures.
2. To giue the sense and vnderstanding of it beeing read, by the Scripture it selfe.
3. To collect a few and profitable points of doctrine out of the naturall sense.
4. To apply (if he haue the gift) the doctrines rightly collected to the life and manners of men, in a simple and plaine speech. (762)

From these *artes praedicandi* it is possible to deduce two quite different models of reading, one for the preachers, the other for their parishioners. The preachers were an extremely heterogeneous lot. Ideally they had attended university (Wood, 82–86) and were knowledgeable in the kinds of logical, rhetorical, and comparative analysis the *artes praedicandi* recommend. But the ideal was infrequently attained; speaking of the beginning of Elizabeth's reign, Herr says, "The quality of the clergy, at least in the beginning of the reign, was very poor. . . . The universities were not able to turn out enough men trained for the priesthood even to begin to fill the vacancies, and so, pressed by the great need, the bishops filled the most crying gaps in the ranks with the next best men they could find, and left the less important vacancies unfilled or in the hands of lay readers" (18–19). Those who had attended university (or even grammar school) would have no real need for such guides, or could, if they wished, read them in the original Latin. The fact that all three were translated into English suggests that the translators recognized that many preachers—presumably the next best men—would have no access to the originals. Indeed, Edward Vernon, who translated Hyperius, says as much in his epistle dedicatory: he translated the book after "calling oftetimes to minde the state of diuers and sundry of the Clergie in this our age, and finding the same either altogether ignorant in the tongues, or els very slenderly seene in the true vnderstanding of them, and therefore very likely to be destitute of such necessary helpes as might further them, as well to the right vnderstanding of the holy Scriptures, as also to the true expounding of them" (sig. A.ii.v). The clergy who were too slenderly seen in Latin to read Hyperius or Perkins in the original cannot have progressed very far in grammar school, and thus would not have learned to read in the way taught there. Lacking an approved model for interpreting and expounding Scriptures, they were in as much need of guidance as their congregations.

What they learned from Hyperius (and more briefly from Perkins and Hemmingsen) was a comparative method of reading pursued within a framework defined by the central tenets of their faith. Without contradicting the analogy of faith, passages were to be understood against a background of other similar passages from the Bible, and (at least in Hyperius) of the interpretations of other writers (62v–63r). A text might or might not mean what it appeared to at first glance, and a faithful interpreter thus had to be wary of being led astray by a too gullible reliance on the letter instead of the spirit. Dark or cryptic passages required the deployment of a whole arsenal of interpretive techniques including the rhetorical and logical analyses taught in grammar schools and the more specifically theological analyses taught at the universities. Complementing interpretation was application; the Scripture had but one literal sense, but this one sense was capable of various applications, and the *artes praedicandi* provided rules for deriving these applications as well. For the preacher, reading was a serious and complicated business, not at all unlike the reading taught in the grammar schools: analytic, intertextual, teleological, and above all, self-conscious, as the preacher had to make his understanding of Scripture conform to certain prescriptions. If his understanding of a scriptural passage did not conform to the analogy of faith, or ignored the circumstances, or contradicted other clear passages, the fault was in him and not in the text.

For the parishioners, on the other hand, reading must have seemed relatively effortless. We may assume that they comprised a wide variety of readers, ranging from the illiterate to the fully literate and educated, though of course each parish might be more homogeneous (in the authorized homilies to be discussed below, Cranmer exhorts the listeners to "knowe God's Worde by diligent hearyng and readyng thereof" [64], and later, "I saie not naie, but a man may prospere with onely hearyng, but he maie muche more prospere with both hearyng and readyng" [65]). Those who were able to read but largely uneducated would have found in the sermons, especially in those that followed the outlines suggested by Perkins or Hyperius, a model for their own reading. The most important aspect of this model was that everything was directed toward a practical goal, the amendment of life; explication of scriptural passages led inexorably to the commonplaces that directed their behavior. Everything was measured and understood by the analogy of faith, which meant that everything read was interpreted in terms of a very strict set of prior expectations; reading was not meant to produce new knowledge but to confirm what was already known (having been already learned from the *Primer* and through the mandated explanations of the Ten Commandments, the Apostles' Creed, and the Paternoster). Within this general expectation, reading would be analytical, breaking a text down into its constituents and considering them separately (and perhaps even reordering them), and inter- or intratextual (comparing the constituents to other similar ones—other similar passages, or stories, etc.). The texts expounded would have a clear and profitable meaning (Hyperius's "nothing hard, wrested, or farre fet") and would always be applicable to the daily life of the parishioners.

What the parishioners would not derive from the sermons they heard was any conception of reading that involved interpretive effort, whether the kind of preparation in divinity Perkins recommends and the application of his rules and consectaries for the understanding of analogical and dark places of Scripture, or the use of the twenty-eight logical and twenty-two theological places that Hyperius applies in deriving the commonplace applications of the scriptural passages. They would not understand the necessity of musing and considering, trying to decide which doctrines a text confirms and which it confutes. For them—if the sermon was successful in its attempt to avoid the hard, wrested, and farre fet— the meaning the preacher derived and confirmed by other places in Scripture would be *natural*, just as the other places used for confirmation would seem to be naturally available; hidden from the hearer would be the consultation of commonplace books, indexes, commentaries, and so forth. They could transfer to their own reading the practical goals of the sermon, and probably apply the analogy of faith and even analyze what they read into increasingly smaller fragments; whether they would be able to exercise the kind of comparative reading that remains one of the characteristics of sermons would depend on their familiarity with the Bible and on the particular Bible they read (see below for a discussion of biblical aids).

But the simpler sort were not entirely at the mercy of their modestly learned preachers. More reliable as a guide to general practice during the period—though in no sense a response to the advice in the *artes praedicandi*, since it predates them—is *CERTAYNE SERMONS OR HOMILIES, Appoynted by the Kynges Majestie to Be Declared and Redde by All Persones, Vicars, or Curates, Every Sondaye in Their Churches Where They Have Cure* (1547). These twelve homilies, originally collected by Cranmer and promulgated during the reign of Edward VI and then reprinted by Elizabeth in 1559, share with *The King's Book* the double aim of instruction and correction, "that thereby [the people] may both learne theyr duetie towardes God, theyr Prince and theyr neyghbours . . . and also to avoyde the manyfolde enormities which heretofore by false doctrine have crept into the churche of God" (56). Standardization was needed because "all they whiche are appoynted ministers have not the gyft of preaching sufficiently to instruct the people which is commytted unto them" (56), the same justification as for the *artes praedicandi*. These homilies were to be preached, in order, every Sunday there was not a sermon (38), and since preaching licenses were required to preach a regular sermon (6), there is reason to believe that they would have reached an extremely wide audience. Moreover, they were to be preached repeatedly—both the Edwardian and the Elizabethan prefaces require that "when the foresayde boke of homilies is redde over, the Kynges [her] Majesties pleasure is that thesame be repeted and redde agayn, in such lyke sorte as was before prescribed" (56, 58)— so any parishioner would have the opportunity to become well acquainted with them. Indeed, so great was Elizabeth's confidence in them that she advised Archbishop Whitgift that they could help solve the pressing shortage of preachers still plaguing the country in 1584: "My meaning is not (that) you should make choice of learned ministers only, for such are not to be found, but of honest, sober, and wise men and such as can read the scriptures and homilies well unto the people" (10).

The homilies provide basic instruction in the doctrines of the church about the misery and salvation of all mankind, faith, good works, love and charity, swearing and perjury, whoredom and adultery, strife and contention, declining from God, the fear of death, obedience, and the reading of the Scriptures (53). The first, "A Fruitfull Exhortation to the Readyng and Knowledge of Holy Scripture," probably by Cranmer himself, contains the most explicit instruction in the art of reading. The reading here contemplated is reading in Hyperius's sense of instruction: it leads to the Christian virtue of charity in the fullest sense for one who is "diligent to reade and in his hearte to print that he readeth" (63). That is, disinterested reading for intellectual satisfaction is not the aim; amendment of life—faith, in the second sense discussed in *The King's Book*—is: "those thynges in the Scripture that be plain to understande and necessarie for salvacion, every mannes duetie is to learne theim, to print theim in memorye, and effectually to exercise theim" (66).

The practical advice about reading comes in a section countering two excuses for not reading the Bible: that one may be led astray through misunderstanding, and that it is too difficult to understand. Cranmer provides guidance about reading without the danger of error:

> Reade it humbly, with a meke and lowly harte, to thintente you maie glorifie God, and not your self, with the knowledge of it; and reade it not without daily praying to God that he would directe your readyng to good effect; and take it upon you to expounde it no further than you can plainly understande it. . . . For humilitie will onely searche to knowe the truthe; it will searche, and will conferre one place with another: and where it cannot fynde the sense, it will praie, it will inquire of other that knowe, and will not presumpteously and rasshely define any thyng which it knoweth not. (65)

As for difficulty, the same humble diligence is the answer:

> If we reade once, twise, or thrise, and understand not, let us not cease so, but still continue readyng, praiyng, askyng of other and so by still knocking, at the last the doore shalbe opened. . . . Although many thynges in the Scripture bee spoken in obscure misteries, yet ther is no thyng spoken under darke misteries in one place, but the selfe same thyng in other places is spoken more familiarly and plainly. (66)

This advice echoes what he had written in his preface to the Bible (called the Great or Cranmer's Bible) issued in 1539. There he quotes Chrysostom on the difficulty of the Scripture:

> Suppose thou understand not the deep and profound mysteries of scripture; yet it cannot be, but that much fruit and holiness must come and grow unto thee by the reading: for it cannot be that

thou shouldest be ignorant in all things alike. For the Holy Ghost hath so ordered and attempered the scriptures, that in them as well publicans, fishers, and shepherds may find their edification, as great doctors their erudition. . . . But the apostles and prophets wrote their books so that their special intent and purpose might be understanded and perceived of every reader, which was nothing but the edification or amendment of the life of them that readeth or heareth it. . . . Take the books into thine hands, read the whole story, and that thou understandest keep it well in memory; that thou understandest not, read it again and again: if thou can neither so come by it, counsel with some other that is better learned. Go to thy curate and preacher; show thyself to be desirous to know and learn: and I doubt not but God, seeing thy diligence and readiness (if no man else teach thee) will himself vouchsafe with his holy Spirit to illuminate thee, and open unto thee that which was locked from thee.[21]

Three (by now familiar) characteristics of the reading process stand out here. The first is simply that reading requires rereading: texts that are clear are reread to imprint their messages on the memory; texts that are mysterious are reread continually in the hopes of illumination. Reading of the Scriptures is, as Lever recommended for reading Bradford's meditations, intensive and meditative, ruminatory even, rather than extensive. Second, the reliance on previous knowledge: one avoids misunderstanding by reading only what seems clear—what accords with the analogy of faith. Whatever does not calls for outside help, secular or divine. The third, a corollary of the second, is that reading is essentially comparative: things expressed darkly in one place are elsewhere clear; to understand them, one must compare them to the clearer statements. It is only a small step from this to Hyperius's reliance on comparison (of texts and authorities) as a determinant of reading.

Cranmer's advice about reading the Bible appeared as part of the front matter for both the Great Bible (1539) and the Bishop's Bible, which succeeded it in 1568 as the version authorized for use in churches. But the most popular version of the Bible during the century, by far, was the Geneva Bible, which went through over 120 editions between its initial publication and the appearance of the King James version in 1611 (compared with seven editions of the Great Bible and twenty-two of the Bishops' Bible).[22] In many of its editions it contained a condensed version of the advice about reading the Scriptures found in the *artes praedicandi* in the form of a table entitled "How to take profite by reading of the Holy Scriptures."[23] In one of the tables made popular by Ramistic approaches to knowledge, it listed seven desiderata for reading the Bible for "who so ever mindeth to take profite by reading scriptures." These include prayer and regular reading, but for our purposes the most important advice comes in the last three sections: the reader is admonished to

5	Refuse all sense of Scripture contrary to the	Articles of Christian faith, conteined in the common Creede [and] First and second table of Gods commandments.
6	Marke and consider the	1. Coherence of the text, how it hangeth together. 2. Course of times and ages, with such things as belong unto them. 3. Maner of speach proper to the Scriptures. 4. Agreement that one place of Scripture hath with an other, whereby that which seemeth darke in one is made easie in an other.
7	Take opportunitie to	Reade interpreters, if he be able. Conferre with such as can open the Scriptures. . . . Heare preaching, and to prove by the Scriptures that which is taught. (Zim, 72).

This advice virtually repeats what is found in the *artes praedicandi* without the elaborate rules for deriving applications of the Scriptures. Here we find the analogy of faith, the comparative reading (both intra- and intertextual), and the consideration of the proper context, in addition to new advice about the proper manner of speech.

All three translations of the Bible contained helps for the reader in the form of marginal notes and commentary which explained difficult passages, sometimes provided doctrinal instruction (in reaction to the argumentative notes in the Geneva Bible, contributors to the Bishops' Bible were warned "to make no bitter notes upon any text or yet set down any determination in places of controversy"[24]), and supplied necessary cross-references. With the assistance of these aids, the untutored reader could understand the basic meaning of the Scriptures and even indulge in a kind of intertextual reading. But this intertextuality was severely restricted, and limited to literal references. Hard or dark places were not referred to clearer statements of the same thought.

In the homilies themselves this type of comparison is not much in evidence. In part this is due to the fact that the homilies are devoted to topics rather than to expositions of specific biblical passages, so there is less opportunity for sustained comparison. Perhaps more important, such comparison is most necessary when the passage being considered is hard or dark, and the comparison can clarify it. Hard or dark places are precisely those which would be avoided by the homilies, which aimed at providing for the population at large a basic introduction to their responsibilities in a Christian commonwealth: "The *Book of Homilies* expounds that Word [contained in the Great Bible], suggests its implications for all people everywhere in terms of the life of active charity and the Christian commonwealth to result from pursuit of that life, in such a way that the people are to be moved to imitate the images given in that Word."[25] Instead, there is a different kind of comparison, more like reminiscence: one text leads to another because they make similar points about the amendment of life. This method is the one Hyperius recommends for the section of the sermon called the "confirmation": "certayne speciall proofes, taken out of the sacred Scriptures" (31r) and "certaine examples or historyes taken out of the sacred Scriptures" (31v) are presented to buttress and amplify the main argument. The second part of the homily "Of the Declinyng from God," for instance, treats Isaiah's parable of the vineyard that God threatens to abandon when it produces wild grapes instead of good ones. The explication is straightforward:

> if we whiche are the chosen vineyarde of God bryng not furth
> good grapes, that is to say, good workes, . . . but rather bryng
> furth wyld grapes, that is to say, sower workes, unsweete, unsavery
> and unfruictfull, then will he pluck away all defence and suffre
> grevous plagues of famyne and battaile, dearth and death, to light
> upon us. (141)

Proofs and histories from the Bible are brought in for amplification: those who rejoice in their liberty to "brynge furht brambles, bryers, and thornes, all naughtynes, all vice" are like the Israelites who "had that they longed for: they had quayles enough, yea, til they were wery of them. But what was the end thereof? Their swete meate had sour sauce" (141). Like the gardener who continues to prune and dig around the vines he thinks may still be productive, God continues to correct those he thinks capable of reformation: the father only stops correcting his child when he has abandoned all hope of rehabilitation. Thus "nothyng should perce our hart so sore and put us in such horrible feare as when we knowe in our conscience that we have grevously offended God and do so continue, and that yet he striketh not, but quietly suffereth us to do the naughtines that we have delight in" (142). That is why David cried out in the Psalms: "Caste me not awaie from thy face and take not thy Holy Spirit from me" (142). Returning to the vineyard, the homilist relates it to passages from 1 Corinthians, Ephesians, Samuel, Luke, Colossians, Isaiah, Ezekiel, Thessalonians, Ecclesiastes, and Hosea.

This practice of gathering many biblical passages in a sermon is so familiar to us that it requires an effort of imagination to distance ourselves from what seems normal practice to recognize that it can provide a model of reading. What is of prime importance in this model is not fidelity to the text (whatever that might be, precisely), but compendiousness. The educated would achieve this by using commonplace books (either commercial or private) and concordances; the uneducated would have to rely on their memories or on marginal references in the Bible. In either case, the text under consideration would be the nexus of a rich web of intertextuality, and reading would require exploring that web.

Another characteristic of reading exemplified in the homilies is one already noted in *The King's Book*—the notion that words have many referents. "An Homilie of Christian Love and Charitie" consists primarily of "a true and playn description of charitie, not of mennes imaginacion, but of the very woordes and examples of our savior Jesus Christ" (120), and the one "Against Swearyng and Perjury" considers various kinds of swearing, lawful and illicit. "An Homilie of Whoredome and Unclennesse" is very clear about polysemy: "By the whiche woorde, adultery, although it bee properly understande of the unlawful commixcion of a maryed manne with any woman beside his wife, or of a wife with any man beside her husbande, yet thereby is signified also all unlawfull use of those partes which bee ordeined for generacion" (174); and it continues to quote Jesus's statement in Matthew that adultery may be mental as well as physical.

Those who for one reason or another had to rely on what they heard in church for their models of reading (i.e., interpreting, comprehending) would thus have learned to conceive of reading in a particular way. The most important characteristic of this method is that it was confirmatory and practical rather than informative, disinterested, or aesthetic: what was read confirmed opinions and beliefs already held; the analogy of faith was the final test of the validity of an interpretation; and the goal of reading was—as Thomas Lever claimed for Bradford's expositions—to "readie [the reader] muche unto the right understanding of Gods worde, and to the right use of Gods workes" (n.p.). This characteristic is of course the most difficult for us to comprehend, and the one least likely to transfer to other kinds of reading. But for religious reading (and I have already argued that for uneducated people most reading would probably be religious in any case) this would be the guiding principle. Guided by the analogy of faith, reading was severely analytical: texts were divided and subdivided, by grammatical, rhetorical, logical, or theological analysis, into smaller and smaller segments which became the focus of attention. The logical conclusion of this process is attention to the individual words, with all their possibilities for polysemy or ambiguity, and this is what occurred. But analysis was always accompanied by comparison, the gathering of relevant parallels, so each segment, even each word, could be the occasion of extended discussion. Characterizing the compendiousness of the Paul's Cross sermons, Millar Maclure says, "Load every rift with ore, and manage it so that almost every word is a rift. The unachievable perfection would have every word of Scripture surrounded by a cloud of glosses, doctrinal and practical: the Scripture bears on everything and everything bears on the Scripture,"[26] and the same approach, if less pronounced, informs the materials I examine here. Finally, for the simpler sort, this model of reading would be tacit and unanalyzed: they would consider it "the way one reads" and would not be conscious of the calculated method recommended by the *artes praedicandi* and followed by the preachers. They would learn from experience what others had learned from instruction.

CHAPTER 5

METHOD AND ART
IN READING

I have argued so far that those who attended grammar school would have learned a method of reading which they would continue to use throughout the rest of their lives, so powerful and omnivorous was it. Those who had learned the rudiments of decoding without much formal education would have encountered in church various kinds of instruction in interpretation without recognizing it as such: for them it would have been explanation of the tenets of religious belief, or a sermon or homily; but without other models for reading, they would perforce have applied these methods of interpretation to their other reading. We turn now to a final source of information about reading, that contained in the numerous books of self-improvement published during the period. None of these books has a title announcing itself as more relevant to our topic than Thomas Blundeville's *The true order and Methode of wryting and reading Hystories* (1574),[1] and it is fitting that we begin with the only book of the period to announce so openly its intention to teach people how to read.

As we have already seen in both the secular and the religious spheres, in Tudor England reading is never entirely theoretical or speculative; it is always preparation for some future action. This general orientation is immediately apparent in Blundeville's book: it is dedicated to the Earl of Leicester because he is one who reads histories "to gather thereof such iudgment and knowledge as you may thereby be the more able, as well to direct your private actions, as to give Counsell lyke a most prudent Counseller in publyke causes, be it matters of warre, or peace" (sig. A.ii.r). The same note is sounded at the end, when Blundeville explains the goal of reading:

> And though we seeke by reading Hystories, to make our selves
> more wyse, aswell to direct our owne actions, as also to counsell
> others, to sturre them to vertue, and to withdrawe them from
> vice, and to beautyfie our owne speache with grave examples,
> when we discourse of anye matters, that therby it may have the
> more authoritie, waight, and credite. (sig. H.ii.v–H.iii.r)

Reading confers both private and public benefits: once we have been improved by our reading, we make our knowledge available to others. But interestingly, Blundeville also provides evidence that this purposeful reading, universally recommended, is sometimes more honored in the breach than in the observance. Just before he commends Leicester for his (correct) method of reading histories, Blundeville glances at those—he calls them "many"—who read "to passe away the tyme" (sig. A.ii.r), and he again refers to them at the beginning of his explanation of reading when he acknowledges that some write histories, not for the proper reasons he is about to explain, but rather "to winne fame to the writer and some to delighte the readers eares that reade only to pass away the time" (sig. F.ii.v).

In Blundeville's view, histories are written for three purposes:

> First that we may learne therby to acknowledge the providence of
> God, whereby all things are governed and directed. Secondly, that
> by the examples of the wise, we may learne wisedome wisely to
> behave our selves in all our actions, as well private as publique,
> both in time of peace and warre.
>
> Thirdly, that we maye be stirred by example of the good to fol-
> low the good, and by example of the evill to flee the evill. (sig.
> F.ii.v–F.iii.r)

The providence of God is rather expeditiously disposed of, primarily because it remains mysterious to mere human intelligence: "And with those accedents which mans wisedome rejecteth and little regardeth: God by his providence useth, when he thinketh good, to worke marveylous effects" (sig. F.iii.r). Reading examples of God's providence will lead the reader to the recognition "that nothing is done by chaunce, but all things by his foresight, counsell, and divine providence" (sig. F.iii.v).

The second and third purposes both fall under the heading of human wisdom, and Blundeville is much fuller in his discussion of this topic, relentlessly dividing and subdividing it in a manner reminiscent of the diagrams made popular by Ramistic approaches to knowledge.

> Humane wisdome hath three principall partes, the first whereof teacheth us rightlye to judge of all thinges, what is to be desired, and what is to be fled. The second, howe and by what meanes we may best attayne to the things which we desire. The thirde teacheth us to take occasion when it is offered and to foresee all peril that may hap. (sig. F.iii.v)

Rightly judging means "to knowe by the examples of others, whyther those thinges which we desire and seeme to us good, be good in deede or not: and secondly what the obtayning thereof will cost" (sig. F.iii.v–F.iv.r); examples are necessary because only they demonstrate clearly that what seems good may lead to great evil and vice versa. Likewise, the cost in terms of "our labour, and traveyle, our expenses, and losse of tyme, also what perilles, displeasures and griefes myght chaunce unto us by having it" (sig. F.iv.v–G.i.r) must be considered, as well as the fact that earthly possessions are necessarily transient.

The most important part of human wisdom, however, is to learn the proper relations between cause and effect:

> It is needefull in reading Hystories, to observe well every thing that hath bene done, by whom, to what ende, and what meanes

142

were used for the accomplishment thereof, and whyther suche
endes by suche meanes, are always, or for the most part, or sel-
dome or never obtayned, and whither all men dyd use therein
lyke meanes or divers, & if divers, which tooke effecte, and which
did not, and what maner of thinges those be, without the which,
the ende cannot be obtayned. (sig. G.i.v–G.ii.r)

One must learn to distinguish accidents from essentials, the universally efficacious means from the locally effective ones, so that
one can obtain what one has correctly learned to desire. And this
inquiry into causes and effects leads directly to three different
methods of reading:

In the observing of meanes to attayne the ende, it is meete to
marke well the order of those meanes, and howe they are linked
togither, which order may proceede three maner of waies, that is,
eyther in beginning wyth the verye first thing that tendeth to any
ende, and so forward from one thing to an other, until you come
to the last, or else contrarywise in beginning with the last meane,
next to the end, and so backewarde from meane to meane untill
you come to the first, or leaving both these waies, you maye take
the thirde, which is to devide all the meanes into their general
kinds, and to consider of all the meanes contayned in every kinde,
apart by themselves. (sig. G.ii.r–G.ii.v)

Just as the religious reader has the authority over the text to reorder
it, the reader of history can choose how he wants to process the
text before him. The history itself is presented in chronological
order (in the opening sentence of his treatise, Blundeville stipu-
lated that "An Hystorye ought to declare the thynges in suche
order, as they were done" [sig. A.iii.r]), but the reader is not entirely constrained by the order of presentation. Rather, his goals in
reading dictate the proper approach.

The first approach is good for initial understanding and is recommended for a first reading. The second approach "is very necessary to judge of every thing, what is well or evill done and to

consider better afterwarde of those thinges, which were not easye to be well considered of at the first" (sig. G.iv.r). Where the first approach is sequential, taking the narrative as a whole, this approach is segmental, dividing the text into a series of cause-effect pairs and subjecting each pair to scrutiny, but it remains within the limits set by the chronology of the text, since the author, reflecting the original facts, has already determined each cause-effect pairing. The reader is empowered to select particular causes and effects for special study, to the end that "you shalbe able quicklye to discerne which meanes bee good, and which be not, to bring anye thing to passe" (sig. G.iv.v).

The third order of reading is essentially what was taught in the grammar schools; its goal is to "reduce all things into a briefe summe, that he may the more easily commit them to memorie" (sig. G.iv.v), and its means is the compilation of a commonplace book:

> And therefore when we finde any such [useful example] in our reading, we must not onely consider of them, but also note them apart by themselves in such order, as we may easily finde them, when soever we shall have neede to use them. And the order of such examples, would not be altogither according to the names of the persons, from whence they are taken . . . but rather according to the matters & purposes whereto they serve. Neyther is it sufficient in this behalfe, to have onely common places of vertues and vices, or of thinges commendable, and not commendable, but other places also besydes them, meete to be applyed to everye one of those partes of observacion, whiche we seeke, which places are to be founde, ordered, and disposed, not before we begin to reade, but whylest we continue in reading, and in observing all kynde of matters every day with better judgement than other. And by considering under what title every example is to be placed (for the ready finding thereof) wee shall greatlye helpe our memorie. (sig. H.iii.r–H.iv.r)

In this section Blundeville refers to the relation between reading and the compilation of a commonplace book. His conception

shares with the grammar school version many assumptions, nota-
bly that the text is to be segmented into smaller units and those
units retained separately for future use, and that the consideration
of what place a particular anecdote illustrates will help focus attention and assist memory (we remember particularly Ascham here).
But Blundeville's version differs in being much more cybernetic, if
we can call it that: instead of relying simply on lists of vices and
virtues, or things commendable and the opposite, the places are
derived from the reading itself in conjunction with observation of
everyday life. The fact that Blundeville has to explain what to
avoid suggests that many people did not avoid it, and this relatively static conception of the commonplace book is indeed the
impression one gets from the educational material examined in
the second chapter. For Blundeville, however, reading provides
ways to conceptualize life and vice versa, and the resulting commonplace book evolves continually in response to pressure from
both. The schoolboys had less opportunity to observe all kind of
matters every day than the adult readers Blundeville is addressing, and so less opportunity for the kind of practical interaction
Blundeville valorizes as his goal.

In the kind of cybernetic commonplace book Blundeville recommends, any firm line between reading and life is erased, since
each tells us what to look for in the other, and this is entirely
consistent with his general view of the utility of reading:

> And though we seeke by reading Hystories, to make our selves
> more wyse, aswell to direct our owne actions, as also to counsell
> others, to sturre them to vertue, and to withdrawe them from
> vice, and to beautyfie our owne speache with grave examples,
> when we discourse of anye matters, that thereby it may have the
> more aucthoritie, waight, and credite. (sig. H.ii.v–H.iii.r)

Just as the line between life and reading is effaced, the split between the self and the other is resolved into a mutual interaction:
one initially reads to improve oneself, but that leads inevitably to
the improvement of others, which requires our own management

of the arts of persuasion whose effect is ultimately dependent on the effect they have on others. Throughout the period the duty of the individual to society is stressed, and here Blundeville, with his alternation between the self and the other, textualizes this reciprocation.

In this section on reading history, Blundeville describes the method of reading but reveals nothing of the expected content of reading, the sorts of things one reads for. What is needed as a complement is the kind of checklist for travellers Albert Meier provided in his guidebook to profitable travelling, which is discussed in the appendix. This Blundeville provides in the first sections of his own book, dealing with the writing of histories, where he proceeds, almost as schematically as Meier did with his lists of questions, to outline what must be included in a proper history. "Hystories," he explains, "bee made of deedes done by a publique weale, or agaynst a publique weale," and "every dede, be it private, or publique must needs be done by some person, for some occasion, in some time, and place, with meanes & order, and with instruments" (sig. A.iv.v). Each of these aspects of the deed is subdivided into its components. First, the deed itself may be composed of many contributory acts, each of which must be considered; likewise it is necessary to determine the principal actor, cause, time, place, means, and instruments. The background of the chief actor must be supplied (his name, family, education, etc.), and especially his power, skill, and activity in accomplishing the deed under consideration. His power consists of his riches, his public authority, and his private estimation; his skill, in his bodily force, his courage, his affections, and his mental habits (sig. B.ii.v–B.iii.v). In a separate section, Blundeville provides more detail on the causes of actions:

And whatsoever enterprise any man taketh in hand, he doth it being mooved and provoked thereunto, eyther by some outwarde principle, or by some inwarde principle, if outwarde, it is eyther by destinie, by force, or by fortune, if inwarde, then it is eyther by

146

nature, by affection, or by choyse and election, and such election springeth eyther of nature, or of some passion of the minde, of custome, or else of the discourse of reason. (sig.C.iii.v–C.iv.r)

One can easily visualize the chart such a paragraph would lead to, with the cause being divided into inward and outward, outward into destiny, force, and fortune, inward into nature, affection, and choice, with four types of the latter (nature, passion, custom, reason) distinguished. Since Blundeville does not amplify his distinctions, many of them remain opaque: what is the difference between being provoked to some action by the inward principle of nature as opposed to electing to do it based on nature? But the impulse is clear: everything is subject to relentless analysis, and the specific categories used are less important than the analytic impulse.

We need not follow Blundeville in detail as he divides and subdivides the time, place, means, and instruments of actions, or the types and parts of military campaigns, to see that what he provides in his instructions for writing histories can also be used as a guide for reading, a checklist for reading not unlike Meier's for travel. The attentive reader, especially the one reading by the second or third method he recommends, will analyze each action into its causes and effects, time, and so forth. The actors will be similarly scrutinized for background, personality traits, political stature, power, influence, in short, for anything that could bear upon any of their actions. The goal is to understand the "proper nature" of things:

and therefore sith in every action there must needs be a dooer, or worker, the hystorie muste first make mention of hym, and then shewe the cause that mooved him to doe, to what intent and ende, in what place, and with what meanes and instruments. And bycause tyme doth accompany all manner of actions, and every action hath his proper and peculier tyme, the writer must give to every action his dewe time accordingly. (sig. F.i.r)

Reflective reading of historical examples (Blundeville warns that "we maye not make over much haste, but rather reade leysurely and with Judgement," [sig. H.ii.v]), with the leisure and judgment to compose a commonplace book organized by the most useful categories, will finally teach us what to desire, what to avoid, and how best to obtain what we desire, and prepare us with the knowledge and the (rhetorical) means to provide guidance for others.

The kind of reading Blundeville recommends contains many of the characteristics we have already seen. It is primarily practical, aimed at some goal other than private edification, typically conceived of as private education for public action or persuasion. It is relentlessly analytic, as each historical event is broken down into causes and effects, times, means, instruments, and so forth, in the attempt to identify universally efficacious means to specific ends. The results of this reading are preserved for future use in a commonplace book, and though Blundeville does not give any explicit directions for intertextual reading, the provision of this book, together with his instructions for identifying accidents, suggest at least a minimal kind of comparative, if not exactly intertextual, reading:

> And bycause we finde manye tymes, that like meanes have bene used to the obtayning of like endes, (as we suppose) & yet not with such like successe, we ought therefore diligently to consider the divers natures of thinges, and the differences of tymes, and occasions, and such like accidents, to see if we can possibly finde out the cause why mens purposes have taken effect at one time, and not at an other. (sig. H.i.r)

The commonplace book differs from those compiled in schools in being more open to the interaction between life and reading, and this reminds us that Blundeville is writing for adults, not children. Thus it is particularly revealing that he emphasizes, in his three methods of reading, the authority of the reader over the text: histories are to be written chronologically, but they need not be read that way. Indeed, they will be most useful if they are not read that way. Most of what students would have absorbed from the practices of the classroom, Blundeville presents as a method equally applicable for adults in their leisure reading.

But there are characteristics of secular and religious reading Blundeville does not address. His suggestion of comparative reading does not entail the kind of intense intratextuality we found in religious reading or the intertextuality, emphasizing language, style, and the close analysis of indebtedness, typical of the classroom. He shows no interest in expression. Since he deals with historical examples, there are no dark passages, nothing that requires any type of allegorical or typological interpretation, and thus no need for anything like the analogy of faith. Like other secular writers, he never concerns himself with whether and how historical examples are applicable to readers, although his discussions of the various components of any historical event (the personalities, powers, settings, occasions, times, etc.) might suggest to a curious reader that the combination of these in any incident is so idiosyncratic that it would never be repeated, and that a historical event could thus provide an example of what to desire or shun, but not of how to obtain what is desired.

I know of no other book from the period that promises in its title to teach people how to read, as does Blundeville's, but many other books, in providing instruction in writing, thereby provided instruction in reading, since what the writer learned to attend to in writing he would notice in reading. In her survey of rhetoric and logic in Shakespeare's time, Sister Miriam Joseph consistently links composition with reading (the title of her first chapter is "The General Theory of Composition and of Reading in Shakespeare's England," and the third section of her book is "The General Theory of Composition and Reading as Defined and Illustrated by Tudor Logicians and Rhetoricians").[2] George Puttenham, author of *The Arte of English Poesie* (1589),[3] recognized this close connection when he claimed that his subject was "not unnecessarie for all such as be willing themselves to become good makeres in the vulgar, or to be able to judge of other mens makings" (159), and his modern editors use him in precisely this way:

> Elizabethan poetry was written primarily for Elizabethans to read and that they did not, in the most concrete sense, read poetry as we do, that indeed the actual reading differed markedly in early- and mid-Tudor times from late-Tudor times, is proved abundantly by the *Arte*. (lxiv)

> This brings us once more to the question of Elizabethan reading and listening. . . . If we suspend judgment as to the value of this pursuit of "applied" rhetorical ornament and substitute for it a sort of detective interest—a nose to smell out the odoriferous flowers of fancy, the jerks of invention—it is possible to approximate the Elizabethan habit. Poets who took so much trouble to follow Art would not wish this Art to be ignored in the reading and would expect their listeners, and still more their readers, to respond with aural and mental agility. (lxxxvi)

Production and reception are images of each other; what the poet learns to produce, the attentive reader learns to perceive and judge. Although he intends to provide a guide for the writing of poetry—"our chiefe purpose herein is for the learning of Ladies and young Gentlewomen, or idle Courtiers, desirous to become skilful in their owne mother tongue, and for their private recreation to make now & then ditties of pleasure" (158)—Puttenham's book is actually a comprehensive introduction to the poetic resources of the English language, providing not only a history of poetry and a discussion of the poetic kinds, but also treatments of prosody, language, style, ornamentation, and decorum. As the reader follows Puttenham's discussions he or she learns more than how to write ditties of pleasure, since Puttenham himself enacts this duality between writing and reading in his examples and commentary, which as samples of his reading are intended to teach others to write. This is evident in the chapter he devotes to "Some vices in speaches and writing" (250–61), where, for instance, he objects to a combination of *tautologia* and *hysteron proteron:*

> *A corrall lippe of hew*

> Which is no good speech, because either he should have sayd no more but a corrall lip, which had bene inough to declare the rednesse, or els he should have said, a lip of corrall hew, and not a corrall lip of hew. (255)

Adding "of hew" is tautologous; placing "corrall" before "lippe" instead of "hew" is a vicious form of *hysteron proteron.* In either case, the reader of the treatise in being warned what to avoid in his own writing is also instructed in what to observe (and condemn) in his reading.

But his critical commentary is not limited to that chapter, and earlier we find an even clearer example of the necessary connection between writing and reading:

> *The tenth of March when Aries received,*
> *Dan Phoebus raies into his horned hed.*

> Intending to describe the spring of the yeare, which every man knoweth of himselfe, hearing the day of March named: the verses be very good the figure nought worth, if it were meant in Periphrase for the matter, that is the season of the yeare which should have bene covertly disclosed by ambage, was by and by blabbed out by naming the day of the moneth, & so the purpose of the figure disapointed, peradventure it had bin better to have said thus:

> *The month and daie when Aries receivd*
> *Dan Phoebus raies into his horned head.*

> For now there remaineth for the Reader somewhat to studie and gesse upon, and yet the spring time to the learned judgement sufficiently expressed. (194)

Writers must consider their readers, leaving them something to contemplate, and here Puttenham as a reader reacts to a periphrasis bungled because it reveals too much and leaves too little for the ingenuity of the reader.

If reading and writing are the two sides of one coin, we can see in *The Arte of English Poesie* a complete guide to reading poetry, a kind of sixteenth-century *Understanding Poetry*. It can also be seen as an adaptation of Erasmus's classroom method for an adult audience. We recall that in Erasmus's presentation of authors, an introduction to the author is followed by a discussion of the pleasures, benefits, origins, and significance of the genre, a close explication of the passage under consideration, comparison with other similar passages, and finally, discussion of its moral implications. Puttenham of course cannot exactly duplicate this procedure, since he is talking of poetry in general rather than a single passage, but it is striking how much of it he does retain. Instead of an introduction to the author, he begins with an introduction to the topic, as the titles for the first two chapters indicate: "What a Poet and Poesie is . . ." and "Whether there may be an arte of our English or vulgar Poesie." He then considers the origins of the genre, arguing that poets were the first priests, prophets, legislators, politicians, philosophers, astronomers, historiographers, orators, and musicians in the world (chapters 3 and 4). A brief history of poetry, showing that all nations use it and chronicling its descent in the West from the Greeks through the middle ages (chapters 5, 6, 7) ends with a consideration of how poetry and poets, revered in antiquity, "be now become contemptible and for what causes" (chapter 8).

The next twenty-two chapters deal with the different kinds of poetry, summarized in the tenth as "The subjecte or matter of Poesie what it is" and subdivided in the following ones into the poetic kinds in which "the gods of the Gentiles were praysed and honored" (12), "vice and the common abuses of mans life was reprehended" (13), "the evill and outragious behaviours of Princes were reprehended" (15), "the great Princes and dominators of the world were honored" (16), "vertue in the inferiour sort was commended" (20), "the amorous affections and allurements were uttered" (22), and how "the solemne rejoysings at the nativitie of Princes children" (225), "the manner of rejoysings at mariages and weddings" (26), "bitter taunts, and privy nips, or witty scoffes and other merry conceits" (27) were treated. The final chapter of the first book is Puttenham's brief history of English poetry.

This first book provides readers and writers with a general introduction to the history and variety of poetry, and the sections devoted to the kinds and to invention (or the sources of poetry) are very much in the spirit of Erasmus's introduction to the background, significance, and pleasure of the passage being explicated. It may not even be entirely fanciful to see in the poetic kinds some echo of Erasmus's advice to explain "the gist of the plot" (*De Ratione Studii*, 683), since each of Puttenham's chapters recounts not only the utility and significance of the kind, but also its typical contents:

> But the chief and principall [matter or subject of poetry] is: the laud honor & glory of the immortall gods (I speake now in phrase of the Gentiles.) Secondly the worthy gests of noble Princes: the memoriall and registry of all great fortunes, the praise of vertue & reproofe of vice, the instruction of morall doctrines, the revealing of sciences naturall & other profitable Arts, the redresse of boistrous & sturdie courages by perswasion, the consolation and repose of temperate myndes, finally the common solace of mankind in all his travails and cares of this transitory life. (24)

In the second and third books we find an adult version of close reading. Erasmus had stressed the importance of meter, and this is the topic of Puttenham's second book, "Of Proportion Poetical," which he subdivides into five topics: "Staffe, Measure, Concord, Scituation and figure" (65). In the chapter devoted to staff (or stanza), he defines the term ("a certaine number of verses allowed to go together and joyne without any intermission, and doe or

should finish up all the sentences of the same with a full period"
[65]), explains the various kinds, and provides some brief history
and personal judgment:

> The fourth [proportion] is in seven verses, & is the chiefe of our
> ancient proportions used by any rimer writing any thing of his-
> torical or grave poeme, as ye may see in *Chaucer* and *Lidgate*. . . .
> The fift proportion is of eight verses very stately and *Heroicke,* and
> which I like better then that of seven, because it receaveth better
> band. (65)

The next two chapters explain meter and English meter, and the
following one sets up some very strict rules for the placement of
the caesura. The sixth chapter deals with rhyme; the next two, with
stress and rhythm; and the ninth, with "how the good Maker will
not wrench his word to helpe his rime, either by falsifying his accent, or by untrue orthographie." The two following chapters return to rhyme to distinguish between close and distant rhyme and
to explain situation, the disposition within a stanza of rhyme and
lines of different length. This leads directly into the longest chapter in the book, "Of proportion by figure," dealing with fifteen
geometrical shapes for poems, including among others, the rhom-
bus, square, triangle, circle, pillar, double triangle, and the oval or
egg. Here he also considers anagrams. The book ends with six
chapters considering the possibility of classical meters in English.

In their introduction to Puttenham's *Arte,* Willcock and Walker
argue that the *Arte* was composed over a period of roughly two
decades, the first book (with the exception of the final chapter on
English poets) and the first eleven chapters of the second dating
from perhaps the late 1560s, while the last chapters of the second
book, the survey of English poetry, and the third book derive from
the 1580s (xliv–liii). This putative dating makes the comparison of
the earlier part of Puttenham's book with George Gascoigne's *Certayne Notes of Instruction Concerning the Making of Verse or Rhyme
in English* (1575) extremely tempting. Gascoigne's short treatise,

prefaced to *The Posies of George Gascoigne, Esquire, corrected, perfected, and augmented by the author,*[4] is similarly addressed to an adult audience, probably more educated than Puttenham's, as the untranslated Latin phrases throughout and the initial statement that it was "written at the request of Master *Eduardo Donati*" (46) indicate. Slightly disorganized (Gascoigne apologizes twice for his "preposterous ordre" [49, 56], and at the end returns to discuss a type of verse he had earlier forgotten: "I had forgotten a notable kind of ryme, called ryding rime . . . but, though it come to my remembrance somewhat out of order, it shall not yet come altogether out of time, for I will nowe tell you a conceipt whiche I had before forgotten to wryte" [56]), the instructions nevertheless cover many of the same points Puttenham had in his first two books.

Gascoigne's instructions fall into two categories dealing generally with invention and execution. His first and most important rule for a poem is to "ground it upon some fine invention. . . . [W]hat Theame soever you do take in hande, if you do not handle it but *tanquam in oratione perpetua,* and never studie for some depth of devise in the Invention, and some figures in the handlyng thereof, it will appeare to the skillful Reader but a tale of a tubbe" (47–48). The second rule is a continuation or extension of this: "Your Invention being once devised, take heede that neither pleasure of rime nor variety of devise do carie you from it: for as to use obscure and darke passages in a pleasant Sonet is nothing delectable, so to entermingle merie jests in a serious mattter is an *Indecorum*" (48). Though not as detailed as Puttenham about the kinds of poetry and their history, Gascoigne agrees with him in putting invention first and sticking to it, and his reference to the skillful reader attentive to the novelty of the invention reminds us that advice for the writer is also advice for the reader. The skillful reader will first scrutinize the invention behind the poem, judging the depth of device and checking that it is both good and fine:

I meane some good and fine devise, shewing the quicke capacitie of a writer: and where I say some *good and fine invention* I meane

that I would have it both fine and good. For many inventions are
so superfine that they are *Vix good.* And, againe, many Inventions
are good, and yet not finely handled. (47)

Gascoigne is not altogether clear on what constitutes a good and
fine invention—"to deliver unto you generall examples it were
almost unpossible, sithence the occasions of Inventions are (as it
were) infinite" (48)—but it appears to be primarily a combination
of originality and novelty while avoiding the merely odd or bizarre
(the superfine).

Then the reader will determine whether the poet has maintained it. The danger is that the poet will be distracted from the
initial invention by an appealing rhyme or dark conceit; the writer
must avoid such temptations because the reader will condemn
them. To avoid "rime without reason" ("my meaning is hereby
that your rime leade you not from your first Invention, for many
wryters, when they have layed the platforme of their invention, are
yet drawen sometimes [by ryme] to forget it or at least to alter it"
[51–52]), he advises that the poet compile lists of rhyming words to
ensure that one not altering the invention will be available (52).
Likewise, he advises that expression should be decorous—"avoyde
prolixitie and tediousnesse" (56)—and challenging:

And asmuch as you may, frame your stile to *perspicuity* and to be
sensible, for the haughty obscure verse doth not much delight,
and the verse that is to easie is like a tale of a rosted horse; but let
your Poeme be such as may both delight and draw attentive readyng, and therewithal may deliver such matter as be worth the
marking. (53)

The emphasis on the reader's reaction in this is striking; the poet
composes with one eye on the reader's probable reaction. To attract his attention, the poem must be founded upon a good and
fine invention; to maintain his interest it must be so executed as to
instruct and delight. Like Puttenham insisting that the reader
must be allowed to exercise his ingenuity, Gascoigne pictures an

active reader asking himself, perhaps unconsciously, whether the invention attracts and the style pleases, and judging the writer's commitment to the initial invention and his ability to avoid tempting distractions.

Gascoigne's assumptions about how readers will react are informative in two ways. They tell us how an active poet conceived of his writing, and more generally, of the situation of writing, in the 1570s; how consciously it could be oriented toward eventual reception. But they also serve as instructions for readers about how they should be reading. The advice for readers here is very general— in the language of the appendix, these are teleological strategies rather than operational ones, since the goal is stressed rather than the means of attaining it—but correspondingly very useful, since they can be applied in every instance.

Gascoigne's second type of instruction is more specific (in the terms of the appendix, operational), dealing with technical matters: "hold the just measure wherewith you begin your verse" (49); "place every worde in his natural *Emphasis* or sound" (49); "thrust as few words of many sillables into your verse as may be" (51); "eschew straunge words, or *obsoleta et inusitata,* unless the Theame do give just occasion" (52–53); "use your verse after thenglish phrase, and not after the maner of other languages" (53); "finish the sentence and meaning at the end of every staffe where you wright staves, and at the end of every two lines where you write by cooples or poulters measure" (56). These bits of advice provide a checklist of strategies for the writer and reader to apply in their activities in a straightforward way: does the poet maintain the original meter? use words in their normal stress? avoid polysyllables and strange vocabulary? maintain English word order? achieve congruity between metrical form and syntactical constructions? One could hardly hope for more concrete expression of the kinds of things readers should observe in their reading.

From both Puttenham and Gascoigne, then, a reader would have learned to read poetry in a particular way. The first thing to be scrutinized was the invention, or conception behind the poem. Puttenham is fuller on the history of the different poetic kinds, and his approach to invention combines two quite different conceptions of the source of poetic inspiration. In the discussion of the more private functions of poetry (lamentations, rejoicings, taunts, love poems) he conceives of something very like the spontaneous overflow of powerful emotions:

> But all the world could not keepe, nor any civill ordinance to the contrary so prevaile, but that men would and must needs utter their splenes in all ordinarie matters also: or else it seemed their bowels would burst, therefore the poet devised a pretty fashioned poeme short and sweete . . . in which every mery conceited man might without any long studie or tedious ambage, make his frend sport, and anger his foe, and give a prettie nip, or shew a sharp conceit in few verses. (53–54)

On the other hand, in his function as priest, prophet, philosopher, legislator, and politician, the poet is more similar to an orator, producing a consciously crafted poem:

> So as next after the honours exhibited to their gods, the Poets finding in man generally much to reprove & litle to praise, made certaine poems in plaine meetres, more like to sermons or preachings then otherwise. (30)

This extremely self-conscious craftsmanship reappears in the courtly poet, who demonstrates his skill by being able to write extemporaneously upon any subject in any metrical form:

> Make me saith this writer to one of the companie, so many strokes or lines with your pen as ye would have your song containe verses: and let every line beare his severall length. . . . Then where you will have your rime or concord to fall, marke it. . . . And bycause ye shall not thinke the maker hath premeditated beforehand any such fashioned ditty, do ye your selfe make one verse whether it be of perfect or imperfect sense, and give it him for a theame to make all the rest upon: if ye shall perceive the maker do keepe the mea-

sures and rime as ye have appointed him, and besides do make his dittie sensible and ensuant to the first verse in good reason, then may ye say he is his crafts maister. (90–91)

Gascoigne, less copious than Puttenham (his work is only a small fraction of the other's length), insists more strongly on the need for originality—good and fine invention—and on avoiding distractions from it.

From both writers the reader would learn to check for consistency in the meter and the placement of the caesura, for congruity between meter and syntax, and for English (rather than French or Latin) word order. From both he would learn to reject strange words, whether inkhorn terms or foreign borrowings, without some special justification (Gascoigne observes, "marie, in some places a straunge worde doth drawe attentive reading," but warns, "but yet I woulde have you therein to use discretion" [53]). From both he would learn to be attentive to the type of meter, but here the two differ in significant ways.

Both introduce the reader to the various kinds of stanzaic patterns, though Gascoigne is fuller in his discussion, mentioning rhyme royal, ballads in six-line stanzas, rondelettes, sonnets, "Dyzaynes and Syxaines" (ten- and six-line stanzas), virelays, four-line stanzas, poulters measure (alternating lines of twelve and fourteen syllables), and finally—the form he forgot and had to add at the end—riding rhyme (couplets) (54–57). Perhaps balancing this, Puttenham devotes a good bit of time to the various geometrical shapes poems could exhibit. Both stress rhyme, with Puttenham assuming that it needs a full explanation ("we make in th' ends of our verses a certaine tunable sound: which anon after with another verse reasonably distant we accord together in the last fall or cadence: the eare taking pleasure to heare the like tune repeated, and to feel his return" [76]). Gascoigne is content to warn of the distraction it offers and to provide practical advice about preparing word lists of rhymes to help in composition (52).

Both introduce caesura, but it is here that the difference in their approaches to metrics begins to appear. Gascoigne defines the term ("certayne pauses or restes in a verse" [54]), says they are at the discretion of the writer, and then offers his opinion about their proper placement (54). Puttenham, on the other hand, is dictatorial in his specifications:

> Therefore in a verse of twelve sillables, the *Cesure* ought to fall right upon the sixt sillable: in a verse of eleven upon the sixt also leaving five to follow. In a verse of ten upon the fourth, leaving six to follow. In a verse of nine, upon the fourth. . . . In a verse of eight just in the middest. . . . In a verse of seaven, either upon the fourth or none at all. . . . in every long verse the *Cesure* ought to be kept precisely, if it were but to serve as a law to correct the licentiousnesse of rymers, besides that it pleaseth the eare better, & sheweth more cunning in the maker by following the rule of his restraint. (75–76)

Willcock and Walker account for this emphasis on caesura by noting that the sections on rhyme and caesura were among the earliest composed, and that Puttenham had by this time achieved no concept of accent and the internal rhythm of a line as constituting part of prosody: "Puttenham recognizes two principles and two only—*number* and *rhyme*" (lxvii). The caesura in the middle of the line was the counterpart of the rhyme at the end of it: "It secured Art in the middle of the line as well as at the end" (lxviii). The three metrical constraints the writer must follow and the reader must recognize are thus line length (in number of syllables), rhyme, and the placement of the caesura.

In the later sections of Puttenham's second book, which Willcock and Walker assign to the 1580s (xlviii–xlix), he begins to approximate our modern conception of English meter based upon stress, but his discussion is so confused, linking English accent uncertainly to Latin and Greek syllable length, that Willcock and Walker almost certainly understate the difficulties when they observe that "a general haziness of context may obscure definition" (lxxi). Puttenham's readers in 1589 might have learned to look for English counterparts of the classical meters (he defines and provides examples of them [120–21]), but it is doubtful whether they would have had much success.

Gascoigne had been much clearer fifteen years earlier. He explained that English has three levels of what he calls "accent"— long, short, and circumflex—and that every word has a natural emphasis or stress pattern (49). English poetry at the time he is writing uses "none other order but a foot of two sillables, whereof the first is depressed or made short, and the second is elevate or made long: and that sound or scanning continueth throughout the verse" (50). Every word must be disposed in meter so its natural emphasis coincides with the metrically required ictus: "place every worde in his natural *Emphasis* or sound, that is to say, in such wise, and with such length or shortnesse, elevation or depression of syllables, as it is commonly pronounced or used" (49). He laments "that wee are fallen into such a playne and simple manner of wryting, that there is none other foote used but one" and anticipates C. S. Lewis's baptism of this kind of poetry as "drab" by noting that "our Poemes may justly be called Rithmes, and cannot by any right challenge the name of a Verse," but he determines "to take the forde as we find it" and lays down the law for his poet: "all the wordes in your verse [must] be so placed as the first sillable may sound short or be depressed, the second long or elevate, the third shorte, the fourth long, the fifth shorte, etc." (50–51).

To illustrate, he explains that *I understand your meaning by your eye* "may passe the musters," but that *Your meaning I understand by your eye*

> is neyther true nor pleasant. . . . The fault of the latter verse is that this worde *understand* is therein so placed as the grave accent falleth upon *der,* and therby maketh *der* in this worde *understand* to be elevated; which is contrarie to the naturall or usual pronunciation. (51)

Monosyllables were considered to have circumflex stress, that is, to be able to bear or not to bear metrical ictus indifferently, so in the first example, *by* is in a metrically stressed position, just as *I* is in the second, while *your* is unstressed in both. Polysyllables, on the other hand, contain an inherently stressed syllable, and placing them so that inherent stress clashes with the metrical requirement of ictus leads to a metrical solecism. Gascoigne's writer and reader, then, would not learn simply to count the number of syllables in a line; instead they would see feet and lines composed of an expected stress (or accent, or emphasis) pattern and words either fitting or failing to fit the expected pattern.

Metrically, then, Gascoigne was far in advance of Puttenham, and his understanding of meter is essentially the same as ours. In the other area in which they differ the opposite was true. Almost in passing, Gascoigne recommends the use of ornamentation: "You may use the same Figures or Tropes in verse which are used in prose . . . but yet therein remember this old adage, *Ne quid nimis*" (52). Puttenham, on the other hand, devotes his entire third book (as long as the first two together) to the topics of language, ornamentation, and decorum, just as the Erasmian teacher spent much of his time in close commentary on the language and ornamentation of the passage in hand. As he turns to ornamentation, we can sense he is entering into his favorite topic:

> As no doubt the good proportion of any thing doth greatly
> adorne and commend it and right so our late remembred proportions doe to our vulgar Poesie: so is there yet requisite to the perfection of this arte, another maner of exornation, which resteth in the fashioning of our makers language and stile, to such purpose as it may delight and allure as well the mynde as the eare of the hearers with a certaine noveltie and strange maner of conveyance, disguising it no litle from the ordinary and accustomed: neverthelesse making it nothing the more unseemely or misbecomming, but rather decenter and more agreable to any civill eare and understanding. (137)

Echoing the Horation *dulce* and *utile,* Puttenham's buzzwords are *eare* and *minde* or *understanding,* and one of the reasons he prefers ornamentation of language to the formal properties of prosody is that it appeals to both the sense and the understanding. It is therefore no surprise that instead of the traditional division of figures into schemes and tropes he introduces a new division: into the *auricular*, which appeal only to the ear ("to satisfie & delight th' eare onely by a goodly outward shew set upon the matter with words, and speaches smothly and tunably running" [142]), *sensable*, which appeal only to the mind ("by certaine intendments or sence of such words & speaches inwardly working a stirre to the mynde" [142–43]), and *sententious*, which appeal to both (159–60). It is also no surprise that although he acknowledges that the third kind of figure is normally limited to the orator (159), he goes on to consider it as proper for the poet on the transparent grounds that poets were the first orators (196).

The figures, in Puttenham's presentation, are the clothing of language; just as a "great Madame of honour" would be "halfe ashamed or greatly out of countenance" to be seen unclothed or garbed only in "plaine and simple apparell," "be they for personage or otherwise never so comely or bewtifull,"

> Even so cannot our vulgar Poesie shew itself either gallant or gorgious, if any lymme be left naked and bare and not clad in his kindly clothes and coulours, such as may convey them somwhat out of sight, that is from the common course of ordinary speach and capacitie of the vulgar judgement, and yet being artificially handled must needes yeld it much more bewtie and commendation. This ornament we speake of is given to it by figures and figurative speaches, which be the flowers as it were and coulours that a Poet setteth upon his language by arte. (138)

Puttenham is trying to inculcate in his readers what he considers the proper attitude toward ornamentation, and though Willcock and Walker are correct in observing that he never directly refers to Puritan attacks on the theater and poetry in general, he does exhibit a certain urbane concern that ornament be given its due. The comparison between poetry and great madames is part of this concern, for the women—no matter how inherently excellent—

appear even better when appropriately attired. Similarly, poetry—whatever the excellence of its invention—will appear to the educated judgment more beautiful and commendable when it is artificially handled. Puttenham realizes that this ornamentation is akin to falsification:

> As figures be the instruments of ornament in every language, so be they also in a sorte abuses or rather trespasses in speach, because they passe the ordinary limits of common utterance, and be occupied of purpose to deceive the eare and also the minde, drawing it from plainnesse and simplicitie to a certaine doublenesse, whereby our talke is the more guilefull and abusing. (154)

But this potentially dangerous similarity between ornament and duplicity can be mitigated in two ways. The first is to relate poetry to courtliness. The simplest way to do this is to stress the playfulness of poetry, to admit that poetry, and especially courtly poetry, is merely a pleasant pastime, the poet being "a pleader . . . of pleasant & lovely causes . . . in the eare of princely dames, yong ladies, gentlewomen and courtiers, . . . and . . . all his abuses tende but to dispose the hearers to mirth and sollace by pleasant conveyance and efficacy of speach" (154–55). This justification is obviously related to his conception of the poet as the consummate craftsman, producing extemporaneously a poem in any metrical pattern on any subject.

On a somewhat deeper level, poetry is intimately related to the purpose of the court because it "teacheth *beau* semblant, the chief posession aswell of Courting as of poesie" (158). As Daniel Javitch has argued in *Poetry and Courtliness in Renaissance England*, "it took the sophisticated sensibility of the court to value and enjoy what seemed to others perversities of language. Puttenham knew that a courtly audience, so alert to the discrepancy between surface and reality in conduct, could only cherish the same effects in poetic discourse."[5] In Javitch's view, the poet is similar to the courtier recommended in Castiglione's *The Book of the Courtier,* whose major achievement is *sprezzatura,* the ability to dissemble the effort required to become universally accomplished. In overtly linking poetry with courtliness, then, Puttenham deflects any criticism of this duplicity in language by allying it with the highest courtly virtue.

Satisfying as this justification appears, particularly because it validates the purpose of poetry in exceeding the vulgar or common understanding and relates poetry to the behavior of the court, Puttenham is not ultimately content to let it go at that. In the section arguing that the poet as well as the orator may use sententious (or rhetorical) figures, he stresses the seriousness of poetry and the epistemological efficacy of the figures:

> And your figures rhetoricall, besides their remembred ordinarie vertues, that is, sententiousness, & copious amplification, or enlargement of language, doe also conteine a certaine sweet and melodious manner of speech, in which respect, they may, after a sort, be said *auricular:* because the eare is no less ravished with their currant tune, than the mind is with their sententiousnes. For the eare is properly but an instrument of conveyance for the minde, to apprehend the sense by the sound. . . . He therefore that hath vanquished the minde of man, hath made the greatest and most glorious conquest. But the minde is not assailable unlesse it be by sensible approches, whereof the audible is of greatest force for instruction or discipline. . . . Therefore the well tuning of your words and clauses to the delight of the eare, maketh your information no lesse plausible to the minde than to the eare. (196–97)

Here the true purpose of the figures, at least the sententious figures, appears: they, and only they, convey the poet's invention to the reader's mind. Unlike the auricular figures, which are merely adornment, however fit, these figures are essential to the social utility of poetry. They are the necessary instruments of the poet in his social role as priest, prophet, legislator, and politician, instructing and disciplining readers. It is no accident that throughout this section, Puttenham repeatedly refers to the poet as a persuader (Willcock and Walker, lxxx).

165

When he discusses the figures themselves, Puttenham is unfailingly engaging: because he is writing for courtiers rather than scholars, he has "devised a new and strange model of this arte, fitter to please the court then the schoole" (159)—the translation of the names of the figures into catchy English phrases, "lovingly designed," as Willcock and Walker put it, "to show some 'kick' or arresting quality in the Greek" (lxxxii)—to help fix them in memory. *Zeugma,* for instance, becomes "the single supply" because one word is used in more than one clause; the single word supplies them all. When the word appears in the first clause, it is *prozeugma,* or "the ringleader"; in the middle, it is *mezozeugma,* or "the middle marcher"; in the last, *hypozeugma,* or "the rerewarder" (163–65). He proceeds systematically through some twenty-one auricular figures, twenty-four sensable ones, and sixty sententious ones, so that by the end the poet has a sizeable inventory of constructions to use in composition and to recognize and appreciate in reading.

Of special interest among the figures are the sensable ones, which "alter and affect the minde by alteration of sence" (178), for in these the opportunity for duplicity and dissimulation Javitch identifies with courtly behavior is most apparent:

> his emphasis on the capacity of figures to convey meaning out of all proportion to words is quite original in terms of English rhetorical theory. Moreover, the singular attention he gives to the possibilities of "darkness" in the artifices of language makes his rhetoric much more concordant with the poetic practice emerging in his age. . . . Puttenham encouraged indirection and ambiguity in language because he realized the pleasures derived from poetry are related to the way it obscures and retards the disclosure of its meaning. (65–66)

Javitch perhaps exaggerates the desire to occlude here, for Puttenham justifies the use of metaphor (or transport) "for necessitie or want of a better word" (178), "for pleasure and ornament" (179), and "to enforce a sence and make the word more signicative"

166

(180), none of which alludes to dissembling. But as he moves from the simpler single-word tropes to the more complicated ones, and then to figures of clauses, Puttenham does emphasize the ability of the poet to dissemble and thus to engage the reader. "[T]he sence is much altered & the hearers conceit strangely entangled by the figure *Metalepsis,* which I call the *farfet*" (183), he writes, and synecdoche ("if we use such a word [as many times we doe] by which we drive the hearer to conceive more or lesse or beyond or otherwise then the letter expresseth") he calls the *quick conceit* because "it seemeth to aske a good, quick, and pregnant capacitie" to understand (185).

Readers, of course, should cultivate such pregnant capacities, especially to understand allegoria (or false semblant), "which is when we speake one thing and thinke another, and that our wordes and our meanings meete not" (186). "The chiefe ringleader and captaine of all other figures" is ubiquitous:

> The use of this figure is so large, and his vertue of so great efficacie as it is supposed no man can pleasantly utter and perswade without it, but in effect is sure never or very seldome to thrive and prosper in the world, that cannot skilfully put [it] in ure. (186)

Under the general heading of allegory Puttenham considers a dozen figures (including enigma, irony, and hyperbole), concluding with periphrasis ("holding somewhat of the dissembler, by reason of a secret intent not appearing by the words, as when we go about the bush, and will not in one or a few words expresse that thing which we desire to have knowen, but do chose rather to do it by many words" [193]) and synecdoche. In all of his discussions there is the assumption that a quick wit will penetrate the dissembling and understand the intent; his reference to the poet who uses circumlocution "to set forth any thing pleasantly and figuratively, yet no lesse plaine to a ripe reader, then if it were named expresly" (195) might usefully serve as a characterization of the ripe reader, who within a courtly setting acts as an arbiter. Puttenham himself exhibits little hesitation in pronouncing judgments (we discuss his treatments of vices of composition shortly); typical is the explanation that "there remaineth for the Reader somewhat to studie and gesse upon, and yet the spring time [the intent of the paraphrase] to the learned judgment sufficiently expressed" (194).

In the discussions above of Harington and the *artes praedicandi* I mentioned the problem of limiting allegorical or figurative readings; Puttenham, with his references to "learned judgment" and the "ripe reader," finesses it by assuming that the courtly poet will express, and the courtly reader will understand, the intended meaning. How far this was so I leave to my own reader to judge from one of Puttenham's examples:

> A pleasant Gentleman came into a Ladies nursery, and saw her for her owne pleasure rocking of her young child in the cradle, and sayd to her:
>
> > *I speake it Madame without any mocke,*
> > *Many a such cradell may I see you rocke.*
>
> Gods passion hourson, said she, would thou have me beare mo children yet, no *Madame* quoth the Gentleman, but I would have you live long, that ye might the better pleasure your friends, for his meaning was that as every cradle signified a new borne childe, & every child the leasure of one yeares birth, & many yeares a long life: so by wishing her to rocke many cradels of her owne, he wished her long life. (183)

Matching the figures are the vices, but they are more ambivalent, as the title of Puttenham's chapter treating them indicates: "Some vices in speaches and writing are always intollerable, some others now and then borne withall by licence of approved authors and custome" (250). Among those universally deplored are *solecism* or "incongruity," the abuse of grammar, *soraismus* or "the mingle mangle," the mixing of foreign words, and *cacosintheton* or "the misplacer," the departure from normal word order (251–53). Puttenham proceeds to list and discuss another dozen, but here the matter becomes more complex, since most of these vices can be, as he indicates, licensed by authority or custom. *Hysteron proteron* or "the preposterous" is discussed both as an auricular figure and as a vice (170, 255), and under *tautologia* or "self saying," he treats abuse of alliteration but then admits that "it doth not ill but pretily becomes the meetre, if ye passe not two or three words in one verse" (254–55). Similarly, the final vice of *amphibologia* or the ambiguous, when the sense may be taken two or more ways, can be either vicious or useful, "when [the maker] doth it for the nonce and for some purpose" (261).

The difficulty Puttenham faces in this section is that since the figures are inherently extraordinary departures from ordinary language, and perhaps even deceptive, it requires something more than simply textbook knowledge to distinguish between a figure and a vice (when is *hysteron proteron* one or the other?) and to decide when a vice is justified either by custom or by purpose. Puttenham is finally interested in providing more than a checklist of figures to allow his poet to dissemble or convince by pleasing the ear; he wants to teach judgment (the ability Erasmus considered of prime importance in teaching the young), which is based on *decorum,* or his English versions of it, "decency," "seemelynesse," "comelynesse," and "pleasant approche" (261–62). This is the final answer to the deceptive nature of figurative language which we considered earlier:

> So albeit we before alleaged that all our figures be but transgressions of our dayly speach, yet if they fall out decently to the good liking of the mynde or eare and to the bewtifying of the matter or language, all is well, if indecently, and to the eares and myndes misliking (be the figure of it selfe never so commendable) all is amisse, the election is the writers, the judgement is the worlds, as theirs to whom the reading apperteineth. (262–63)

In this penultimate chapter, the balance Puttenham has previously maintained between the reader and the writer ("all such as be willing themselves to become good makers in the vulgar, or to be able to judge of other mens makings" [159]) shifts almost entirely to the reader: "the election is the writers, the judgment is the worlds," and the good liking of the ear and mind is the final test of propriety.

It is therefore of primary importance that the ear and mind be educated in judgment. Unlike the figures, judgment cannot be taught by precept: "by reason of the sundry circumstances, that mans affaires are as it were wrapt in, this [*decencie*] comes to be very much alterable and subject to variety" (263). It depends on the speaker, the hearer, the place and time of speaking, and the subject; it involves not only the language used but all qualities of voice and gesture (263–66). It can be learned only by experience, and so Puttenham devotes the longest chapter of his book to a series of examples of decency in language and behavior, partly "for the solace they may geve the readers, after such a rable of scholastical precepts which be tedious," but more because "olde memories are very profitable to the mind, and serve as a glasse to look upon and behold the events of time, and more exactly to skan the trueth of every case that shall happen in the affaires of man" (264). The reader who reads this chapter in the way Blundeville recommended, considering and reconsidering the examples, looking for what they have in common and how they differ, will achieve "a learned and experienced discretion" and become a fit judge, since "he who can make the best and most differences of things by reasonable and wittie distinction is to be the fittest judge or sentencer of [*decencie*]" (263). The judgment the reader learns to exercise is especially necessary because the poet, like Castiglione's courtier, uses art to disguise art: the poet is to be commended for both his natural inspiration and his use of the arts of language:

> Therefore shall our Poet receave prayse for both, but more by knowing of his arte then by unseasonable using it, and be more commended for his naturall eloquence then for his artificiall, and more for his artificiall well desembled, then for the same overmuch affected and grossely or undiscretly bewrayed, as many makers and Oratours do. (307)

170

A learned and experienced discretion must learn to see through the well-dissembled artifice to draw the distinction between the artificial, the natural, and the artificial disguised so as to appear natural. To do this, he must understand and control the poet's craft so he can read from the inside, and judge as the poet writes: "first to devise his plat or subject, then to fashion his poeme, thirdly to use his metricall proportions, and last of all to utter with pleasure and delight" (306).

The reader of Puttenham (and to a lesser extent, simply because he is less detailed, Gascoigne) would have learned to do this. Neither can provide much specific guidance in judging invention, since like the opportunities for decorum it is limitless, but Gascoigne, in his comments about good and fine invention and the necessity of maintaining the initial invention, provides some guidelines. Both discuss metrical proportion in enough detail to make a reader proficient in English meter, though as we have seen, Puttenham's reader would be severely limited in dealing with verse composed after 1570 or so. And Puttenham, through his long discussion of language and its ornaments and his education in judgment and decorum, enables his reader to identify a wide range of figures and judge their effectiveness. Finally, both recognize the paramount importance of the reader, though Puttenham puts it better: "the election is the writers, the judgment is the worlds."

In both writers, the emphasis is on single texts—neither suggests anything approaching intertextuality or comparative reading—and local effects: the foot or line for metrics, the short passage for figures. Invention encompasses the whole of the poem, but neither is able to discuss it in detail, and even something like decorum is limited to one incident or figure. Even an essentially extended figure like allegoria, which Puttenham compares to a perpetual metaphor ("and because such inversion of sense in one single worde is by the figure *Metaphore,* of whom we spake before, and this manner of inversion extending to whole and large speaches, it maketh the figure *allegorie* to be called a long and perpetuall Metaphore" [187]) is exemplified, almost necessarily, by short examples, the longest being six lines.

As informative and exemplary as they are for us in reflecting Tudor modes of reading, it is questionable whether Gascoigne and Puttenham reached especially large audiences in their own day. Gascoigne's treatise was prefixed to *The Posies of George Gascoigne, Esquire, corrected, perfected, and augmented by the author,* which appeared in 1575 with another edition in the same year, and then was included in *The whole woorkes of G. Gascoigne,* which had two editions. Puttenham was apparently never reprinted until the modern editions. So the audience for the advice Gascoigne and Puttenham provide cannot be compared to the number of people in congregations around the country who heard the expositions of the Paternoster, Ten Commandments, and Creed in church. On the other hand, a truly popular book, Angel Day's *The English Secretary,*[6] provided a basic introduction to rhetoric and writing for the masses. This book, which went through at least eleven printings between its appearance in 1586 and 1635 (Alston, "Note," n.p.), was the most popular of the English versions of the *artes epistolaria* or guides to letter writing. Robert O. Evans, one of its modern editors, attributes this popularity to "the fact that it is at once the most systematic and simplest of the rhetorical analysis [*sic*] of figures" (ix), and even R. C. Alston, who claims that the work is of interest "principally for the history of English prose-style," perhaps unwittingly identifies it as a rhetoric when he notes that it "was very popular, more so than any other sixteenth-century rhetoric" ("Note"). But a reader less fixated on the figures might well attribute its popularity more to the many sample letters it contains dealing with delicate daily situations, especially the letters currying favor, rebuking inferiors, or expostulating with superiors. For instance, *"An example of an Epistle Expostulatorie from an inferiour Gentleman to his farre better in degree, authoritie and calling,"* attempts to convince a nobleman that he should pay the fair price of 1,600 pounds for a farm rather than the 970 pounds he has actually paid (Book 2, 27–30), and the "Epistle

172

expostulatorie touching certaine injuries betweene two friends," together with the "answere defensorie," "A reply to the said answere Defensorie," and "A second answere" (Book 2, 19–26), form an engrossing series. The impression that the letters are the cause of the book's popularity is strengthened when one realizes that a section of the introduction that appeared in the first edition warning against imitation of examples was excised in later editions:

> in this matter of writing Epistles, nothing is more disordered, fonde, or vaine, then for anye one, of a thing well done, to take forth a precident, and think to make him selfe thereof a common platforme for every other accident . . . much like unto a foolish Shoemaker, that making his shoes after one fashion, quantitye and proportion: supposeth the same forthwith of abilitie fit to serve every mans foot. (Alston, 4)

As Evans suggests, "[t]he student had simply to select one [letter] suitable to the occasion and copy it, making whatever emendations he thought necessary and personalizing it to suit his particular situation" (vi).

The practical applications of such a book were obvious, and it is this immediate utility that distinguishes it from the Latin versions of the *artes epistolaria* such as Erasmus's *De Conscribendis Epistolis*[7] and similar works by Vives, Macropedius, and Hegendorphinus used as textbooks in grammar schools. Written in Latin, these were of use only to those who had already mastered that language, and the model letters they proposed tended to be based on classical models (especially Cicero) and to deal with classical topics: Erasmus suggests that the teacher seek topics for practice letters "in the stories of the poets or the historians, unless, as may well happen, some novelty is provided by contemporary events" (24) or in "commonplaces made up for the occasion or taken from the classical authors" (27). As exercises for schoolboys, these letters were designed to develop powers of invention and expression, just as the other compositions done in the classroom. Day's audience and goal were quite different; his letters deal with everyday situations, often delicate ones, and—being written in English—are directed toward those who had not mastered Latin and learned in grammar school to write practice letters "from Cicero encouraging Milo to bear exile with a brave heart" or "discouraging Cato from the study of Greek, to which he aspired in his old age" (Erasmus, 25–26). He wishes to help the "unlearned" (but apparently literate), "knowing how greevous it is to participate their most secreate causes to an other, and to laye up their chiefest trust in the affiaunce of an others credite" (Alston, 3) when they have to have others compose their letters for them.

Day's book, in its fullest version (the 1599 edition which Evans edited), consists of an introduction to epistles, detailing the types and parts of letters, with explanations and examples of twenty-two kinds of letters, their parts and rhetorical figures identified marginally; a discussion of over ninety figures; and a concluding discussion "of the parts, place and office of a secretary." "A Table shewing the principal matters contained in the first part of this Booke" at the end allowed readers to locate examples of the kinds of letters they needed without rereading the entire volume. Day recognized the interdependence between reading and writing I have been stressing—what one learns to produce, one learns to recognize—and so in his introduction he stresses that he has included the figures for those who are "farre more curious of imitation and studie of the best":

> so besides the furtherance continuallie atchieved by the often use of reading, shall herein be greatlie holpen, in that for the self same purpose, and to the intent the learner maie aswell in his native tongue, know the right use of figures and Tropes heretofore never by him understoode, as also to discerne and use them, out of others and in his own writings. (Book 1, 9)

Reading by itself is a useful education, but without specific instruction it is not clear what to read for, what to discern. To learn the right use and appreciation of the figures, the reader must be instructed in their use and effects, and so Day has

at the latter end of this booke, gathered together all such Figures
and Tropes heretofore needeful and convenient, and there by sundrie familiar examples expressed their uses and severall effects. In
diligent conceit and adverting whereof, the use unto the practiser
shall in short time bee found greatlie available, by the benefit
thereby attained. (Book 1, 9–10)

For Day as for the other writers of the period, nature is aided by
art or method; natural inclination is improved by practice (the
often use of reading, diligent conceit, and adverting to the figures)
and method (the explanation of the figures). It is possible to succeed by nature, but even those especially gifted can benefit from
cultivation:

to the end that they who (being unlearned, & having a pretie
conceit of invention of themselves) have heretofore unknowingly
done well, may see how with skill and discretion hereafter to pursue the same, & the ignorant also here of whose reach hath not
been so ample as others, may be thereby informed what unto well
doing is most consonant and agreeing. (sig. A.4.r)

The fortunate few who have unknowingly deployed figures in
their own writing, or recognized their power in reading, will learn
how to identify them consciously and judge their right use; others
will learn at least something of decorum.

Day's discussion of the figures is thoroughly traditional; he divides figures into tropes and schemes, explaining clearly that "Betweene a Trope and a Scheme the difference is, that the Trope
changeth the signification. . . . The Scheme hath no change of
signification" (Book 2, 77). He then defines and provides examples
of tropes of words (metaphor, synecdoche, etc.), tropes of sentences (allegory, irony, etc.), syntactical schemes (zeugma, paren-
thesis, etc.), and rhetorical schemes (anaphora, epizeuxis, etc.).
His discussions are not as detailed as Puttenham's, and he seldom
gives more than two examples of a figure, but this final discussion
of the figures, which Evans so much emphasizes, is only part of

175

the education Day provides in rhetoric. For almost every sample letter, he indicates in the margin the figures used, the apex being achieved in an example of a vehement comminatory (or threatening) letter in which twenty figures are identified in twenty-seven lines of text. The attentive reader—the one who is far more curious of imitation and study of the best—can move back and forth between the letters and the discussion of the figures, matching the definitions and examples in the discussion with the examples in the letters to gain a measure of control over their use. Not incidentally, in so doing he will be learning to identify the figures himself, even where there is no marginal assistance.

Although modern readers, and even his two modern editors, tend to value Day for his discussion of rhetoric, we should be aware that this is not the topic Day himself stresses most. In his book, he first defines what epistles are and then discusses the three "principall points" to be respected in all letters: "Aptness of wordes and sentences, . . . Brevity of speach, . . . Comliness in deliverance" (Book 1, 2). Aptness of speech, in turn, consists "in choice and good termes, in skilful and proper applications of them according to their true meanings, in wel sorting and fitting them, to their severall purposes" (Book 1, 2). Brevity of speech is not simply a matter of length, but of *necessary* length: "Necessarie speeches, I do account whatsoever is set downe, for the plaine and open deliverie of every occasion, to the intent the minde of the writer, and what he pursueth may aptly and in good and ready sort be conceived" (Book 1, 3). Comeliness of deliverance is decorum, the fitting of the writing to the circumstances of the writer, the reader, and the topic, and Day devotes several pages to two examples of indecorum, one caused by inattention to the station of the reader, the other due to "affectation of words," a misapplication of terms (Book 1, 5–8).

After this discussion of language and style, Day turns to the "habite and parts of an Epistle," distinguishing between general or familiar letters, written to friends, and those special letters, "bearing in them a resolute purpose and intendment seriously to discourse upon, to answere, mitigate or avoid any certain matter or causes, importing the present affairs whereupon the direction is framed" (Book 1, 8–9). Special epistles (he had earlier listed some of their varieties: "Hortatorie, Dehortatorie, Laudatorie, Vituperatorie, Suasorie, Petitorie, Monitorie, Accusatorie, Excusatorie, Consolatorie, Invective and such like" [Book 1, 3]) are more like orations, and in composing them the writer must be attentive to invention, disposition, and "eloquution," which he had already treated under aptness of words (Book 1, 9). As a help to "eloquution," he mentions in passing the table of tropes and figures at the end of the book. Related to elocution is decorum of style, and he discusses the three styles (sublime, humile, and mediocre) in relation to the subject matter of the letter. In disposition special letters are like orations, with an exordium, narration or proposition, confirmation, confutation, and peroration (Book 1, 11). Finally, all letters have salutations, closings, subscriptions, and "outwarde directions" or addresses, the many varieties of each Day explores in some detail (Book 1, 11–19).

Before he turns to example letters, he returns to consider in more detail the various kinds of letters and their relations with each other. Of special letters there are three main classes, the demonstrative, deliberative, and judicial, each with numerous subclasses: of demonstrative, there are descriptorie, laudatorie, and vituperatorie; of deliberative, hortatorie, dehortatorie, swasorie and disswasorie, conciliatorie, reconciliatorie, petitorie, consolatorie, monitorie, reprehensorie, and amatorie; of judicial, accusatorie, excusatorie, expostulatorie, purgatorie, defensorie, exprobatorie, deprecatorie, and invective (Book 1, 20–21). Even familiar letters have their varieties: narratorie, nunciatorie, gratulatorie, remuneratorie, jocatorie, objurgatorie, mandatorie, and responsorie (Book 1, 22). While he admits that these classes overlap—"how can I exhort, counsell, advise, withdraw, commend, admonish or reprehend, if therin I set not forth what is worthie or unfit" (Book 1, 21)—they do have some pedagogical value: "for ease of the learner, and to the end that he may with more readines find out what best fitteth and beseemeth the cause hee hath in handling, they bee thus drawne forth as you see in so many particular distinctions" (Book I, 22).

Before the reader encounters any sample letters, then, Day has prepared him to see them in a certain way. First, whatever is read will not simply be a letter, but a particular type of letter, laudatory, accusatory, amatory, and so forth. Day makes no reference to commonplace books, but the same impulse toward classification (not to say pigeonholing) is evident: no letter is an altogether original creation; it is rather another token of a well-known type, a categorization emphasized by the discussion of the sample letters in the rest of the book, where an explanation of the general type precedes each letter. Indeed, for the book to be useful in providing practical guidance to the would-be writer, he must know what type of letter he wants to write so he can locate relevant examples either in the table of matters at the back of the book or in the running heads at the top of each page, as Day advises in his opening address to the reader: "Now for the readier finding of those *Epistles,* as each of their kindes are suted forth in sundrie *Examples:* Peruse but the head of every page and there you shall find what in the same page is contained" (sig. A.4.r). As I suggest in the second chapter, the basic question the reader learns to ask is not "What is this?" but "What is this an example of?"

Once the type is identified, its parts can be predicted: the oratorical divisions of exordium, narration or proposition, confirmation, confutation, and peroration for the special letters, a long narration for the familiar ones. Whatever the type, the careful reader will pay special attention to mechanics: aptness of words and sentences, apposite brevity, and decorum with respect to persons and topic. The marginal notations and the discussion of the figures at the end of the book will predispose the reader to identify various forms of ornamentation, but in the general discussion at the beginning of the book, Day devotes more attention to aptness of words and sentences, making it clear that the figures are only one part of eloquence, which is itself one of the three major aspects of any composition (along with invention and disposition). The neophyte writer runs a much greater risk of attracting unfavorable attention, and thereby thwarting his purpose, by indecorous language than by missing the opportunity for an elegant epizeuxis.

Finally, of course, the purpose of reading is practical preparation for future action. This is clearest in the chapter dealing with "Epistles Responsorie," which instructs the writer to forego the normal structure of an epistle and answer the points of the original letter in the order in which they were raised, merely alluding to them rather than repeating them at length for the sake of brevity. But responses and answers are scattered throughout the book (roughly a fifth of the ninety-three letters fall into this category), and they serve as a reminder that the book and all its advice are intensely practical, even utilitarian. The connection between reading and writing here is covert but pervasive, since one often writes in response to what has been read. The orations and letters schoolboys composed were preparation for a distant future; Day's sample letters prepare his readers to handle daily exigencies, and it is reasonable to assume that many consulted his book in reaction to a particularly pressing situation.

In this, Day differs slightly from Blundeville, Gascoigne, and Puttenham: their books were also overtly preparatory for future writing (as the titles of the first two announced), but it is difficult to conceive of them being consulted as reference collections of specific models for emulation. Their examples invite contemplation; Day's, replication. For this reason, the covert education in the method of reading Day provides may well have been less effective, as his readers leafed through his pages in search of a letter responding to a situation similar to their own instead of digesting fully his "platforme or method." We can only hope that most avoided the "example of an epistle Deprecatory, pleasantly written to answere a former Letter," which includes the following paragraph:

> The compasse of your writing, according to the measure it
> beareth, being so much mystical, as that the grossnesse of my wit

cannot well conceive of, having drawne thereinto as it seemeth, the very quintessence of those well performed partes, that in your person are refiant, maketh me post off the answere, till by a more deepe consideration I may better conforme me unto it. Wherein I must confesse in very deed, that all that may be within or without, over or under, or besides master B., you have to the uttermost strained. (Book 2, 57)

CHAPTER 6
CONCLUSION

ertain characteristics of reading reappear in all the sources
we have surveyed. The first, and most important, is the
utilitarian or preparatory nature of reading. For the Tudors, reading was always preparation for something else, ranging
from the relatively concrete need to answer a letter or compose a
poem on demand to the more general amendment of life that was
the purpose of religious reading, and the preparation for a life in
society requiring the ability to discern the proper course of action
in a particular situation and to convince others of it. But it must be
stressed that this is a very utilitarian conception, rather unlike
Mortimer Adler's justification for reading: "Reading . . . is a basic
tool in the living of a good life" and for liberal education (which
for him is also reading; the full title of his book is *How to Read a
Book: The Art of Getting a Liberal Education*): "it enriches us. It
makes men of us. It makes us able to lead the distinctively human
life of reason."[1] The Tudors could hardly quarrel with this statement, but I suspect that to Erasmus and Vives and Ascham it
would seem a reasonable but flabby justification; they were interested in making the life of reason operational by inculcating in the
reader or student enough examples from the past so he could
discern the proper course of action in any situation, and enough
examples and phrases from the past so he could convince others of
the proper action he had discerned. The distinctive life of reason
for them was lived in a society to which those living a good life
were expected to contribute. In his frustrated attempts to become
a politician, Gabriel Harvey perhaps best suggests the goal—"activity, present bold activity."

Of course, this activity was differently conceived in different spheres. Angel Day, George Gascoigne, and George Puttenham have the most immediately utilitarian view of it in the sense that the expected outcome of reading is limited in scope (composing letters or poems) and temporally contiguous to the reading itself. Longer term effects were sought in the religious sphere, where the amendment of this life prepared for the next, and in educational writings of various sorts (including Blundeville), where the preparation is for a future indefinitely deferred and difficult or impossible to specify the contours of. But as Harvey—the consummate student throughout his life—reminds us, everything, including advice on diet and exercise, is useful preparation for whatever might come. The Tudors were ants, not grasshoppers.

Reading as preparation for future action is clearly a teleological goal, but there are hints throughout the writers we have examined about how it might be made operational, most obviously in the rules for deriving applications of texts in the *artes praedicandi*. As I have already suggested, these are attempts to formalize the ubiquitous assumption that historical examples can provide guidance for readers, despite the fact that the historical conjunction of circumstances is so unique that the reader will never be in precisely the same situation as Cicero or David. Blundeville's advice to distinguish between universal and contingent causality is a similar attempt, but it must be seen as teleological rather than tactical because it never instructs the reader how to make the distinction. Much of Gascoigne's more specific advice is fairly operational, and Day's sample letters provide perhaps the most transparent and specific patterns for imitation.

The second characteristic of reading we encounter everywhere is its radically analytical nature, in two senses. First, in breaking a work down into smaller segments; the impression one gets from the writers we have surveyed is that a Tudor reader would never read something as long as a chapter straight through, preferring to pause after an anecdote or other section (probably not a paragraph, since they are not consistently indicated in texts of the period) to practice analytical reading in the second sense of performing various operations on the text. Primary among these is close attention to language and style, obviously important for the letter writer, the schoolboy, and the aspiring poet but also necessary for those reading for religious edification, whose full comprehension would be dependent on recognizing the semantic variability of the terms they read. Duplicating the Ciceronian emphasis on contextualizing in legal (or academic) disputes, religious reading also required close attention to various aspects of the context: the speaker, the addressee, the time and circumstances.

In dealing with the language of the text we find a good deal of specific tactical advice: Erasmus's comments on the aspects of language worthy of note provide a checklist for the teacher not unlike Meier's guide to travel, and Ascham explains in similar detail how to compare two passages. Perkins's list of aspects of the circumstances to be scrutinized is similarly detailed, and his consectaries, together with the rules for deriving applications of scriptural stories in Hyperius and Hemmingsen, supply the religious reader with fairly precise instructions about how to generalize from a given text.

Hardly less important as a characteristic of reading is what I have been calling intertextuality (or the counterpart in the religious context, intratextuality). The poet and the letter writer need not worry excessively about literary affiliations (though Puttenham fulminates against what he sees as plagiarism, and Day at least implicitly encourages some modest plagiarism on the part of the reader), but other readers must. For the religious reader intratextuality is important because texts may be literal or figurative, and the only way to determine which is to compare their apparent meanings with the analogy of faith or other places already known to be literal. For the student or reader of history, with their commonplace books, comparison or conference is equally important: the schoolboy learns from comparison how to vary a theme or improve on it and collects examples for future use, while the reader of histories must compare similar stories to learn both what is to be desired and how to obtain it efficiently.

Except for Perkins, who provides a number of consectaries for reconciling apparent contradictions in Scripture, specific instructions for comparative reading in the religious sphere are not extensively developed, since the authors of the *artes praedicandi* assume that the general goal of comparative reading is to illuminate dark passages and that clear examples for that purpose can always be found either elsewhere in Scripture itself or in the texts comprising the analogy of faith. Ascham's method of comparing authors is fully operational, since he specifies the steps to be followed, but advice about the compilation of commonplace books, whether in the classroom or study, is necessarily teleological, since the most useful places cannot be completely specified in advance, and Blundeville's conception of a commonplace book based on the interaction between life and reading raises this limitation to a principle.

A fourth characteristic of reading in the period is that it is generally confirmatory rather than exploratory, though this is perhaps determined by the nature of these books as educational. Although Gascoigne and Puttenham praise invention, there is everywhere the unstated assumption that one will never read anything inherently novel. This is most clear (and most crucial) in the religious sphere, where the analogy of faith specifies the parameters within which comprehension can occur; anything unanticipated is unacceptable. As we have seen, this provides a useful guide for limiting allegorical readings (or applications, as the Reformers would prefer to call them), but even in the secular sphere there is an implicit analogy of faith: when Erasmus delights in the various applications of the story of Socrates's death, it would never occur to him to see it as an example of a generally meaningless universe where things happen by chance or human whim. The fables of Aesop and the stories of the poets (including Ariosto and Spenser) may demand allegorical interpretations, but the general contours of those readings are implicitly set in advance. And in Angel Day, most of the text itself is set in advance, as readers find a letter they can alter slightly to fit their own circumstances.

Commonplace books generally promote this tendency; the theorists may agree that the relevant places cannot be exhaustively specified in advance, but with the sole exception of Blundeville, whose more dynamic conception of the commonplace book I have already discussed, it is difficult to conceive of teachers encouraging real creativity. The entire conception of a commonplace book is that whatever the student reads will be an example of a preexisting place; as I have said before, the kind of question this encourages in reading is not "What does this mean?" but "What is this an example of?" Students were expected to find examples of moral behavior to emulate and immoral behavior to avoid; the authors studied in the classroom were chosen for qualities (purity of expression and thought) the teachers knew and expected the students to learn. Invention was not the discovery of something truly novel, but rather the rediscovery of what somebody else had already written or the recombination of pieces already available, the nosegay composed of the odoriferous flowers of others.

Beyond these similarities, of course, there are important differences. Those reading in preparation for writing—students, would-be poets, letter writers—would pay more attention to language and style, carefully noting the structure of argument and its expression, especially the use of the figures. And since reading was often not an immediate prelude to writing, they would form the habit of reading this way in general. Those reading for amendment of life would be less concerned with the means of expression and would stress arriving at proper (and multiple) applications of passages. The more utilitarian the reading, the less likely it was to involve comparison and conference of other texts.

The view I have been urging is that different classes of readers internalized different sets of teleological and operational strategies for use in their reading. To return to Bourdieu's arresting metaphor (discussed in the appendix), it is tempting to see the teleological strategies as the constituents of a map of reading, while the operational strategies form the individual paths through the terrain represented on the map. But this is not altogether accurate: the operational strategies provide a repertoire of means from which individual readers may have chosen their favorites. Just as the styles of authors can be identified by their favorite constructions, transformations, and diction, so any reader would presumably select some subset of the available operational strategies for repeated use. Instead of being acutely sensitive to all the figures Puttenham and Day list, for instance, it is not unreasonable to assume that different readers might find their attention consistently attracted by three or four dozen favorites. Intertextuality is obviously a function of the texts which are available for comparison, and this leads to differences in both quality (religious readers tend to look to the Scriptures, secular readers to the classical tradition) and quantity (not every secular reader has Harvey's background). Even the rules for deriving commonplaces or applications of scriptural texts seem, at least to us, to invite selection: would any reader consistently utilize all twenty-eight of Hyperius's logical places and all twenty-two of the theological ones?

Even making allowance for this necessary process of selection in the actual reading of individual readers, I have been presenting a somewhat idealized view of reading. We have already seen references to inattentive readers (in Blundeville), hearers (in J. F.), and even teachers (in Erasmus and Palsgrave), and while it is tempting to dismiss them as people whose performance does not match their competence, the number of references in the period to those who read without understanding, or who read primarily to criticize the writer, suggests that an important segment of the reading public did not always pursue the kind of constructive reading I have been cataloguing. Even Bacon, immediately before his famous (though hardly original) distinction between the books to be tasted, swallowed, and chewed and digested, had made the point: "Reade not to Contradict, and Confute; Nor to Beleeve and Take for granted; Nor to Finde Talke and Discourse; But to weigh and Consider."[2] In this study, we have seen examples of all four of Bacon's categories of readers: those who read to find talk and discourse are the students and the readers of Blundeville and Day, Gascoigne and Puttenham, and more generally, those whose grammar-school educations prepared them for participation in the affairs of state. Religious readers seek to believe and take for granted. The better students—and Harvey is a prime example, both in his pedagogical approach in the *Ciceronianus* and in his own reading—would move beyond mere language and learn to weigh and consider matter.

But with the exception of the *artes praedicandi*, which recognized the necessity of redargutive sermons for the purpose of combatting false doctrine, we have seen little of contradiction and confutation. The sixteenth century, and more especially the Elizabethan era, was a contentious one, and there were undoubtedly many contentious readers. But there was no theory of disputatious reading, nor any training for it (apart from the standard training in dialectic[3]); some readers chose this path through the map of reading. And we can be fairly sure that they exhibited many of the standard Tudor characteristics of reading when they contended, reading small sections, analyzing them minutely, comparing them to other texts.

One particular form of contentious reading is suggested by a different sense of Bacon's finding talk and discourse: topical reading, with its identification of specific contemporary referents for fictional or historical characters and events. The most famous instance of this is probably the presentation of a play about Richard II (perhaps Shakespeare's) to Essex's supporters on the eve of his rebellion, with the obvious identification of Elizabeth with Richard and Essex with Bolingbroke, but the number of nervous prefaces throughout the period warning (and perhaps thereby inviting) readers not to apply them incorrectly testify to how common an occurrence this was.[4] In an important sense, this kind of applied reading is the goal of all reading instruction in the period: as we have seen, the entire educational program of reading as preparation for social participation encouraged this kind of application, as did the advice (and specific rules) of the religious writers about finding applications of scriptural stories. In an even more practical sense, Day's letters offered models for immediate application. Puttenham in *The Arte of English Poesie* specifically identifies the purpose of comedy and tragedy as "the good amendment of man by discipline and example" (32)—comedy treating the commons, tragedy the nobility—which can only be accomplished by application of fictional or historical examples to current events, and he goes further in his characterization of the eclogue, the purpose of which he sees as "not . . . to counterfait or represent the rusticall manner of loves and communication: but under the vaile of homely persons, and in rude speeches to insinuate and glaunce at greater matters, and such as perchance had not been safe to have disclosed in any other sort" (38; quoted in Patterson, 29).

But as we have seen in the previous discussions of Harington on allegory and Puttenham on metaphor, there was little operational advice extant about how the reader was to determine which greater matters were being glanced at: the fit reader was expected to know. The religious writers had been more specific with their consectaries and rules for deriving commonplaces or applications from Scripture, but these were so general that most of the interpretation on any specific occasion was still left to the ingenuity of the reader: if the example of David, for instance, could be generalized to any ruler or any person, who was to decide whether to apply it to a particular ruler or person? Sensitivity to the parallels between historical or fictional and contemporary situations was constantly stressed in both secular and religious instruction, and it would have been the exception rather than the rule for someone to have escaped internalizing it. Thus the extremely useful guidelines for topical reading Annabel Patterson derives from passing mention in a letter of John Chamberlain and from comments and prefaces by Ben Jonson (47–48, 57–58) are codifications for present-day readers of what for the Tudors was so deeply ingrained that it went without saying. What the Tudors had learned was vigilance for topical allusion, not the content of any particular reference.

Finally, we should return to the pleasure of the text. Despite the plethora of titles with either *pleasure* or *delight* in them (e.g., *The Palace of Pleasure* [1566], *A Petite Palace of Pettie His Pleasure* [1576], *A Handful of Pleasant Delights* [1584], and *Breton's Bower of Delights* [1591]), I would argue that Tudor readers generally lacked what we might think of as a purely aesthetic approach to literature; for them the *dulce* was inextricably linked to the *utile*. For us, the pleasure (or *jouissance*) of the text exists as an independent value, and we can conceive of categories of books like beach reading, page turners, and so forth that exist primarily to afford pleasure or to kill time. For the Tudors, pleasure certainly existed, but not independently; its link with utility was so well established as to be in the category of what goes without saying, and so the very word had a different meaning. This was true even of the genres that we might think of as most obviously intended for the marginally literate—the street ballad and the pamphlet. Recent studies of both emphasize their moral or practical utility; Natascha Wurzbach observes of the street ballad, "It was the didactic observations involved, especially the moral guidance, which served to justify the existence of an entertainment literature that was as popular and widespread among the people as it was despised by contemporary men of letters,"[5] and Sandra Clark echoes this sentiment in *The Elizabethan Pamphleteers*.[6]

Throughout the period, there are allusions to reading practices apparently directed primarily at pleasure that are clearly considered dubious by the authors: we have already seen Blundeville's disparaging reference to those who read only to pass away the time, and John Lyly, in the sarcastic preface to *Euphues and His England* addressed "To the Ladies and Gentlewomen of England," describes a mode of reading that may or may not have been fairly popular:

> It resteth, Ladies, that you take the paines to read it, but at such times as you spend playing with your little Dogges, and yet will I not pinch you of that pastime, for I am content that your Dogges lye in your laps, so *Euphues* may be in your hands, that when you shall be wearie of reading of the one, you may be ready to sport with the other. . . . Yet after dinner, you may overlook him to keep you from sleepe, or, if you be heavie, to bring you a sleepe.[7]

Harvey, with his marginal reminders about good physic, would have cringed, but Lyly is after all only poking fun: "better it were to hold *Euphues* in your hands . . . then to sowe in a clout, and

189

prick your fingers, when you begin to nod" (9). Perhaps fun is not the proper term, since the preface is a document in the history of antifeminism:

> You chuse cloth that will weare whitest, not that will last longest, coulours that looke freshest, not that endure soundest, and I would you woulde read bookes that have more shewe of pleasure, then ground of profit, then should *Euphues* be as often in your hands, being but a toy, as Lawne on your heads, being but trash, the one will scarce be liked after once reading, and the other is worne out after the first washing. (9–10)

The glimpses of inattentive reading we get in Blundeville and Lyly, while suggestive, seem to me to support my main point: Lyly and Blundeville believe in one kind of reading, and while they recognize other methods, they think of them as imperfect approximations or even counterfeits of "real" reading, indulged in only by those stigmatized by their gender or lack of intellectual seriousness. Through them the preferred mode of reading—serious, attentive, repetitive, teleological, containing more ground of profit than show of pleasure—is clearly visible.

On the other hand, there are numerous references to pleasure without any specific link to utility throughout the period which seem to be wholeheartedly endorsed by their authors, but these, when examined closely, seem to me to assume the close connection between the two. Consider the dedication of Painter's *Palace of Pleasure:* "Wherein also be intermixed pleasant discourses, merry talk, sporting practises, deceitful devices, and nipping taunts to exhilarate your Honor's mind."[8] Painter here echoes typical advice included in the rhetorics of the period, as for instance in Thomas Wilson's popular *The Art of Rhetorique, for the Use of All Such as are Studious of Eloquence* (1553),[9] which has been called "the greatest Ciceronian rhetoric in English":[10]

> The next parte that [the orator] has to plaie, is to chere his gestes, and to make them take pleasure, with hearyng of thynges wittily

190

devised, and pleasauntly set furthe. Therfore every Orator should
earnestly laboure to file his tongue, that his woords maie slide
with ease, and that in his deliveraunce, he maie have such grace,
as the sound of a lute, or any suche instrument doeth geve. . . .
Thirdly, such quicknesse of witte must be shewed, and such pleas-
aunt sawes so well applied, that the eares maie finde muche delite,
whereof I will speake largely, when I entreate of movyng laughter.
And assuredly, nothyng is more nedeful, then to quicken these
heavie loden wittes of ours, and muche to cherishe these our lom-
pish and unweldie natures, for excepte men finde delight, thei
will not long abide: delight theim and wynne them; werie theim,
and you lose theim for ever. (26–27)

And even Puttenham, after discussing the primary subjects or
occasions of poetry (such as "the laud honour & glory of the
immortall gods. . . . the worthy gests of noble princes" [24]), seems
to allow pure pleasure, not unlike the sound of a lute or other
musical instrument:

finally the common solace of mankind in all his travails and cares
of this transitorie life. And in this last sort being used for recreation onely, may allowably beare matter not always of the gravest,
or of any great commoditie or profit, but rather in some sort,
vaine, dissolute, or wanton, so it be not very scandalous & of evill
example. (24)

To understand these sentiments in their contemporary setting,
however, it might be useful to consider probably the most famous
statement of this sort, from Sidney's *The Defense of Poesy*:

For [the poet] doth not only show the way, but giveth so sweet a
prospect into the way as will entice any man to enter into it. Nay,
he doth, as if your journey should lay through a fair vineyard, at
the very first give you a cluster of grapes, that, full of that taste,
you may long to pass further. . . . he cometh to you with words set
in delightful proportions, either accompanied with, or prepared

for, the well-enchanting skill of music; and with a tale forsooth he cometh unto you, with a tale which holdeth children from play and old men from the chimney corner.[11]

Here the emphasis is solidly on the physical pleasures of poetry (whether read or heard), conceived in terms of taste and sound, but Sidney is not referring to the *jouissance* of the text for its own sake; his description of the sensuous attraction of poetry comes as part of the argument that the poet is more effective than the philosopher because he moves the hearer instead of simply instructing him in abstractions: "And, pretending no more, [the poet] doth intend the winning of the mind from wickedness to virtue: even as the child is often brought to take the most wholesome things by hiding them in such other as have a pleasant taste" (613). Pleasure is only prelude to instruction: "glad they will be to hear the tales of Hercules, Achilles, Cyrus, Aeneas; and, hearing them, must needs hear the right descriptions of wisdom, valure, and justice" (613).

Poetry, according to Sidney, is so constituted that delight has as its inevitable companion profit, and even those who seek only the former cannot help finding the latter:

For even those hard-hearted evil men who think virtue a school name, and know no other good but *indulgere genio,* and therefore despise the austere admonitions of the philosopher, and feel not the inward reason they stand upon, yet will be content to be delighted—which is all the good-fellow poet seemeth to promise— and so steal to see the form of goodness, which seen they cannot but love ere themselves be aware, as if they took a medicine of cherries. (613)

The medicine of instruction is so well hidden by the sugar coating of delight that it is ingested unawares, and in reconsidering Painter and Puttenham we observe the same principle of unconscious instruction being assumed. Painter had already mentioned the examples, both good and bad, contained in the stories he includes in his collection *Palace of Pleasure,* and he continues in his preface to justify the scenes which "seem to intreat of unlawful love and the foul practices of the same" by the standard argument that they serve as warnings against immorality and examples of what is to be avoided. He ends with the stirring peroration, "All which may render good examples, the best to be followed and the worst to be avoided, for which intent and purpose be all things good and bad recited in histories, chronicles, and monuments by the first authors and elucubrators of the same" (Painter, 673). The simple interpretive strategy of seeing everything good as a positive example and everything evil as a negative one immediately renders anything moral and instructive, potentially useful, and so it is only the truly worst examples, beyond all possibility of recuperation, that Puttenham would rule out—"so it [the matter] be not very scandalous & of evill example" (Puttenham, 24). Thus even Puttenham, in his allowance of poetry for no further purpose than recreation, seems to be subscribing to the same notion: there is no pure pleasure; instead it is always linked (through the subject matter) to examples of good or evil. For recreation and solace we can focus our attention more on the delight than on the profit (as his frequent anecdotes illustrate), but we must remember that we are also always learning something, perhaps unawares, and therefore must avoid what is absolutely evil. If reading were in fact purely for recreation, like the music of a lute or the taste of a cherry, the content wouldn't matter, and scandalous and evil examples would be licit.

My argument has been that the connection between delight and profit was so deeply ingrained in this period that it became one of the background assumptions, something that went without saying, just as it was possible more recently to refer to the id and thereby (without specific mention) invoke the whole Freudian trinity. So, for instance, when Bacon begins "Of Studies" by observing that "Studies serve for Delight, for Ornament, and for Ability. Their Chiefe Use for Delight, is in Privatenesse and Retiring" (292), we should not automatically assume that reading privately for delight meant for Bacon what it means for us (or that it has a univocal meaning even for us). To practice a purely aesthetic reading, one must have a model, and nowhere in the material we have surveyed is such a model available: in Tudor terms, there was no method or art of aesthetic reading. Individual readers (Barthesians and Derrideans before their time) might stumble into it, and writers (of ballads, jest books, and the like) might even pander to it, but it was considered a transgression from the true purpose of reading, and readers and writers both recognized that they had left the path of reading and were wandering in a perhaps alluring but ultimately dangerous wilderness. For Tudor readers, there was pleasure to be had from the text, but it derived partly from their ability to appreciate language well deployed (i.e., in accordance with the dictates of rhetoric), partly from the analytical and comparative operations they had learned to perform on it, and partly from their firm conviction that reading would lead to the improvement of the individual and thus of the society.

APPENDIX

NOTES

INDEX

THE HISTORICAL
RECONSTRUCTION
OF READING

I n an interesting paper on the use of metaphor in setting social
policy, Donald A. Schon observes that, in opposition to the
dominant view that "the development of social policy ought
to be considered as a problem-solving enterprise," he has

> become persuaded that the essential difficulties in social policy
> have more to do with *problem setting* than with problem solving,
> more to do with ways in which we frame the purposes to be
> achieved than with the selection of optimal means for achieving
> them. . . . When we examine the problem-setting stories told by
> the analysts and practitioners of social policy, it becomes apparent
> that the framing of problems often depends upon metaphors un-
> derlying the stories which generate problem setting and set the di-
> rections of problem solving.[1]

It may seem strange to frame a consideration of the historical
reconstruction of reading with reference to social policy, but it
seems to me fitting in a number of ways. First, reading is inherently a social problem (as the media continue to remind us),
though as I argue, it is social in a rather special way. Second,
Schon's emphasis on problem setting rather than problem solving
seems to me to provide a necessary framework for research: there
are many possible approaches to a historical study of reading, and

any inquiry can assay only one of them. I will try to be as clear as possible about the problem I am setting out to solve, but I realize at the outset that others would have chosen different problems to try to solve. Third, his emphasis on generative metaphors reminds us (as has a good deal of recent work in cognitive science[2]) how much of our understanding is metaphorical: we continually *see as,* assimilating what we understand less well to what we understand better. Any attempt at historical reconstruction is radically metaphorical in this sense, for we are forced to understand something forever alien and technically unreconstructable in terms of what we understand from our present experience. In particular, I assume (metaphorically) that reading in Tudor England was similar in some respects to reading today, and that various concepts applicable to the study of comprehension today can also be applied to the comprehension of people dead for several hundred years. This is standard historical practice, but we should not for that reason forget its metaphorical nature.

More specifically, any inquiry is framed in terms of what Schon calls the generative metaphor that sets the problem. In my case this metaphor is what Michael Reddy, in a classic article, identified as the "toolmakers paradigm."[3] The standard conception of language, Reddy argues, is mediated by the conduit metaphor, according to which linguistic entities (words, phrases, sentences, paragraphs, texts) are containers into which thoughts, ideas, and emotions are placed by a writer or speaker; the containers are then sent (by sound waves or inscriptions) to a reader or hearer, who simply extracts the thoughts, ideas, or emotions from their linguistic containers. To illustrate how pervasive this conceptualization of communication is, Reddy originally collected some 140 examples of constructions in English that reflect this view (e.g., "It is very difficult to put this concept into words," #14, p. 312; "I missed the idea in the sentence completely," #68, p. 315; cf. "I couldn't get anything out of that article").

The conduit metaphor so completely structures our thinking about communication that it is difficult or impossible to escape it, primarily because it is "largely determined by the semantic structures of the language itself" (285) and because "the logic of the framework runs like threads in many directions through the syntactic and semantic fabric of our speech habits" (297). But to provide a different perspective, Reddy suggested the "toolmakers paradigm," in which individuals inhabit similar but not identical environments (one with lots of trees, one relatively stony, one marshy) and can only communicate by means of small sheets of paper containing instructions for constructing useful implements. Since the toolmakers cannot visit each others' environments, they never realize how different they are, so one's instructions for making a rake out of wood to rake leaves appear to another (who lives in the stony environment, with only stone to work with, and only stone to manipulate) to be suggestions for making a tool with a rather different design—more like a pick—for digging up stones, and to the third (the marsh dweller) to describe what we would call a hoe—something useful in a marshy environment. Each toolmaker, assuming the communication was serious, tries to construct out of indigenous materials a tool useful in the surrounding environment, but since the environments and materials are different, the resulting tools are necessarily different as well (292–95).

Conceiving of communication in this way illuminates a number of aspects of it: its radically subjective nature (the inhabitants cannot visit each others' environments, just as speakers and hearers cannot enter each others' minds); the possibility (indeed, almost certainty) of what would be seen in the conduit metaphor as miscommunication; and—perhaps most important—the amount of construction necessary for understanding any communication. As Reddy explains,

> Both models offer an explanation of the phenomenon of communication. But they come to totally different conclusions about what, in that phenomenon, are more natural states of affairs, and what are less natural, or constrained, states. In terms of the conduit metaphor, what requires explanation is failure to communicate. Success appears to be automatic. But if we think in terms of the toolmakers paradigm, our expectation is precisely the op-

posite. Partial miscommunication, or divergence of readings from a single text, are not aberrations. They are tendencies inherent in the system, which can only be counteracted by continuous effort and by large amounts of verbal interaction. (295)

Reddy is primarily interested in contemporary problems of communication, but the toolmakers paradigm has obvious consequences for those studying the history of reading as well. The most important of these is to emphasize the point about radical subjectivity I have already made: in this study I have attempted to make sense from the perspective of my own (mental) environment of messages sent from a quite different environment several hundred years ago, and even though the senders of those messages shared little of our contemporary anxiety about failure of communication, we cannot avoid being aware of how uncertain an enterprise it is. Hardly less important is the realization that reading—as a form of communication—is an active constructive process, not a relatively passive retrieval of information that has been placed into a text by a writer.

This view of reading corresponds with much contemporary reading theory, particularly with those views emphasizing the cognitive or transactive aspects of reading. As Kenneth S. Goodman explains in outlining what he characterizes as "a unified theory of reading":

In a transactional view, the writer constructs a text through transactions with the developing text and the meaning being expressed. The text is transformed by the process and so are the writer's schemata (ways of organizing knowledge). The reader also constructs a text during reading through transactions with the published text and the reader's schemata are also transformed in the process through the assimilation and accommodation Piaget has described.[4]

The transactions involved in reading are discussed in more detail below; here it is sufficient to emphasize that in this view, reading (or hearing) is as active a process of construction as writing (or speaking):

> In the productive generative processes (speaking and writing) a text is generated (constructed) to represent the meaning. In the receptive processes (listening and reading) meaning is constructed through transactions with the text and indirectly through the text with the writer. Both generative and receptive processes are constructive, active, and transactional. (80)

Instead of simply packaging meanings already achieved, as the conduit metaphor would encourage us to believe, writers actively construct meaning, reading and reconsidering (Goodman's term is transacting) what has already been written to modify or amplify it, considering what needs to be added or how to construct a smooth transition to an important point yet to be made. In Reddy's example, the writer is struggling to explain as clearly as possible how to construct the tool he has invented. The reader also struggles, not simply to extract information from the containers in which it has been placed, but to use various cues in the text to construct a meaning. And in those instances in which reading assumes what Paul Grice has termed the Cooperative Principle,[5] the reader additionally assumes that the author in fact meant to convey a particular meaning, and in attempting to reconstruct that meaning, the reader interacts with the author.

Goodman's model of reading is a conscious attempt to integrate knowledge about reading from a number of fields (80), and as such it echoes a number of contemporary approaches to literary interpretation, especially those of Norman N. Holland, Stanley E. Fish, and the structuralist approach outlined by Jonathan Culler in *Structuralist Poetics*. The cognitive strategies Goodman describes are very similar to the interpretive strategies Stanley E. Fish has provocatively described as methods "not for reading (in the conventional sense) but for writing texts, for constituting their properties and assigning their intentions."[6] Emphasizing (some would say hopelessly exaggerating) the kind of constructivist account found in Goodman, Fish argues that even what might be thought of as the basic constituents of a text are the result of a reader's construction: "formal units are always a function of the interpretive model one brings to bear; they are not 'in' the text" (164). The lines of prose texts, for example, "end" just as convincingly at the right margin as do lines of poetry, but readers ignore the line endings in prose and pay attention to those in poetry; the physical stimulus is the same, but an interpretive strategy creates a significant characteristic of a text (available for interpretation in various ways) in one instance and not in the other. Similarly, whether (apparently objective) linguistic characteristics (e.g., phonological or syntactic patterns) are noticed—and thus in a sense created—depends on the kind of attention the reader deploys: "the distinctive features that make articulation and reception possible are the product of a system of differences that must be *imposed* before it can be recognized: the patterns the ear hears (like the patterns the eye sees) are the patterns its perceptual habits make available" (166).

Norman N. Holland has recently proposed a refinement of the idea of interpretative strategies by distinguishing between those which are relatively tight and accepted as normal by all members of a culture and those which are looser, more open to contention, and which serve to define interpretive communities within a culture.[7] Examples of the former, which Holland calls " 'not otherwise' cultural codes," are linguistic structures:

> No member of our culture would normally hear the sound [red] as a form of the verb "to go." In reading, no member of our culture would normally read *r* other than as *r*, as *g*, for example, or *n*. No member of our culture would normally think that *4* really means five. (35)

The same applies to shared cultural symbols (such as stop signs, flags, and so forth) and institutions (e.g., department stores): those who do not share the cultural understanding are "not normal": according to Holland, "Such schemata constitute cultural norms, and in that strict sense they are 'norm-al'" (34). On the other hand, many decisions could be otherwise—"it is customary, it is even 'norm-al' for people to disagree in our culture about political, aesthetic, and even factual matters" (35)—and these are the result of what Holland calls "canons" rather than codes. The meanings of words (as opposed to the simple identification of which word is exemplified) are quite variable, as are religious, political, and aesthetic judgments; canons define interpretive communities within a given culture (35–38).

In Holland's model there are two further levels. The most basic is the level of physical perception depending on human capabilities, which Holland characterizes as "physiological feedback loops, close to raw, unmediated, unprocessed sensations, mere transductions" (34); all people share this. The highest level is individual identity, which is one person's construction of the theme and variations that define another person (26–31). Moving from the most basic level of physiological feedback through the codes and canons to the identity is thus a progression from what is shared to what is individual, from what constitutes a person to what constitutes a member of a particular culture, of a particular group (or groups) within that culture to what constitutes an individual.

Unfortunately, Fish and Holland tend not to specify in any detail what interpretive strategies, codes, and canons are, preferring to provide illustrative examples for the reader to extrapolate from. This hiatus is filled, at least in part, by Jonathan Culler's work with what he variously calls "interpretive strategies" (134), "conventions for reading literary texts" (118), "expectations with which one approaches lyric poetry" (162), and "interpretive operations" (162).[8] Culler's approach is explicitly modelled on Noam Chomsky's seminal work in linguistics, which he calls "an attractive methodological analogy" (122), especially on the distinction between linguistic competence (what a speaker-hearer knows about language, represented as an internalized system of rules) and performance (how that knowledge is used on specific occasions) (122–24).[9] Culler argues that instead of elucidating individual works of literature, the goal of a structuralist poetics should be to characterize "literary competence"—"the underlying system which makes literary effects possible" (118). And the linguistic analogy demands that this system be conceived of in terms of mentally represented rules or formal operations that can be tested for their correctness (122).

What makes Culler's interpretive strategies so useful is that they are relatively explicit: in discussing why a short newspaper story can be read differently when it is presented as a poem, Culler identifies

> the expectations with which one approaches lyric poetry, the conventions which govern its possible modes of signification: the poem is atemporal . . . it is complete in itself . . . it should cohere at a symbolic level . . . it expresses an attitude . . . its typographic arrangements can be given spatial or temporal interpretations. (162)

The second half of *Structuralist Poetics* is largely an explication of these and similar conventions, and "Semiotics as a Theory of Reading" goes on to demonstrate that they (or their results) can be observed in published interpretations of Blake's "London."[10]

It is perhaps useful to distinguish, as Culler does not, two distinct kinds of conventions: teleological, or goal-oriented (or strategic), and operational, or process-oriented (or tactical). The conventions cited above are all teleological: they tell the reader what to look for, what to expect in a poem, much as the advice to control the center in a chess game specifies a goal rather than a discrete set of steps by which to attain it. Others are more operational, for instance, the "basic models" of unity: "the binary opposition, the dialectical resolution of a binary opposition, the displacement of an unresolved opposition by a third term, the four-term homology, the series united by a common denominator, and the series with a transcendent or summarizing final term" (174). These models are still partially goal-oriented—they do not explain how a reader is to decide which one applies on a given occasion—but there is an attempt to relate the goal "unity" to the specific configurations that exemplify it. Even more clearly operational is his discussion of "Distance and Deixis," where he claims that the reader recognizes "from the outset that such deictics [first- and second-person pronouns, anaphoric articles and demonstratives, adverbials of place and time, verb tenses] are not determined by an actual situation of utterance but operate at a certain distance from it. . . . The deictics do not refer us to an external context but force us to construct a fictional situation of utterance" (165–66). This must be read, I think, as an operational instruction: do not interpret deictics as you normally would; the *I* in a poem is not to be identified with the author, and other deictics like *now* and *here* do not refer to the situation of reading, as they would if somebody in the same room uttered them. Both types of strategies are important: the teleological ones specify what counts as an acceptable interpretation of a text, and the operational ones tell you how to achieve it.

These interpretive strategies are the counterparts in literary studies of a number of insights in the field of cognitive science, the intersection of linguistics, psychology, computer science (particularly artificial intelligence), and philosophy. The most important stems from the straightforward observation that we only very infrequently face any situation innocently; usually—and certainly for a situation that has been encountered before—we have a set of fairly precise expectations about what will be encountered in it: the people, the physical setting and props, the norms of behavior, and the aims of the whole undertaking.[11] Schank and Abelson, in a classic work in the field, refer to these organized sets of expectations as "scripts":

A script is a structure that describes appropriate sequences of events in a particular context. A script is made up of slots and requirements about what can fill those slots. The structure is an interconnected whole, and what is in one slot affects what can be in another. . . . Thus, a script is a predetermined, stereotyped sequence of actions that defines a well-known situation. (41)

David E. Rumelhart, who refers to these sets of expectations as "schemata," emphasizes their private nature:

> it is useful to think of a schema as a kind of informal, private, un-articulated theory about the nature of the events, objects, or situations we face. The total set of schemata we have available for interpreting the world in a sense constitutes our private theory of the nature of reality.[12]

What is encountered in any particular restaurant, store, or classroom is comprehended against this background, which allows us to make sense of both the expected and the unexpected, and which provides a yardstick for deciding what is distinctive enough about a given occasion to make it tellable—the menu presented in a strange way, the peculiar decor or service, the unusual arrangement of desks, and so on. It also supplies "default values" that allow us to fill in information lacking in an experience, so for instance if from our perspective a room has only one or two walls visible, we assume that the other walls (and ceiling, floor, etc.) also exist.

Scripts or schemata for reading are the larger structures into which the individual interpretive strategies, codes, and canons of Holland and Culler are organized. The relation between the strategies and the scripts is mediated by what Ray Jackendoff calls "preference rules."[13] Chomskyan linguistics, dealing with competence, is primarily concerned with decisions of a yes-no variety, especially with the question of whether a particular string is grammatical or not. In dealing with actual performance, however, judgments are often less clearly categorical: in a famous experiment William Labov presented his subjects with a continuum of cuplike containers in which the height-width ratio was varied and asked them to decide whether a given exemplar was a cup, a vase, or a bowl. Different results were obtained when handles were added to the containers, indicating interacting principles of classification, one dealing with the relation between the height and the width of the example, the other with the presence or absence of a handle (1983, 137). In cases like this, there is no one right answer, nor even an obvious categorical one; instead, graded responses are found, with respondents identifying some examples as clearly belonging to one or another category and other examples as intermediate or indeterminate where subjects simply aren't sure about their judgments.

To account for these graded judgments, Jackendoff, building on earlier work in Gestalt psychology, suggests the use of preference rules, which give rise to preferred, rather than categorical, judgments. When two rules reinforce each other, the judgment is stronger; when two are in conflict, the judgment is uncertain. Jackendoff lists as the "symptoms of preference rule systems":

(1) judgments of graded acceptability and family resemblance;
(2) two or more rules, neither of which is necessary, but each of which is under certain conditions sufficient for a judgment;
(3) balancing effects among rules that apply in conflict; (4) a measure of stability based on rule applications; (5) rules that are not logically necessary used as default values in the face of inadequate information. (1983, 152)

He has identified these symptoms in a number of areas in psychological inquiry, including phonology, semantics, syntax, pragmatics, vision, and musical perception (Lerdahl and Jackendoff, 307–28; 1983, 135–57), and has suggested the use of preference rules to "accomplish what psychological systems do well but computers do very badly: deriving a quasi-determinate result from unreliable data" (1983, 157).

It seems to me that Holland's canons and the interpretive strategies discussed by Fish and Culler are most usefully considered preference rules which guide, without fully determining, judgment. In some situations, only one rule will be applicable, or two or more rules will reinforce each other, and the reader will be relatively sure of the judgment. In others, however, several rules will be applicable, and conflict between them is an inevitable possibility. Thus to return to Culler's basic models of unity, in any given case it will not be immediately obvious whether three terms should be seen as a dialectical resolution of a binary opposition, the displacement of an opposition by a third term, a (short) series united by a common denominator, or a series with a transcendent final term. Each model is a preference rule that organizes experience in one way, and which one is applied on a particular occasion will depend in part on a person's general preferences (Jackendoff observes that "interpersonal differences are characteristic of preference rule systems in general" [1983, 152]) and in part on the influence of other preference rules, which might reinforce one or another of the choices. But we must remember that there are basic physiological rules which all humans share, and that the cultural codes Holland identifies may not be representable as preference rules.

Preference rules and scripts interact interestingly in reading: as I have demonstrated with contemporary readers, interpretive strategies are subject to some kind of further teleological organization.[14] Even though they use very similar interpretive strategies, different readers have different expectations about what constitutes a successful interpretation of a text and different ways of arriving at that interpretation. It is this overall organization which guides their reading and—perhaps more importantly—indicates when a satisfactory conclusion has been reached. Preference rules reflect, in a way that interpretive strategies do not, the effortful nature of interpretation, as readers try to apply favored rules in a given situation, seeking favored organizations and relations; in short, preferring particular kinds of interpretations.

The most revealing way to conceptualize reading, then, might be as radically constructive, a script-like organization of preferred interpretive strategies which operate on the information supplied by the physiological rules and cultural codes to arrive at preferred kinds of interpretations (which themselves will be related to the reader's identity). The physiological rules are given by biological heredity, while the cultural codes and the interpretive canons derive from education, both the formal education supplied by schools and informal education based on the models one has encountered. Whether given by biology or derived from cultural examples, however, all this knowledge is mentally represented individually in each person, and it is these individual mental representations that guide behavior; whatever their own views about the matter, the toolmakers are forever imprisoned in their own environments. To return to Culler's models of unity, a particular reader might prefer thesis-antithesis-synthesis as a general model of organization, while another favors a series of examples summarized by a common denominator; both will have a number of specific strategies that allow them to select material from the text and interpret it so as to arrive at the desired conclusion. But to choose one or the other, both readers will have to agree that there are three entities to be organized, and these will be the result of codes or physiological rules.

Most readers of this book are likely to be relatively (if not obsessively) self-conscious about reading in general, and about their own reading in particular, and to them it will seem only natural to conceive of reading in terms of interpretive strategies, to assume that different modes of reading are appropriate for different texts and occasions, that one may choose to resist the imperatives of the text, and so forth. To gain some perspective on the way those less preoccupied with literacy are apt to consider reading it is illuminating to consider a similar intellectual achievement about which highly literate people tend not to be curious. The perfect candidate, it seems to me, is numeracy, which is mastered by most people in grade school and thereafter considered a strictly instrumental skill devoid of any interest in its own right.[15] Numeracy includes knowing the necessary basic relations—the addition and multiplication tables, which are memorized and then in most people simply retained in the form in which they were learned— and the operations using those relations, including specific methods for adding, subtracting, multiplying, and dividing. In theory, there are quite different methods for doing all of these, ranging from notational variants (to take subtraction as an example, one may "borrow" either by reducing the next column in the minuend by one or by increasing the next column in the subtrahend by one) to quite large conceptual differences, for example those embodied in the set-theoretic approach once known as the new math. And clearly, numeracy can be modelled by the same kinds of strategies I have already discussed, ranging from the cultural codes—nobody would interpret *4* as five—to individual preference rules about adding from the bottom up, the top down, or skipping around a column to add numbers that total multiples of ten first. But the important consideration is that most people, having learned one method of subtraction or addition, persist in it for the rest of their lives, never conceiving that there could be another way of doing it. Subtraction is subtraction, and there's an end on it. Those who are old enough to remember the new math will recall the dismay parents exhibited when they discovered their children doing "subtraction" in an entirely new and incomprehensible way, and—even more surprisingly—getting the same answers: it never occurs to most people that there could be any variation in overlearned skills—those that are learned to the point of being automatic. Even those who in calculating consciously add a one to a column of figures (either mentally or in writing) have little idea why they do so: that is the way they were taught, and since it leads to the right answer, that is the way to do it. Period. More astute numerators may, of course, develop methods of estimation and approximation that are used in specific circumstances, but they account for only a very small proportion of those who know how to add and subtract.

My working assumption is that learning to read in the Tudor period was radically different from learning to read today. It was much more similar to learning to add and subtract today: those who either graduated from or spent a good deal of time in grammar schools would have been exposed to a single monolithic method of reading so constantly that they would have difficulty in conceiving of (let alone using) any other. Reading, at least in the school situation, was treated (as is numeracy today) instrumentally, as a skill used to achieve other goals. Today we pay little conscious attention to our arithmetic methods because we are primarily interested in the answers they allow; for the Tudors, reading was instrumental to some other goal, usually preparing to write or orate. For students in the Tudor educational system, reading, not being an end in itself, would attract little conscious attention, and the only alternatives to the standard method of reading most students could conceive of would be at best imperfect imitations or approximations of the kind of reading they had learned, and at worst, simply incorrect. But most would not even consider the possibility of alternatives: the method of reading they learned in youth would simply be retained and practiced for the rest of their lives. (Again, perspective may be gained by considering our own response to an answer of 31 to the sum 15+17; most of my readers, I suspect, consider it simply wrong, not a correct answer in a slightly different system, i.e., base 11 rather than base 10). And, as today, social instruction in reading becomes internalized as individual cognitive representations.

Most of the educational theorists of the period agreed that youth was the time for rote learning and that what was learned in youth was retained for the rest of life.[16] Erasmus argues in *De Pueris Institutendis,* which was translated into English by Richard Sherry and published together with his *Treatise of Schemes and Tropes* in 1550, that children should be exposed to moral and educational experiences in their earliest ages: "Nature has given small children as a special gift the ability to imitate—but the urge to imitate evil is considerably stronger than the urge to imitate the good. . . . nothing clings more tenaciously than something that is poured into empty minds."[17] Thus it is of the first importance that the earliest examples be the best examples; parents who provide bad examples, inadvertently exemplifying vanity, intemperance, or the love of war, irreparably corrupt their children (308). Teachers, on the other hand, can use this natural predisposition to imitation and retention to begin the work of a moral education, for children are naturally attracted to such stories as the moral apologues of Aesop, "which present serious moral lessons in the guise of humorous sketches," or ancient fables, "which cast such an enticing spell upon children's ears that even adults will derive a great deal of benefit from these stories, not only for the study of language, but also as a guide to practical thinking, and as a source of good vocabulary" (336). Although Erasmus is here speaking of very young children, the same argument applies to those who are older, especially if they have had the kind of moral upbringing he recommends: what is learned earliest remains the foundation of everything that comes later.

Richard Mulcaster, whose long tenure as the master of the Merchant Taylor's School perhaps entitles him to especial respect as one whose practical experience equals his theoretical acuity, observes that "in the little young souls, first we find, capacity to perceive that which is taught them, and to imitate the foregoer. . . . We find also in them as a quickness to take, so a fastness to retain: therefore their memory would straight way be furnished with the very best, seeing it is a treasury."[18] Ascham's famous distinction between quick wits and hard wits ("Quick wits commonly be apt to take, unapt to keep. . . . Hard wits be hard to receive but sure to keep" [21, 24]) sophisticates Mulcaster's understanding, as does his insistence that one of the qualities necessary for a successful student is good memory (29). But he is equally notable for his insistence that the bad habits encouraged by the present educational system last forever:

> And in learning farther his *syntaxis,* by mine advice he shall not
> use the common order in common schools for making of Latins,
> whereby the child commonly learneth, first, an evil choice of
> words . . . , then, a wrong placing of words, and, lastly, an ill framing of the sentence, with a perverse judgment, both of words and
> sentences. These faults, taking once root in youth, be never or
> hardly plucked away in age. (13)

Similarly, his justification for not having children speak Latin is that bad habits acquired in youth are extremely difficult to unlearn (16–17). As Erasmus had written, "What matters at the outset is not how much knowledge you acquire, but how sound it is" (*De Conscribendis,* 193).

These habits acquired in youth form the basis of the social practice I have tried to describe in this book. Although it is relatively clear *how* to describe reading in terms of the schematized organization of preference rules I discuss above, it is not at all clear *what* constitutes evidence of reading. This is a problem even in contemporary studies once one steps outside the controlled conditions of the laboratory. Jonathan Culler, for instance, examines both his own intuitions and published interpretations,[19] David Bleich uses readers' written reflections about what they have read,[20] Norman Holland discusses past reading experiences,[21] I have studied protocols of what readers do while they are reading,[22] and Stanley Fish analyzes a fictionalized version of his own reading.[23]

Studying the processes of readers dead for hundreds of years necessarily requires a somewhat different approach. Clearly, the many comparative demographic studies that seek to establish basic literacy levels by obtaining signature rates on documents of various kinds offer little to work with,[24] and detailed examinations of individual ability to read such as those included in Johansson's studies of the catechetical registers in Sweden offer little information beyond success or failure at rote memorization.[25] Margaret Spufford's illuminating studies of the acquisition of literacy alert us to the myriad methods of becoming literate but are less informative about how that ability was used.[26] There is also a good deal of information about the various contexts of reading available in the works by Robert Darnton, Roger Chartier, and others in "the history of reading." But as Darnton clearly illustrates in his study of Jean Ranson, knowledge of library contents, book construction and circulation, and readers' letters to authors and publishers provides practically no information about the essentially private experience of reading, the process through which marks on the page become thoughts in the mind,[27] and even Carl B. Kaestle's impressive *Literacy in the United States: Readers and Reading since 1880* is more valuable for its synthesis of the information available about the context of reading—measures of literacy, surveys of reading, and studies of available materials—than about its content.[28]

On the other hand, there is, in the historical record, a mass of anecdotal information about examples of reading—Gabriel Harvey's various marginalia (recently subjected to a very illuminating analysis by Anthony Grafton and Lisa Jardine),[29] William Tem-

ple's logical analysis of Sidney's "Apology,"[30] the marginal annotations of an early reader of the *Faerie Queene*,[31] and even E. K.'s
comments on "The Shepheardes Calendar," to mention only a
few—which could serve as the basis for analysis. But all these share
two limitations: first, they are products of reading rather than the
process that led to those products, and thus provide only indirect
evidence about the process: what could one conclude about the
processes our own contemporaries use in subtracting if the only
evidence available were the answers to subtraction problems? And
they are not even products in the sense of veridical reports of the
process, for constraints of various kinds (including the space available in margins) affect their form and content. Second, they are
merely anecdotal, intriguing and illuminating to be sure, but suspect in their typicality. For both reasons, these anecdotes serve
more properly as tests or illustrations of a theoretical practice of
reading derived from other sources than as the sole basis for such a
theory, and I have used them in precisely this way.

The limitations of any printed evidence about reading processes
is evident if we consider what can be concluded from what seems
an incontrovertible piece of evidence about reading in the United
States fifty years ago: a book called *How to Read a Book*. Mortimer
Adler and Charles Van Doren's bestseller provides guidelines for
becoming a "demanding reader," one who routinely asks four
questions: "What is the book about as a whole? What is being said
in detail, and how? Is the book true, in whole or part? and What of
it?"[32] These four questions define four stages of "analytical reading," which is described in terms of a set of rules designed to force
the reader to confront the text in various ways. Each rule is explained in detail, so the reader is provided a recipe or checklist for
successful analytical reading.

From the perspective of an inquiry into reading practices, one
could hardly hope for anything better: a method is clearly set out
in operational terms; both the goals and the steps leading to those
goals are clear (especially in the revised edition, from which I have
quoted). And yet, even such a clear exposition provides only am-

biguous evidence about the actual reading practices of readers: the book proves that at least somebody could conceive of reading in the recommended fashion, and suggests that at least two people—the authors—in fact read that way, at least part of the time. But the fact that the book had to be written—and read—suggests that not everybody was already an analytical reader: if everybody already read the way Adler advises, they would have no use for it. As Adler says in his first sentence, "This is a book for readers who cannot read" (3). Thus even so promising a source provides contradictory evidence, testifying to at least two kinds of reading—the one recommended, which can be described in some detail, and another kind, which can be described only as a negative complement.

Faced with this problem, I have attempted to solve it by examining, as much as possible, the institutions that provided models for successful reading, and have relied on specific examples of reading as illustrations or tests of the process I have derived. These models—schematized organizations of preferentially applied interpretive strategies—provide the kind of bridge we need between external information about historical contexts and traces of reading and the inherently private activity of reading a particular text. Jon Klancher's conclusion that we should not attempt to reconstruct the reading practices of the past, though he presents it as a recognition of otherness, is simply a counsel of despair:

> To the largest questions—how did readers understand the texts they read? how were those texts used?—historical evidence offers few and scattered answers. These cultures remain, despite their occasional similarity to reading cultures of our own time, distinctly opaque insofar as we cannot penetrate the minds of all those readers who left no mark of their understandings, no trace of the doubtless ingenious ways they must have recombined, retranslated, or simply resisted the interpretive and ideological patterns framed by their texts. We ourselves need to resist the ambition to reclaim those lost understandings in some consummate act of historical recovery.[33]

215

As we have already seen, even today when we have other readers available for scrutiny, we cannot penetrate their minds; they remain forever opaque to us. We may not be able—ever—to witness a reader in the act of reading, but we may well be able to specify the strategies that reader used, or was likely to use. And the assumption that past readers were interested in recombining, retranslating, or resisting texts is surely a projection of our own practices onto the past: not only do we have models for these varieties of manipulating texts, we have institutional rewards for applying them. Whether these conditions were present in Tudor England is a question I have explored in the preceding chapters; as we have seen, there is good evidence for the practices of recombining and retranslating but not of resisting, and I take it as an object lesson that Klancher, so sensitive to the differences between the past and present, should so easily assume that a practice we value highly would also have been prized in the past. Again, for the sake of perspective we might turn to numeracy: my own readers should ask themselves how much they "recombined, retranslated, or simply resisted" the methods of arithmetic they had learned the last time they faced an addition or subtraction problem, perhaps in balancing a checkbook or preparing a tax return.

Those unable to resist the ambition to reconstruct past reading practices will find themselves more seriously challenged by James L. Machor's warning:

> Because literary texts are made meaningful within a field consisting not just of interpretive strategies but also intersecting ideologies, epistemic frames, and material conditions, the historical study of response must guard against the assumption that interpretive strategies, on their own, determine the dynamics of reading.[34]

In fact, Grafton and Jardine's study of Harvey referred to above reveals just such effects: Harvey annotated his copy of Livy on three different occasions, with quite varied results: "a single text could give rise to a variety of goal-directed readings, depending on the initial brief" (31; see also 35–44). While it is undoubtedly true that circumstances affect the course of a reading, lending greater salience to some aspects of a text than others, their effect is distinctly limited, simply because readers can only deploy interpretive strategies they have already learned. Ideology, epistemic frames, and material conditions may affect at most which strategies readers use, or which they use most frequently, but they cannot inculcate new strategies, and it is more likely that they will encourage readers to select particular aspects of the text for processing by means of preexisting strategies. From the point of view of overall interpretations or readings—what Machor calls meaningfulness—circumstances may appear to have an enormous effect, and this may be true of the dynamics of reading as well, but from the point of view of interpretive strategies, of the processes a reader uses in constructing an understanding of the text, their influence is severely limited.

In stressing the interpretive strategies themselves rather than, say, their temporal deployment or the result of that deployment, I am conscious of the danger of becoming too schematic, of inflicting on practice, as Bourdieu says in *Outline of a Theory of Practice*, "a much more fundamental and pernicious alternation . . . constitut[ing] practical activity as an *object of observation and analysis, a representation*" (2). Echoing the common linguistic distinction between competence and performance and valorizing the latter as practice, he introduces the striking metaphor of maps and paths:

> So long as he remains unaware of the limits inherent in his point of view on the object, the anthropologist is condemned to adopt unwittingly for his own use the representation of action which is forced on agents or groups when they lack practical mastery of a highly valued competence and have to provide themselves with an explicit and at least semi-formalized substitute for it in the form of a *repertoire of rules*. . . . It is significant that "culture" is sometimes described as a *map*; it is the analogy which occurs to an outsider who has to find his way around in a foreign landscape and who compensates for his lack of practical mastery, the prerogative of the native, by the use of a model of all possible routes. (2)

217

The native, on the other hand, navigates by means of paths:

> The logical relationships constructed by the anthropologist are
> opposed to the "practical" relationships—practical because con-
> tinuously practised, kept up, and cultivated—in the same way as
> the geometrical space of a map, an imaginary representation of all
> theoretically possible roads and routes, is opposed to the network
> of beaten tracks, of paths made ever more practicable by constant
> use. (37–38)

Disheartening as it is to anthropologists to be perpetual outsiders, that is the obvious lot of those who deal with historical
documents. But in (necessarily) adopting the cartographic stance,
we may be reassured by the realization that Tudor theorists and
readers themselves assumed it—even valued it—in their writing.
Consider an interesting but by no means unique pamphlet by
Albertus Meierus entitled *Certaine briefe and speciall instructions
for gentlemen, merchants, students, . . . marriners, &c. Employed in
service abrode, or anie way occasioned to converse in the kingdomes,
and govermentes of forren Princes* (1589).[35] In his dedication to Sir
Francis Drake, Philip Jones, the translator, explains that the book
is needed because many travel without benefitting from it, as did
the son of the wise man of Naples, who returned from his travels
to "report that he had seene men, women, wals, houses, woods,
and medowes, but of the state, manners, lawes, government, and
natures of the people, his simple wit could make no reasonable
answere" (A.2.v–A.3.r). The reason that travel did not sufficiently
broaden this naive traveller is that he lacked a method to guide his
sightseeing:

> There is no man, although but of meane and ordinary insight in
> the state of things, that is ignorant of the great necessity and com-
> moditie of Methods, and directions to men of all qualities: inso-
> much, that whoever undertaketh any course or profession without
> it, is like to the foolish youth, that would needs prove a Latinist
> without his Grammar, or to the mad Architect, which went about

to set up a house without his rule and compasse, both whose beginnings were confused, and their conclusions ridiculous. (A.2.v)

This book presents the method of travelling so that "if our men
will vouchsafe the reading, portage, and practise of this pamphlet
of notes . . . the thicke mistes of ignorance, and harde conception
will soone be scattered, and the same converted into a quicke
sight, and illumination of the senses, so that the traveller (although in that course a Novice) after his ranginges and peregrina-
tions, shall retire him selfe a man of skill" (A.3.r).

Jones's introduction provides good evidence of something very
like schema theory extant in Elizabethan England. Untutored observation is unprofitable: in order to see what is valuable, one must
be taught what to look for. The reference to the grammar can
hardly be seen as an early foreshadowing of linguistic or literary
competence, but it does testify to a remarkably similar conception:
just as Latin grammar is necessary for the Latinist, so a grammar of
travel is necessary to the traveller. Knowledge, whether linguistic
or topographical, can be expressed as a sequence of rules. Or, to
use Jones's other metaphor, proper practice requires the proper
tools, and for mental practices, like observing other countries,
those tools are the mental ones contained in "this pamphlet of
notes." In either case, some mediating presence is necessary to
convert innocent observation, which leads only to "the thicke
mistes of ignorance, and harde conception," into "quicke sight,
and illumination of the senses." The influence of Ramism is obvious here, especially in Jones's references to "method," and the
Ramistic use of schematic displays of knowledge in dichotomous
tables is clearly relevant to the question of schemata, but this is too
large a topic to explore in this appendix.[36]

The pamphlet itself provides a set of precisely formalized rules;
organized into twelve sections, ranging from cosmography and
astronomy, through the political and ecclesiastical states, to histories and chronicles, it furnishes the observant traveller with a
checklist for informed observation. Each section typically contains
between twenty and thirty instructions about things to notice,

such as "Whether the place be Mediterrane, or the part of a Continent" (3.1), "Whether it be a citie, towne, village, or what else" (4.1), "The usuall nature and times of the spring, summer, Autumne, and winter, in that region" (6.1), and "Ingenious epigrams, sonets, epitaphs, orations, poems, speeches, verses, adages, proverbs, and other scholasticall and learned exercises, the fruits of good wits" (10.10). Most of the observations seem to be useful primarily as military intelligence, in keeping with the generally nationalistic tone of the dedication, but in their number and specificity they bear eloquent testimony to the need for strategies in understanding: the untutored eye sees but does not understand; for "quick sight and illumination of the senses" some method is necessary.

In his insistence on a method for travelling, Meier simply provides one example of the preoccupation in the sixteenth century with the question of "method" or "art" and the relation of the method or art to the use made of it on various occasions. Here, toward the beginning of the century, is Vives:

> Wherefore an art is defined for us as a collection of universal rules brought together for the purpose of knowing, doing, or producing something. . . . The practice of an art is nothing but the carrying out of its precepts: that indeed is the part of the pursuer of the art, and the precepts are his instruments rather than those of the art itself. The end of the artificer is the carrying out of its precepts. The end of the art is always a very excellent work which will surely be the result of that action if nothing prevents, e.g. the end of the medical art is health, but that of the doctor is the application of drugs according to the rules of the art. Thus that which is for the art itself only the means, viz. the precepts, is, for the practitioner of the art, the end, and for this cause neither art nor artist can be deprived of their separate ends.[37]

In this conception there is none of Bourdieu's criticism of rules; indeed, Vives assumes that it is only by the help of rules that the practitioner can perfect his practice. If anything in Vives's conception of art corresponds to Bourdieu's mapless paths, it is the inventors of art, those who "brought [the arts] forth without art, but were instructed by a certain unusual force of nature, aided by their own diligence and practice. Thus from the practice of Cicero and Demosthenes, rhetorical precepts were gained; poetry from Homer and Virgil" (88). In these originating geniuses, practice preceded art, but for everybody else, art—that is, a series of rules—is necessary to guide practice.

To illustrate that this conception of the relation between art or method (composed of rules) and practice was common during the period, we may compare two brief references later in the century, both illustrating by their titles how popular reference to art or method had become. The first is from Dudley Fenner's *The Artes of Logicke and Rhetorike* (1584): "An art is the orderly placing of rules, whereby the easiest being first set down, and then the harder, the perfect way of learning anything is fully set down."[38] The second is from William Kempe's *The Education of Children in Learning: Declared by the Dignity, Utility, and Method thereof* (1588):

> [A]ll knowledge is taught generally both by precepts of art and also by practice of the same precepts. They are practiced partly by observing examples of them in other men's works, and partly by making somewhat of our own; and that first by imitation, and at length without imitation. So that perfection of the art is not gotten at the first, but *Per numeros veniunt ista gradusque suos.* Wherefore first the scholar shall learn the precepts: secondly, he shall note the examples of the precepts in unfolding other men's works: thirdly, to imitate the examples in some works of his own: fourthly and lastly, to make somewhat alone without an example.[39]

In neither Fenner nor Kempe is there any hesitation to resort to rules (which Kempe calls "precepts"), and while it would be possible to see their goal as the development of a practice without explicit rules—a path rather than a map—it is much more likely that they would conceive the mastery they expect their students to achieve as rule-governed, simply because that is what an art is.

Finally, we should consider George Puttenham's *The Arte of English Poesie*:

> Then as there was no art in the world till by experience found out, so if Poesie be now an Art, and of all antiquity hath been among the Greeks and Latins, and yet were none until by studious persons fashioned and reduced into a method of rules and precepts, then no doubt may there be the like with us. . . . If again Art be but a certain order of rules prescribed by reason, and gathered by experience, why should not Poesie be a vulgar Art with us? (5)

By the time of Puttenham, late in the century, the conception of an art or method as a set of rules for a particular practice has become so commonplace that he can refer to it in passing as part of a larger argument (that poetry in English can be methodized as easily as poetry in Latin and Greek). More importantly, this conception of an art has become so ingrained that Puttenham, as we have seen in the fifth chapter, ends his treatise with a consideration of when the poet (or maker) should disguise his use of rules:

> But for that in our maker or Poet which rests only in device and issues from an excellent sharp and quick invention, holpen by a clear and bright phantasie and imagination, . . . even as nature herself working by her own peculiar virtue and proper instinct and not by example of meditation or exercise as all other artificers do, is then most admired when he is most natural and least artificial: and in the feats of his language and utterance, because they hold aswell of nature to be suggested as by art to be polished and reformed. Therefore shall our Poet receive praise for both, but more by knowing of his art than by unseasonable using it, and be more commended for his natural eloquence than for his artificial, and more for his artificial well dissembled than for the same over-much affected and grossly or undiscreetly bewrayed, as many makers and Orators do. (307)

In Puttenham's view, poetic inspiration and expression belong to different faculties: inspiration—what the poet shares with nature and even God ("It is therefore of poets thus to be conceived, that if they be able to devise and make all these thing of them selves, without any subject or verity, that they be [by manner of speech] as creating gods" [4])—is more highly valued than the kind of imitation that other artificers must practice, and thus most admired when most natural and genuine. Expression, on the other hand, though suggested by nature is polished by art (or rules), and therefore must be judged by both. But that art which dissembles itself is the most praiseworthy.

Considering reading or interpretation in its widest sense an art or method has led me to reconstruct its precepts or universal rules into a map of possibilities, a way for us as outsiders to conceptualize the parameters of reading in an earlier era. Any Tudor reader would have favorite beaten paths which he followed in pursuing his own reading, his own selection and applications of the precepts and universal rules that constitute the art; in short, his own scripts. Or, as Vives says, "an art does not regard the separate cases, but all in common, which are bound together by that method by which the art teaches; whilst, what the artificer does is concerned with separate cases" (24–25). In this book, I have been interested in the art; what the artificers—i.e., the readers—did on specific occasions has served as a check on the more general strategies I attempt to isolate.

NOTES

1. INTRODUCTION

1. Roger Ascham, *The Schoolmaster,* ed. Lawrence V. Ryan (Ithaca: Cornell University Press for the Folger Shakespeare Library, 1967), 35–36.

2. Erving Goffman, *The Presentation of Self in Everyday Life* (New York: Anchor, 1959); Stephen J. Greenblatt, *Renaissance Self-Fashioning: From More to Shakespeare* (Chicago: University of Chicago Press, 1982).

3. Derek Attridge, *Peculiar Language: Literature as Difference from the Renaissance to James Joyce* (Ithaca: Cornell University Press, 1988), 18. Margaret W. Ferguson, *Trials of Desire: Renaissance Defenses of Poetry* (New Haven: Yale University Press, 1983), 11, 138, 161.

4. David Javitch, *Poetry and Courtliness in Renaissance England* (Princeton: Princeton University Press, 1978), 50.

5. Frank Whigham, *Ambition and Privilege: The Social Tropes of Elizabethan Courtesy Theory* (Berkeley and Los Angeles: University of California Press, 1984); Heinrich Plett, "Aesthetic Constituents in the Courtly Culture of Renaissance England," *New Literary History* 14 (1982–83), 597–621, esp. 605–12; Louis Montrose, " 'Eliza, Queene of Shepheardes,' and the Pastoral of Power," *Renaissance Historicism,* ed. Arthur F. Kinney and Dan S. Collins (Amherst: University of Massachusetts Press, 1987), 34–63, esp. 34–35; and Louis Montrose, "Of Gentlemen and Shepherds: The Politics of Elizabethan Pastoral Form," *ELH* 50 (1983): 415–59.

6. The second chapter of Attridge's *Peculiar Language,* "Nature, Art, and the Supplement in Renaissance Literary Theory: Puttenham's Poetics of Decorum," is a slight reworking of "Puttenham's Perplexity: Nature, Art, and the Supplement in Renaissance Poetic Theory," *Literary Theory/Renaissance Texts* (Baltimore: Johns Hopkins University Press, 1986), 257–79.

7. Jonathan V. Crewe, "The Hegemonic Theater of George Puttenham," *Renaissance Historicism,* ed. Arthur F. Kinney and Dan S. Collins (Amherst: University of Massachusetts Press, 1987), 94.

8. Rosemary Kegl, " '*Those Terrible Aproches': Sexuality, Social Mobility, and Resisting the Courtliness of Puttenham's* The Arte of English Poesie," *ELR* 20 (1990): 184.

9. Louis Montrose, "The Elizabethan Subject and the Spenserian Text," *Literary Theory/Renaissance Texts,* ed. Patricia Parker and David Quint (Baltimore: Johns Hopkins University Press, 1986), 306.

10. Attridge, *Peculiar Language*, 17.

11. George Lakoff, *Women, Fire, and Dangerous Things* (Chicago: University of Chicago Press, 1987), 266; cf. Ray Jackendoff, *Semantics and Cognition* (Cambridge: MIT Press, 1983), 23–29.

12. For discussions of this approach, called "methodological individualism," see Fred D'Agostino, "Chomsky's Individualism," *Chomsky's System of Ideas* (Oxford: Clarendon, 1986), 11–60; and John O'Neill, ed., *Modes of Individualism and Collectivism* (London: Heinemann, 1973). David Bromwich's *Politics by Other Means: Higher Education and Group Thinking* (New Haven: Yale University Press, 1992), provides an interesting exploration of a similar approach to a different problem.

13. Pierre Bourdieu, *Outline of a Theory of Practice,* trans. Richard Nice (1972; Cambridge: Cambridge University Press, 1990), 78.

14. Clifford Geertz, "Thick Description: Toward an Interpretive Theory of Culture," *The Interpretation of Cultures* (New York: Basic, 1973), 3–30.

15. Walter J. Ong, S. J., "The Writer's Audience is Always a Fiction," *Interfaces of the Word* (Ithaca: Cornell University Press, 1977), 58.

16. See Noam Chomsky, "A Framework for Discussion" and "The View Beyond: Prospects for the Study of the Mind," both in *Language and Problems of Knowledge* (Cambridge: MIT Press, 1988), 1–34 and 133–70.

17. See the classic discussion in Noam Chomsky, *Aspects of the Theory of Syntax* (Cambridge: MIT Press, 1965), 3–9, and the fuller consideration in the first three chapters of Chomsky, *Language and Mind,* enlarged ed. (New York: Harcourt Brace Jovanovich, 1972), 1–99.

18. In his discussion of "The Fetish of Recreation," Frank Whigham notes that "The evidence suggests that courtiers were indeed so serious as to be continually and resolutely purposeful in their pastimes. They played because play was in fact work, play would take them to the top or keep them there; they knew that because their play would be taken seriously, they too must take it so" (92).

19. Robert Darnton, "Toward a History of Reading," *Princeton Alumni Weekly 87* (8 April 1987): 19; another version appeared as "First Steps Toward a History of Reading" in the *Australian Journal of French Studies* 23 (1986): 5–30, and in *The Kiss of Lamourette: Reflections in Cultural History* (New York: W. W. Norton, 1990), 154–87.

2. EDUCATION AND READING IN TUDOR ENGLAND

1. Edmund Coote, *The English Schoole-Maister,* ed. R. C. Alston (Menston: The Scolar Press, 1968), sig. A.iii.r. For a general survey of preliminary schooling, see T. W. Baldwin, *William Shakespere's Petty School* (Urbana: University of Illinois Press, 1943).

2. T. W. Baldwin, *William Shakespere's Small Latin and Lesse Greeke,* vol. 1 (Urbana: University of Illinois Press, 1944), 163.

3. Richard Mulcaster, *Positions,* ed. Robert Henry Quick (London: Longmans, Green, 1888), 31.

4. Jo Ann Hoeppner Moran, *The Growth of English Schooling 1340–1548* (Princeton: Princeton University Press, 1985), 216–19.

5. For a good overview see Anthony Grafton and Lisa Jardine, *From Humanism to the Humanities* (Cambridge: Harvard University Press, 1986). See also Joan Simon, *Education and Society in Tudor England* (Cambridge: Cambridge University Press, 1966); and R. R. Bolgar, *The Classical Heritage and Its Beneficiaries* (Cambridge: Cambridge University Press, 1954), chaps. 7 and 8.

6. Brian Street, *Listening for the Text* (Baltimore: Johns Hopkins University Press, 1990), 23.

7. Erasmus, *De Copia,* trans. and ed. Betty I. Knott, *De Ratione Studii,* trans. and ed. Brian McGregor, *Collected Works of Erasmus: Literary and Educational Writings 2* (Toronto: University of Toronto Press, 1978), vol. 24.

8. Erasmus, "A Declamation on the Subject of Early Liberal Education for Children" (*De pueris statim ac liberaliter instituendis declamatio*), trans. and ed. Beert C. Verstraete, *Collected Works of Erasmus: Literary and Educational Writings 4* (Toronto: University of Toronto Press, 1985), vol. 26.

9. Erasmus, *Convivium Religiosum,* trans. Craig R. Thompson, *The Colloquies of Erasmus* (Chicago: University of Chicago Press, 1965), 46–78.

10. Erasmus, *De Conscribendi Epistolis,* translated and annotated by Charles Fantazzi, *Collected Works of Erasmus: Literary and Educational Writings 3,* ed. J. K. Sowards (Toronto: University of Toronto Press, 1985), vol. 25.

11. Roger Ascham, *The Schoolmaster,* 139.

12. Juan Luis Vives, *De Tradendis Disciplinis,* trans. by Foster Watson as *Vives: On Education* (1913; Totowa: Rowman and Littlefield, 1971), 105.

13. Erasmus, *Parabolae sive similia,* translated and annotated as "Parallels" by R. A. B. Mynors, *Collected Works of Erasmus: Literary and Educational Writings 1* (Toronto: University of Toronto Press, 1978), vol. 23.

14. John Brinsley, *Ludus Literarius or The Grammar Schoole* (1627), ed. E. T. Campagnac (Liverpool: Liverpool University Press, 1917), 188.

15. Joel B. Altman, *The Tudor Play of Mind: Rhetorical Inquiry and the Development of Elizabethan Drama* (Berkeley and Los Angeles: University of California Press, 1978), 132.

16. William Kempe, *The Education of Children in Learning: Declared by the Dignity, Utility, and method Thereof* (1588), in *Four Tudor Books on Education,* ed. Robert D. Pepper (Gainesville: Scholars' Facsimiles & Reprints, 1966), 233.

17. *William Temple's Analysis of Sir Philip Sidney's Apology for Poetry,* ed. and trans. John Webster (Binghamton: Center for Medieval and Early Renaissance Studies, State University of New York, 1984).

18. Abraham Fraunce, *The Lawiers Logicke,* ed. R. C. Alston (Menston: The Scolar Press, 1969), 120v–124r.

19. Dudley Fenner, *The Artes of Logicke and Rhetorike*, in *Four Tudor Books on Education*, ed. Robert D. Pepper (Gainesville: Scholars' Facsimiles & Reprints, 1966), 143–80. For discussion, see Sister Miriam Joseph, *Shakespeare's Use of the Arts of Language* (1947; New York: Hafner, 1966), 44–53.

20. *The Comedy of Acolastus Translated from the Latin of Fullonius by John Palsgrave*, ed. P. L. Carver, EETS 202 (London: Oxford University Press, 1970), 4.

21. *Gabriel Harvey's* Ciceronianus, ed. Harold S. Wilson, trans. Clarence A. Forbes, University of Nebraska Studies in the Humanities 4 (Lincoln: University of Nebraska Press, 1945), 87.

22. See R. C. Alston's "Note" in his edition of *A Short Introduction of Grammar* (1549), by William Lily and John Colet (Menston: The Scolar Press, 1970).

23. John Crowe Ransom, "Art Worries the Naturalists," *Kenyon Review* 7 (1945): 282–99; cited by Jonathan Culler, *Structuralist Poetics* (Ithaca: Cornell University Press, 1975), 171.

24. Charles Hoole, *A New Discovery of the Old Art of Teaching School*, ed. R. C. Alston (Menston: The Scolar Press, 1969).

25. Thomas Blundeville, *The True Order and Methode of Writing and Reading Hystories* (London: W. Seres, 1574), sig. H.iii.r.

26. Mortimer Adler and Charles Van Doren, *How to Read a Book: The Art of Getting a Liberal Education*, rev. ed. (1940; New York: Simon and Schuster, 1972), 340–41.

3. TUDOR READERS READING

1. Harold S. Wilson, "Introduction" to *Gabriel Harvey's* Ciceronianus, 20.

2. Virginia F. Stern, *Gabriel Harvey: His Life, Marginalia, and Library* (Oxford: Clarendon, 1979).

3. *Letter-Book of Gabriel Harvey*, ed. Edward John Long Scott (London: Camden Society, 1884).

4. Harold S. Wilson, "Gabriel Harvey's Method of Annotating His Books," *Harvard Library Bulletin* 2 (1948): 344–61.

5. *Gabriel Harvey's Marginalia*, collected and edited by G. C. Moore Smith (Stratford-upon-Avon: Shakespeare Head Press, 1913), 113–14. All references to Harvey's marginalia are to this volume unless otherwise noted.

6. Anthony Grafton and Lisa Jardine, " 'Studied for Action': How Gabriel Harvey Read His Livy," *Past and Present* 129 (Nov. 1990): 46–48.

7. Eleanor Relle, "Some New Marginalia and Poems of Gabriel Harvey," *RES*, ns. 23 (1972): 409.

8. Caroline Ruutz-Rees, "Some Notes of Gabriel Harvey's in Hoby's Translation of Castiglione's *Courtier* (1561)," *PMLA* 25 (1910): 610.

9. Lynn Staley Johnson, *The Shepheardes Calendar: An Introduction* (University Park: Pennsylvania State University Press, 1990), 7.

10. Edmund Spenser, *The Shepheardes Calendar,* in *The Variorum Edition of the Minor Poems,* vol. 1, ed. Charles Grosvenor Osgood and Henry Gibbons Lotspeich, assisted by Dorothy E. Mason (Baltimore: Johns Hopkins University Press, 1943), 7. All citations to the poem and its apparatus are to this edition.

11. Robert McNulty, "Introduction," *Ludovico Ariosto's* Orlando Furioso, *translated into English Heroical Verse by Sir John Harington (1591)* (Oxford: Clarendon, 1972), xxv. All citations to Harington are to this edition; McNulty's "Introduction" is numbered in roman, Harington in arabic, numerals. References to the poem are by canto and line. In this discussion I have profited from Anne T. Sampson's seminar paper, "Harington's Ariosto: A Model for Reading."

12. Sir Philip Sidney, "An Apology for Poetrie," in *Elizabethan Critical Essays,* ed. G. Gregory Smith (Oxford: Clarendon, 1904), 172.

13. Townsend Rich, *Harington and Ariosto: A Study in Elizabethan Verse Translation* (New Haven: Yale University Press, 1940), 147.

14. Simon Cauchi, "The 'Setting foorth' of Harington's Ariosto," *Studies in Bibliography* 36 (1983): 137–68, 159.

15. T.G.A. Nelson, "Sir John Harington and the Renaissance Debate Over Allegory," *SP* 82 (1985): 361.

4. READING IN A RELIGIOUS SETTING

1. Baldwin, *Shakespere's Petty School,* 79.

2. F. E. Brightman, *The English Rite* (London: Rivingtons, 1921), 778–86.

3. *King Henry's Primer,* in *Three Primers put Forth in the Reign of Henry VIII* (Oxford: Oxford University Press, 1848), 442.

4. Alan Fager Herr, *The Elizabethan Sermon: A Survey and a Bibliography* (1940; New York: Octagon, 1969), 13–14.

5. Louis B. Wright, *Middle-Class Culture in Elizabethan England* (Chapel Hill: University of North Carolina Press, 1935), 228.

6. Thomas Lever, "A Preface shewing the true understanding of God's word." *Godly Medititions uppon the ten Commandments, the Articles of the fayth, and the Lordes prayer,* by John Bradford (London: William Seres, 1567), sig. A.iii.r–A.iii.v.

7. Introduction by T. A. Lacey to *A necessary Doctrine and Erudition for any Christian Man (The King's Book)* (London: Society for Promoting Christian Knowledge, 1932), 3.

8. Bishop of Rochester, *The Manual Of Prayers, or The Primer, in English,* in *Three Primers put Forth in the Reign of Henry VIII* (Oxford: Oxford University Press, 1848), 389.

9. *Certayne Sermons or Homelies,* ed. with an introduction by Ronald B. Bond (Toronto: University of Toronto Press, 1987), 55–56.

10. Norman Wood, *The Reformation and English Education* (London: George Routledge and Sons, 1931), 138–39.

11. In *Three Reformation Catechisms: Catholic, Anabaptist, Lutheran,* ed. Denis Janz (New York: Edward Mellen, 1982), 196–97.

12. J. F., *A most breefe manner of Instruction, to the principles of Christian Religion* (London: Hugh Singleton, n.d.).

13. J. W. Blench, *Preaching in England in the Late Fifteenth and Sixteenth Centuries* (New York: Barnes and Noble, 1964), 59.

14. W. Fraser Mitchell, *English Pulpit Oratory from Andrewes to Tillotson* (London: Society for Promoting Christian Knowledge, 1932), 32–33.

15. *The Diary of John Manningham,* ed. Robert Parker Sorlien (Hanover, NH: University Press of New England, 1976).

16. William Perkins, *The Art of Prophecying,* in *[Works] A golden chaine: or, the description of theology* (Cambridge: J. Legate, 1609), 731–62.

17. Neils Hemmingsen, *The Preacher,* trans. John Horsfall, ed. R. C. Alston (1574 [T. Marsh, London]; Menston: The Scolar Press, 1972).

18. Andreas (Gerhardt) Hyperius, *The Practice of Preaching,* trans. John Ludham (London: Thomas East, 1577).

19. Frederic W. Farrar, *History of Interpretation* (1886 [Dutton]; Grand Rapids: Baker Book House, 1961), 327.

20. In *The Work of William Tyndale,* ed. G. E. Duffield (Philadelphia: Fortress, 1965), 340–41.

21. "A Prologue or Preface," *The Works of Thomas Cranmer,* ed. Rev. John Edmund Cox, Parker Society, vol. 16 (Cambridge: Cambridge University Press, 1846), 120.

22. Lloyd E. Berry, "Introduction," *The Geneva Bible: A Facsimile of the 1560 Edition* (Madison: University of Wisconsin Press, 1969), 14.

23. Rivkah Zim, "The Reformation: The Trial of God's Word," *Reading the Text: Biblical Criticism and Literary Theory,* ed. Stephen Prickett (Oxford: Blackwell, 1991), 72, 121.

24. S. L. Greenslade, "English Versions of the Bible, 1525–1611," *The West from the Reformation to the Present Day,* vol. 3 of *The Cambridge History of the Bible,* ed. S. L. Greenslade (Cambridge: Cambridge University Press, 1963), 159–60.

25. John N. Wall, "Godly and Fruitful Lessons: The English Bible, Erasmus' Paraphrases, and the Book of Homilies," *The Godly Kingdom of Tudor England,* ed. John E. Booty (Wilton: Morehouse-Barlow, 1981), 126.

26. Millar Maclure, *The Paul's Cross Sermons 1534–1642* (Toronto: University of Toronto Press, 1958), 159.

5. METHOD AND ART IN READING

1. Thomas Blundeville, *The true order and Methode of wryting and reading Hystories* (London: William Seres, 1574).

2. Sister Miriam Joseph, *Shakespeare's Use of the Arts of Language.*

3. George Puttenham, *The Arte of English Poesie,* ed. Gladys Doidge Willcock and Alice Walker (1936; Cambridge: Cambridge University Press, 1970).

4. *The posies of George Gascoigne, Esquire, corrected, perfected, and augmented by the author,* in G. Gregory Smith, ed., *Elizabethan Critical Essays,* vol. 1 (Oxford: Clarendon, 1904), 46–57.

5. Javitch, *Poetry and Courtliness in Renaissance England,* 66.

6. There are two modern editions of *The English Secretary.* R. C. Alston edited the first (1586) edition (Menston: The Scolar Press, 1967); Robert O. Evans, the fourth (1599) (Gainesville: Scholars' Facsimiles & Reprints, 1967). I have generally quoted from the fuller 1599 edition and identify quotations from the 1586 edition as "Alston."

7. Erasmus, *De Conscribendis Epistolis,* 1–254.

6. CONCLUSION

1. Adler and Van Doren, *How to Read a Book,* vii, viii.

2. Francis Bacon, *The Essays 1625* (Menston: The Scolar Press, 1971), 292. This is a reproduction of a copy in the Bodleian.

3. See Altman's *The Tudor Play of Mind* for an extended argument that Renaissance students were trained specifically to argue on both sides of an issue.

4. For discussion of the events surrounding Essex's Rebellion, see Richard Dutton, *Mastering the Revels: The Regulation and Censorship of English Renaissance Drama* (Houndsmills: Macmillan, 1991), 117–41. The question of topical reference is obviously related to censorship; see especially Annabel Patterson, *Censorship and Interpretation: The Conditions of Writing and Reading in Early Modern England* (Madison: University of Wisconsin Press, 1984). For a different view of theatrical censorship, see Janet Clare's *"Art made tongue-tied by authority": Elizabethan and Jacobean Dramatic Censorship* (Manchester: Manchester University Press, 1990).

5. Natascha Wurzbach, *The Rise of the English Street Ballad, 1550–1650,* trans. Gayna Walls (Cambridge: Cambridge University Press, 1990), 65–66.

6. Sandra Clark, *The Elizabethan Pamphleteers: Popular Moralistic Pamphlets, 1580–1640* (London: Athlone, 1983). Her study is confined, as her subtitle indicates, to popular moralistic pamphlets. For her, however, this distinguishes these pamphlets from strictly "moral or religious" ones (33) and, she continues to explain, "The desire for entertainment alone explains the popularity of such forms as the romance and the jestbook, but it is always entertainment combined with instruction" (35). In her later discussion, she observes that "some topics which are used as the main subject of a pamphlet very frequently, almost inevitably, give rise to moral reflections of a particular kind, as if the topic and the reflections were closely connected, not just in the minds of one or two individuals, but in the commonest habits of thought of the time" (211). For an earlier discussion of the close relation between pleasure and utility, see Wright's *Middle Class Culture in Elizabethan England.*

7. John Lyly, preface to *Euphues and his England,* in *The Complete Works of John Lyly,* ed. R. Warwick Bond, vol. 2 (Oxford: Clarendon, 1967), 8–9.

8. William Painter, *Palace of Pleasure,* in *The Renaissance in England,* ed. Hyder E. Rollins and Herschel Baker (Boston: D. C. Heath, 1954), 673.

9. Thomas Wilson, *Arte of Rhetorique,* ed. Thomas J. Derrick (New York: Garland, 1982).

10. Wilbur Samuel Howell, *Logic and Rhetoric in England, 1500–1700* (Princeton: Princeton University Press, 1956), 98.

11. Sir Philip Sidney, *The Defense of Poesy,* in *The Renaissance in England,* ed. Hyder E. Rollins and Herschel Baker (Boston: D. C. Heath, 1954), 613.

APPENDIX

1. Donald A. Schon, "Generative Metaphor: A Perspective on Problem-Setting in Social Policy," *Metaphor and Thought,* ed. Andrew Ortony (Cambridge: Cambridge University Press, 1979), 255.

2. See Ortony, ed., *Metaphor and Thought;* George Lakoff and Mark Johnson, *Metaphors We Live By* (Chicago: University of Chicago Press, 1980); Lakoff, *Women, Fire, and Dangerous Things;* Mark Johnson, *The Body in the Mind: The Bodily Basis of Meaning, Imagination, and Reason* (Chicago: University of Chicago Press, 1987); George Lakoff and Mark Turner, *More Than Cool Reason: A Field Guide to Poetic Metaphor* (Chicago: University of Chicago Press, 1989); Mark Turner, *Death is the Mother of Beauty: Mind, Metaphor, Criticism* (Chicago: University of Chicago Press, 1987), and *Reading Minds: The Study of English in the Age of Cognitive Science* (Princeton: Princeton University Press, 1991).

3. Michael J. Reddy, "The Conduit Metaphor—A Case of Frame Conflict in Our Language About Language," *Metaphor and Thought,* ed. Andrew Ortony (Cambridge: Cambridge University Press, 1977), 284–324.

4. Kenneth S. Goodman, "Unity in Reading," *Becoming Readers in a Complex Society,* ed. Alan C. Purves and Olive Niles (Chicago: National Society for the Study of Education, 1984), 80.

5. H. P. Grice, "Logic and Conversation," *Speech Acts,* vol. 3 of *Syntax and Semantics,* ed. P. Cole and J. L. Morgan (New York: Academic, 1975), 41–58.

6. Stanley E. Fish, "Interpreting the *Variorum,*" *Is There a Text in This Class?* (Cambridge: Harvard University Press, 1980), 171.

7. Norman N. Holland, *The Critical I* (New York: Columbia University Press, 1992), 34–35.

8. Jonathan Culler, *Structuralist Poetics* (Ithaca: Cornell University Press, 1975).

9. See Chomsky, *Aspects of the Theory of Syntax,* 3–4. For a more recent discussion, see his *Language and Problems of Knowledge.*

10. Jonathan Culler, *The Pursuit of Signs* (Ithaca: Cornell University Press, 1981), 47–79.

11. For good introductions, see Roger C. Schank and Robert P. Abelson, *Scripts, Plans, Goals, and Understanding* (Hillsdale: Lawrence Erlbaum Associates, 1977); and John Haugeland, *Artificial Intelligence: The Very Idea* (1985; Cambridge: MIT Press, 1990).

12. David E. Rumelhart, "Understanding Understanding," *Understanding Reading Comprehension,* ed. James Flood (Newark, DE: International Reading Association, 1984), 3.

13. See Ray S. Jackendoff, *Semantics and Cognition* (Cambridge: MIT Press, 1983), 128–58, and *Consciousness and the Computational Mind* (Cambridge: MIT Press, 1987), 143–48; and Fred Lerdahl and Ray Jackendoff, *A Generative Theory of Tonal Music* (Cambridge: MIT Press, 1983), 39–43, and *passim.*

14. See Eugene R. Kintgen, *The Perception of Poetry* (Bloomington: Indiana University Press, 1983), 140–64, and "Expectations and Processes in Reading Poetic Narratives," *Empirical Studies in the Arts* 4 (1986): 79–95; and Eugene R. Kintgen and Norman N. Holland, "Carlos Reads a Poem," *College English* 46 (1984): 478–93.

15. Willcock and Walker suggest the comparison in their "Introduction" to *The Arte of English Poesie* by George Puttenham without developing it: "A well-educated modern reader may confess without shame to momentary confusion between *Hypozeuxis* and *Hypozeugma,* but to his Elizabethan prototype the categories of the figures were, like the multiplication tables, a part of his foundation" (lxxv). For interesting discussion, see Chomsky's comments on "the number faculty" in *Language and Problems of Knowledge,* 167–69 and 181–85; and the discussion of addition in Raphael Salkie, *The Chomsky Update: Linguistics and Politics* (London: Unwin Hyman, 1990), 102–06.

16. For a general survey, see Gerald Strauss, "The State of Pedagogical Theory c. 1530: What Protestant Reformers Knew About Education," *Schooling and Society,* ed. Lawrence Stone (Baltimore: Johns Hopkins University Press, 1976), 69–94, esp. 79–84.

17. Erasmus, *De pueris,* 308–09.

18. Richard Mulcaster, *Positions,* ed. Robert Herbert Quick (London: Longmans, Green, 1888), 27.

19. Jonathan Culler, *Structuralist Poetics* (Ithaca: Cornell University Press, 1975).

20. David Bleich, *Readings and Feelings* (Urbana: NCTE, 1975); and *Subjective Criticism* (Baltimore: Johns Hopkins University Press, 1978).

21. Norman Holland, "UNITY IDENTITY TEXT SELF," *PMLA* 90 (October 1975): 813–22; and *5 Readers Reading* (New Haven: Yale University Press, 1975); and "Reading Readers Reading," *Researching Response to Literature and the Teaching of Literature,* ed. Charles R. Cooper (Norwood, N.J.: Ablex, 1985), 3–21.

22. Kintgen, *The Perception of Poetry.*

23. Stanley E. Fish, "Literature in the Reader: Affective Stylistics," *Is There a Text in This Class?* (Cambridge: Harvard University Press, 1980), 21–67.

24. The best single study remains David Cressy, *Literacy and the Social Order*

(Cambridge: Cambridge University Press, 1980). See also Cressy's "Levels of Illiteracy in England 1530–1730," *Historical Journal* 20 (1977): 1–23, reprinted in *Literacy and Social Development in the West, A Reader*, ed. Harvey J. Graff (Cambridge: Cambridge University Press, 1981), 105–24; and the discussions and voluminous references in Harvey J. Graff, *The Legacies of Literacy* (Bloomington: Indiana University Press, 1987), esp. 95–106 and 151–63.

25. Egil Johansson, "The History of Literacy in Sweden," *Literacy and Social Development in the West, A Reader*, ed. Harvey J. Graff (Cambridge: Cambridge University Press, 1981), 151–82, reprinted from *Educational Reports, Umea* (Umea, Sweden: Umea University and School of Education), No. 12 (1977): 2–42.

26. Margaret Spufford, "First Steps in Literacy: The Reading and Writing Experiences of the Humblest Seventeenth-Century Spiritual Autobiographers," *Literacy and Social Development in the West*, ed. Harvey J. Graff, 125–50, reprinted from *Social History* 4 (1979): 407–35.

27. Robert Darnton, "Readers Respond to Rousseau," in *The Great Cat Massacre and Other Episodes in French Cultural History* (New York: Basic, 1984), 215–56. See, also by Darnton, "What Is the History of Books?" *Daedalus* 111 (summer 1982): 65–83, and "Toward a History of Reading," 19–24, 30; the same problems are evident in Roger Chartier's extremely illuminating *The Cultural Uses of Print in Early Modern France*, trans. Lydia G. Cochrane (Princeton: Princeton University Press, 1987). See especially "Urban Reading Practices, 1660–1780," 183–239, in which he considers many aspects of reading but never actually confronts the processes by which marks on the page become thoughts in the mind. See also Carl F. Kaestle, "The History of Literacy and the History of Readers," *Review of Research in Education* 12 (1985): 11–53.

28. Carl F. Kaestle, *Literacy in the United States: Readers and Reading since 1880* (New Haven: Yale University Press, 1991).

29. Grafton and Jardine, " 'Studied for Action,' " 31–78. See also two preliminary articles by Anthony Grafton, "Gabriel Harvey's Marginalia: New Light on the Cultural History of Elizabethan England," *Princeton University Library Chronicle* 52 (autumn 1990): 21–24; and " 'Discitur ut agatur': How Gabriel Harvey Read His Livy," *Annotation and its Texts*, ed. Stephen A. Barney (New York: Oxford University Press, 1991), 108–29; see also Moore Smith, ed., *Gabriel Harvey's Marginalia*.

30. *William Temple's Analysis of Sir Philip Sidney's* Apology for Poetry, ed. and trans. Webster.

31. Graham Hough, *The First Commentary on the* Faerie Queene (np., 1964).

32. Adler and Van Doren, *How to Read a Book*, 46–47.

33. Jon P. Klancher, *The Making of English Reading Audiences, 1790–1832* (Madison: University of Wisconsin Press, 1987), 174.

34. James L. Machor, "Historical Hermeneutics and Antebellum Fiction: Gender, Response Theory, and Interpretive Contexts," *Readers in History*, ed. James L. Machor (Baltimore: Johns Hopkins University Press, 1993), 63.

35. Albertus Meierus, *Certaine briefe and speciall instructions for gentlemen, mer-*

chants, students, . . . marriners, &c. Employed in service abrode, or anie way occasioned to converse in the kingdomes, and govermentes of forren Princes, trans. Philip Jones (London: J. Woolfe, 1589).

36. See Walter J. Ong, S. J., *Ramus, Method, and the Decay of Dialogue* (Cambridge: Harvard University Press, 1958); and Lisa Jardine, *Francis Bacon, Discovery and the Art of Discourse* (Cambridge: Cambridge University Press, 1974), esp. chap. 1.

37. Vives, *De Tradendis Disciplinis,* 24.

38. Fenner, *The Artes of Logicke and Rhetorike,* 151.

39. Kempe, *The Education of Children in Learning,* 223.

INDEX